Our Daily Bread

Devotional Collection

Discovery House is affiliated with Our Daily Bread Ministries, Grand Rapids, Michigan.

ISBN of Rich Brown edition: 978-1-62707-480-3

ISBN of Purple Rose edition: 978-1-62707-481-0

Printed in Italy
First printing in 2016

Quiet Time with God

Keeping a daily appointment with God is a vital part of the Christian life. The more time we spend with God—reading His Word, conversing with Him in prayer, meditating on thoughts from His Word—the better we get to know Him and the more our lives begin to reflect His image and His truth.

These selections from the popular *Our Daily Bread* devotional encourage this daily discipline with short devotional readings for each day of the year.

Each *Our Daily Bread* reading is based on a Scripture passage and developed around a relevant story or illustration that helps to illuminate the truth of God's Word.

We hope that this yearly devotional will encourage you to keep those daily appointments. And may it give you spiritual guidance along the way as it helps to make the wisdom of the Bible understandable and accessible.

Better or Worse?

Read: 2 Timothy 3:1–5, 10–17

Continue in what you have learned and have become convinced of. —v. 14

At the beginning of each new year, experts give their predictions about the economy, politics, weather, and a host of other topics. Will there be war or peace? Poverty or prosperity? Progress or stagnation? People everywhere are hoping that this year will be better than last, but no one knows what will happen.

There is, however, something we can be certain about. A guest speaker at my church suggested that when we ask if the world will get better or worse, the answer is "Yes, to both!"

Paul told Timothy, "There will be terrible times in the last days. . . . Evildoers and impostors will go from bad to worse, deceiving and being deceived. But as for you, continue in what you have learned and become convinced of, because you know those from whom you learned it" (2 TIM. 3:1,13–14).

The inspired Word of God instructs, corrects, and encourages us as we follow God's path (vv. 16–17). J. B. Phillips described the Scriptures as our "comprehensive equipment" that prepares us fully for all branches of God's work.

As the spiritual darkness of our world grows deeper, the light of Christ shines more brightly through all those who know and love Him. Jesus is our joy and hope—today, tomorrow, and forever! *DAVID MCCASLAND*

Heavenly Father, the trouble in this world can divert our eyes from you. Thank you for your Word that helps us stay focused. May we find our delight in your love and share it with others today.

The powers of evil around you are no match for the power of Jesus within you.

Where Are You?

Read: Genesis 3:1–10

The Lord God called to the man, "Where are you?" —v. 9

The two teenage boys heard the sound of their parents' car and panicked. How would they explain the mess in the house? Their father's instructions had been clear that morning before he and their mother drove out of town: no parties, no rowdy friends. But the unruly friends came and the boys allowed them to stay, despite their father's warning. Now the house was in a jumble and the boys were tipsy and disheveled. In fear, they hid.

That was how Adam and Eve must have felt after they had chosen to disobey God and then heard the sound of Him approaching. In fear, they hid themselves. "Where are you?" God called (GEN. 3:9). Adam responded, "I heard you in the garden, and I was afraid because I was naked; so I hid" (v. 10). Sin makes us feel afraid and naked, and we become vulnerable to even more temptation.

God is still calling to people: "Where are you?" Many run away, trying to hide from Him or drown out the sound of His voice. Yet we cannot hide from God; He knows exactly where we are. Rather than hide in fear, we can respond in this way: "God, have mercy on me, a sinner" (LUKE 18:13).

LAWRENCE DARMANI

Would you be free from the burden of sin?
There's power in the blood, power in the blood;
Would you over evil a victory win?
There's wonderful power in the blood.
JONES

The only place to hide sin is under the blood of Christ.

I Am Redeemed!

Read: Psalm 40:8–10

Sing to the Lord, praise his name; proclaim his salvation day after day. —Psalm 96:2

One day when Ann was visiting her husband in the hospital, she began talking with a caregiver who was assisting him. Ann enjoys engaging people in conversation wherever she is, and she also looks for ways to talk to people about Jesus. Ann asked the caregiver if he knew what he wanted to do in the future. When he said he wasn't sure, she suggested that it's important to know God first so He can help with such decisions. He then pulled up the sleeve of his shirt to reveal "I am redeemed!" tattooed across his arm.

They realized that they shared a mutual love for the Lord Jesus Christ! And both had found ways to show their faith in the One who died to give us life.

The title of an old song by Steve Green says it best: "People need the Lord." It's up to us to find ways to share "the good news" with them (PS. 40:9 NKJV). Not everyone feels comfortable talking to strangers, and there is no one-size-fits-all method. But God will use our personalities and His light in us to spread His love.

"I am redeemed!" Let's allow God to guide us to find ways to tell others about Jesus Christ, our Redeemer! *DAVE BRANON*

Redeemed, how I love to proclaim it!
Redeemed by the blood of the Lamb;
Redeemed through His infinite mercy—
His child, and forever I am.
CROSBY

The good news of the gospel is too good to keep to ourselves.

JANUARY 4

The Beautiful Bride

Read: Revelation 19:4–9

The wedding of the Lamb has come, and his bride has made herself ready. —v. 7

I have officiated at a lot of weddings. Often planned according to the dreams of the bride, each of the weddings has been unique. But one thing is the same: adorned in their wedding dresses with hair beautifully done and faces aglow, brides steal the show.

I find it intriguing that God describes us as His bride. Speaking of the church, He says, "The wedding of the Lamb has come, and his bride has made herself ready" (REV. 19:7).

This is a great thought for those of us who have become discouraged about the condition of the church. I grew up as a pastor's kid, pastored three churches, and have preached in churches all over the world. I've counseled both pastors and parishioners about deep and troubling problems in the church. And though the church often seems unlovable, my love for the church has not changed.

But my reason for loving the church has changed. I now love it most of all for whose it is. The church belongs to Christ; it is the bride of Christ. Since the church is precious to Him, it is precious to me as well. His love for His bride, as flawed as we may be, is nothing less than extraordinary!

JOE STOWELL

Lord, we look forward to the day when we will be
robed in the fine linens of purity and join you at the
marriage supper of the Lamb.
Until then, remind us to love your bride
and to live beautifully for you.

Since Christ loves His bride, the church, so should we.

Assembly Required

Read: Philippians 4:4–13

Do not be anxious about anything, but . . . present your requests to God. —v. 6

When our daughter and her fiancé began receiving wedding presents, it was a happy time. One gift they received was a bench cabinet that had to be assembled—and I volunteered for the task because they already had so much to do to prepare for the wedding. Although it took a couple of hours, it was much easier than expected. All of the wooden pieces were precut and predrilled, and all the hardware for assembly was included. The instructions were virtually foolproof.

Unfortunately, most of life isn't that way. Life doesn't carry with it simple instructions, nor do we find all of the necessary parts in hand. We face situations with no clear idea of what we're getting into or what it will take to pull it off. We can easily find ourselves overwhelmed with these difficult moments.

But we need not face our burdens alone. God wants us to bring them to Him: "Do not be anxious about anything, but in every situation . . . present your requests to God. And the peace of God . . . will guard your hearts and your minds in Christ Jesus" (PHIL. 4:6–7).

We have a Savior who understands and offers His peace in the midst of our struggles.

BILL CROWDER

Stayed upon Jehovah, hearts are fully blest—
Finding, as He promised, perfect peace and rest.
HAVERGAL

The secret of peace is to give every anxious care to God.

Mistakes Made Beautiful

Read: Luke 22:39–51

[Jesus] touched the man's ear and healed him. —v. 51

Early in his career, jazz player Herbie Hancock was invited to play in the quintet of Miles Davis, already a musical legend. In an interview, Hancock admitted being nervous but described it as a wonderful experience because Davis was so nurturing. During one performance, when Davis was near the high point of his solo, Hancock played the wrong chord. He was mortified, but Davis continued as if nothing had happened. "He played some notes that made my chord right," Hancock said.

What an example of loving leadership! Davis didn't scold Hancock or make him look foolish. He didn't blame him for ruining the performance. He simply adjusted his plan and turned a potentially disastrous mistake into something beautiful.

What Davis did for Hancock, Jesus did for Peter. When Peter cut off the ear of one of the crowd who had come to arrest Jesus, Jesus reattached the ear (LUKE 22:51), indicating that His kingdom was about healing, not hurting. Time after time Jesus used the disciples' mistakes to show a better way.

What Jesus did for His disciples, He also does for us. And what He does for us, we can do for others. Instead of magnifying every mistake, we can turn them into beautiful acts of forgiveness, healing, and redemption.

JULIE ACKERMAN LINK

Lord, you understand how prone we are to make selfish and foolish mistakes. Forgive us and restore us. Please, for your name's sake, use even the worst aspects of our lives for your glory.

Jesus longs to turn our mistakes into amazing examples of His grace.

Where Can I Help?

Read: Galatians 6:1–10

As we have opportunity, let us do good to all people, especially to those who belong to the family of believers. —v. 10

Last winter our city was hit by an ice storm. Hundreds of ice-heavy tree limbs cut into power lines, leaving thousands of homes and businesses without electrical power for days. Our family kept basic energy coming into the house through a generator, but we were still unable to cook meals. As we set out to find a place to eat, we drove for miles past closed businesses. We finally found a breakfast restaurant that had not lost power, but it was packed with hungry customers who were in the same fix as we were.

When a woman came over to take our order for food, she said, "I'm not really an employee of this restaurant. Our church group was having breakfast here, and we saw how the staff was overwhelmed with so many customers who came in. We told the restaurant management we would be willing to help by waiting on tables if it would ease the burden and help people to get fed."

Her willingness to serve reminded me of Paul's words: "As we have opportunity, let us do good to all" (GAL. 6:10). In light of the many needs around us, I wonder what could happen if we all asked God to show us opportunities to serve Him and help others today. *DENNIS FISHER*

Dear Lord, show us where and how we might serve others and ease their burdens. Give us hearts of love and compassion that reflect your love. Then help us to take action.

We follow the example of Christ when we serve people in need.

Extraordinary Showers

Read: Ezekiel 34:25–31

There will be showers of blessing. –v. 26

What do fish, tadpoles, and spiders have in common? They have all fallen from the sky like rain in various parts of the world. Fish fell on the Australian town of Lajamanu. Tadpoles pelted areas of central Japan on multiple occasions. Spiders showered down on the San Bernardo Mountains in Argentina. Although scientists suspect that the wind plays a part in these intriguing showers, no one can fully explain them.

The prophet Ezekiel described a far more extraordinary downpour—a shower of blessing (EZEK. 34:26). Ezekiel spoke of a time when God would send blessings like rain to refresh His people. The Israelites would be safe from enemy nations. They would have enough food, be liberated from slavery, and be freed from shame (VV. 27–29). These gifts would revive Israel's relationship with God. The people would know that God was with them, and that "they, the Israelites, are [His] people" (V. 30).

God blesses His modern-day followers too (JAMES 1:17). Sometimes blessings abound like rain; sometimes they trickle in one by one. Whether many or few, the good things we receive come with a message from God: *I see your needs. You are mine, and I will care for you.* *JENNIFER BENSON SCHULDT*

"There shall be showers of blessing"—
this is the promise of love;
there shall be seasons refreshing,
sent from the Savior above.
WHITTLE

Daily blessings are daily reminders of God.

Love Letter

Read: Psalm 119:97–104

Oh, how I love your law! I meditate on it all day long. –v. 97

Each morning when I reach my office, I have one simple habit—check all my e-mails. Most of the time, I'll work through them in a perfunctory fashion. There are some e-mails, however, that I'm eager to open. You guessed it—those from loved ones.

Someone has said that the Bible is God's love letter to us. But perhaps on some days, like me, you just don't feel like opening it and your heart doesn't resonate with the words of the psalmist: "Oh, how I love *your* law!" (PS. 119:97). The Scriptures are "*your* commands" (v. 98), "*your* statutes" (v. 99), "*your* precepts" (v. 100), "*your* word" (v. 101, emphasis added).

A question by Thomas Manton (1620–1677), once a lecturer at Westminster Abbey, still holds relevance for us today. He asked: "Who is the author of Scripture? God. . . . What is the end of Scripture? God. Why was the Scripture written, but that we might everlastingly enjoy the blessed God?"

It is said of some people that the more you know them the less you admire them; but the reverse is true of God. Familiarity with the Word of God, or rather the God of the Word, breeds affection, and affection seeks yet greater familiarity.

As you open your Bible, remember that God—the One who loves you the most—has a message for you. *POH FANG CHIA*

Oh, may I love Thy precious Word,
may I explore the mine,
may I its fragrant flowers glean,
may light upon me shine!
HODDER

Knowing the Bible helps us know the God of the Bible.

Too Late to Change?

Read: John 3:1–8, 13–16

How can someone be born when they are old? –v. 4

There are sayings in many languages about the difficulty of changing long-established habits. In English, "You can't teach an old dog new tricks." In French, *"Ce n'est pas a un vieux singe qu'on apprend a faire la grimace"* (You can't teach an old monkey how to pull a funny face). In Spanish, *"El loro viejo no aprende a hablar"* (An old parrot can't learn to speak).

When Jesus told Nicodemus that he must be "born again" to "see the kingdom of God," he replied, "How can someone be born when they are old? . . . Surely they cannot enter a second time into their mother's womb to be born!" (JOHN 3:3–4). Professor and author Merrill Tenney suggests that Nicodemus was saying, in effect, "I acknowledge that a new birth is necessary, but I am too old to change. My pattern of life is set. Physical birth is out of the question and psychological rebirth seems even less probable . . . . Is not my case hopeless?"

Jesus's reply included these words, "For God so loved the world that he gave his one and only Son, that whoever believes in him shall not perish but have eternal life" (v. 16). That is the offer of new life and a new beginning for anyone, young or old.

Whatever our age or situation in life, with God's power, it's not too late to change.

DAVID MCCASLAND

Father, old habits are hard to break,
new ones are harder to learn,
and sometimes we don't want to do either.
Thank you for your faithfulness to continue teaching us
new ways, your ways.

Because God is powerful, change is possible.

What's Your Motto?

Read: Luke 12:4–7, 22–32

Don't be afraid; you are worth more than many sparrows. –v. 7

Grug Crood, the dad of a caveman family in an animated movie, believes that there's no safe place beyond their cave. They huddle together at night so he can protect them. He thinks his teenage daughter should give up her adventurous side because it can only lead to danger. His motto for his family is "Never *not* be afraid." In other words, "*Always* be afraid."

Jesus often told His followers the opposite: "Don't be afraid." He said that to Simon when He called him to follow Him (LUKE 5:10). When Jairus, a synagogue leader whose daughter was dying, came to Him, Jesus reassured him with those same words of care (8:50).

Luke 12 records Jesus telling His disciples not to be afraid when He taught them how God cared for them much more than for the sparrows (v. 7). And after His resurrection, Jesus told the women who came to the tomb, "Do not be afraid" (MATT. 28:10).

Fear is a universal feeling. We have concerns about loved ones, our needs, and the unknown future. How can we learn to have faith? The Lord has given us a foundation on which to build our confidence in Him: "He Himself has said, 'I will never leave you nor forsake you.' So we may boldly say: 'The Lord is my helper; I will not fear' " (HEB. 13:5–6 NKJV). *ANNE CETAS*

Father, life in this world can sometimes be scary.
Thank you for the promise that your love and care will
never be taken away from us. When fear seems overwhelming,
help us to remember your promises.

The love of God frees us from the prison of fear.

A Storyteller

Read: Colossians 1:13–23

Once you were alienated from God . . . . But now he has reconciled you. —vv. 21–22

In the years following the American Civil War (1861–1865), Union Major General Lew Wallace served as a governor of the New Mexico territories; New Mexico not yet having been admitted as a state. His work there put him in contact with many of the characters that make up the Wild West's near-mythic history, including Billy the Kid and Sheriff Pat Garrett. It was here that Wallace wrote what has been called by some "the most influential Christian book" of the 19th century, *Ben-Hur: A Tale of the Christ.*

Wallace witnessed the worst impact of sin on humanity as he saw the violence of the Civil War and the Wild West. In life and in his best-selling book, Wallace understood that only the story of Jesus Christ has the power of redemption and reconciliation.

For the follower of Christ, the climax of our lives was the moment God "rescued us from the dominion of darkness and brought us into the kingdom of the Son he loves, in whom we have redemption, the forgiveness of sins" (COL. 1:13–14). Now we have the privilege of being storytellers of God's wonderful redemption. *RANDY KILGORE*

Lord, please take control of my words today.
Fill me with your words of love and grace.
Use them to turn some heart toward you.
I can do nothing without you.

The difference Christ makes in your life is a story worth telling.

JANUARY 13

Out of the Darkness

Read: Psalm 77:1–15

I cried out to God . . . . What god is as great as our God? –vv. 1, 13

I don't know what desperate situation gripped Asaph, the writer of Psalm 77, but I've heard, and made, similar laments. Over the past dozen years since I lost my daughter, many others who have experienced the loss of a loved one have shared with me heartbreaking sentiments like these:

Crying out to God (v. 1). Stretching empty arms heavenward (v. 2). Experiencing troubling thoughts about God because of horrible circumstances (v. 3). Enduring unspeakable trouble (v. 4). Cowering under the feeling of being cast aside (v. 7). Fearing failed promises (v. 8). Fearing a lack of mercy (v. 8).

But a turnaround occurs for Asaph in verse 10 through a recollection of God's great works. Thoughts turn to God's love. To memories of what He has done. To His marvelous deeds of old. To the comfort of God's faithfulness and mercy. To reminders of God's wonders and greatness. To His strength and redemption.

Despair is real in this life, and answers do not come easily. Yet in the darkness—as we remember God's glory, majesty, power, and love—our despair can slowly subside. Like Asaph, we can rehearse God's acts, especially the salvation He brought through Jesus, and we can return to where we once were—resting gratefully in His mighty love. *DAVE BRANON*

Lord, we cannot fathom the depth of your character
or the wisdom of your actions when trouble visits us.
Help us to inch our way back into your arms through a rehearsal of
your goodness and a recollection of your glorious love.

Remembering the past can bring hope to the present.

JANUARY 14

It's Worth It

Read: 2 Corinthians 11:24–33

If I must boast, I will boast of the things that show my weakness. —v. 30

"I can't do it," Robert said, throwing his pencil down in despair. "It's just too hard!" Reading, writing, and spelling seemed impossible to our dyslexic 9-year-old. At last, a solution was offered. But it was tough. We had to do reading and spelling practice with him for 20 minutes every evening—without exception. Sometimes we just didn't feel like doing it, and at times we despaired of seeing progress. But we were committed to getting Robert's reading age and his chronological age to match, so we battled on.

After 2½ years, all the tears and struggles seemed infinitely worthwhile. Robert learned to read and spell. And we all learned patient endurance.

The apostle Paul suffered all sorts of hardships as he pursued his goal of sharing the good news of Jesus with those who had never heard. Persecuted, beaten, imprisoned, and misunderstood, sometimes he faced death itself (2 COR. 11:25). But the joy of seeing people respond to his message made it all worthwhile.

If you feel that the task God has called you to is too hard, remember that the spiritual lessons and joy that are wrapped up in the journey may seem hidden at first, but they are certainly there! God will help you find them. *MARION STROUD*

Sometimes we learn that hardships were blessings in disguise,
that earnest work and faith in God were proven to be wise.
HESS

The journey is as important as the destination.

Kindness Gone Viral

Read: Mark 10:13–16

Let the little children come to me, and do not hinder them, for the kingdom of God belongs to such as these. —v. 14

News of a simple act of kindness on a New York subway has gone around the world. A young man, head covered by a hooded sweatshirt, fell asleep on the shoulder of an older passenger. When someone else offered to wake the young rider, the older man quietly said, "He must have had a long day. Let him sleep. We've all been there." Then he let the tired fellow rider sleep on his shoulder for the better part of the next hour, until the older man gently eased away to get up for his stop. In the meantime, another passenger snapped a photograph and posted it on social media, and it went viral.

The man's kindness seems to resonate with what we all long for—the kindness that reflects the heart of God. We see this gentleness in Jesus when His friends tried to protect Him from the noise and bother of little children. Instead, Jesus insisted on taking the little ones in His arms and blessing them (MARK 10:16). In the process, He invited all of us to trust Him like a little child (vv. 13–16).

Jesus lets us know that all of us are safe in His presence. Whether awake or asleep, we can lean on Him. When we're exhausted, He provides a safe place for us to rest.

MART DEHAAN

Under His wings, I am safely abiding, though the night deepens
and tempests are wild; still I can trust Him—I know He will keep me,
He has redeemed me and I am His child.

CUSHING

God is a safe resting place.

You Had to Act

Read: John 7:37–46

No one ever spoke the way this man does. –v. 46

A US congressman, John Lewis, was 23 years old when he participated in the historic 1963 civil rights "March on Washington" led by Dr. Martin Luther King Jr. Half a century later, journalist Bill Moyers asked Lewis how he was affected by Dr. King's "I Have a Dream" speech that day. Mr. Lewis replied, "You couldn't leave after hearing him speak and go back to business as usual. You had to do something, you had to act. You had to move. You had to go out and spread the good news."

Many who encountered Jesus found it impossible to remain neutral about Him. John 7:25-46 records two different reactions to Jesus. While "many in the crowd believed in him" (v. 31), the religious leaders tried to silence Him by sending temple guards to arrest Him (v. 32). The guards were likely present when Jesus said, "Let anyone who is thirsty come to me and drink. Whoever believes in me, as the Scripture has said, rivers of living water will flow from within them" (vv. 37–38). The guards returned without Jesus and were asked, "Why didn't you bring him in?" (v. 45). They answered, "No one ever spoke the way this man does" (v. 46).

The words of Jesus compel us to act, and to move, beyond business as usual. *DAVID MCCASLAND*

So let our lips and lives express the holy gospel we profess;
so let our works and virtues shine, to prove the doctrine all divine.
WATTS

Jesus's death forgave my past sins and inspires my present obedience.

Leaving It Behind

Read: John 4:9–14, 27–29

Then, leaving her water jar, the woman . . . said to the people, "Come, see a man who told me everything I ever did. Could this be the Messiah?" —vv. 28–29

In the year or so after our teenage son got his driver's license and started carrying a wallet, we got several calls from people who had found it somewhere. We cautioned him to be more careful and not leave it behind.

Leaving things behind, though, is not always a bad thing. In John 4, we read about a woman who had come to draw water at a well. But after she encountered Jesus that day, her intent suddenly changed. Leaving her water jar behind, she hurried back to tell others what Jesus had said to her (vv. 28–29). Even her physical need for water paled in comparison to telling others about the Man she had just met.

Peter and Andrew did something similar when Jesus called them. They left their fishing nets (which was the way they earned their living) to follow Jesus (MATT. 4:18–20). And James and John left their nets, boat, and even their father when Jesus called them (vv. 21–22).

Our new life of following Jesus Christ may mean that we have to leave things behind, including those that don't bring lasting satisfaction. What we once craved cannot compare with the life and "living water" that Jesus offers.

CINDY HESS KASPER

Now none but Christ can satisfy, none other name for me;
there's love and life and lasting joy, Lord Jesus, found in Thee.

MCGRANAHAN

Christ showed His love by dying for us; we show ours by living for Him.

The Wonder of Sight

Read: Psalm 139:7–16

I praise you because I am fearfully and wonderfully made; your works are wonderful, I know that full well. —v. 14

On the livescience.com website, I read something pretty amazing: "If you were standing atop a mountain surveying a larger-than-usual patch of the planet, you could perceive bright lights hundreds of miles distant. On a dark night, you could even see a candle flame flickering up to 30 miles (48 km) away." No telescopes or night-vision goggles needed—the human eye is so profoundly designed that even long distances can be spanned with clear sight.

This fact is a vivid reminder of our amazing Creator, who designed not only the human eye but also all of the details that make up our expansive universe. And, unlike anything else in creation, God has made us in His own image (GEN. 1:26). "In His image" speaks of something far greater than the ability to see. It speaks of a likeness to God that makes it possible for us to be in relationship with Him.

We can affirm David's declaration, "I praise you because I am fearfully and wonderfully made; your works are wonderful, I know that full well" (PS. 139:14). Not only have we been given eyes to see, but we have also been made so that, in Christ, one day we will see Him! *BILL CROWDER*

Lord, how Thy wonders are displayed wherever I turn my eye,
if I survey the ground I tread or gaze upon the sky!
WATTS

All of God's creation bears witness to Him as our great Creator.

God's Refreshing Word

Read: Isaiah 55:8–11

[My word] . . . will not return to me empty. –v. 11

When I was a boy, our family would occasionally travel across Nevada. We loved the desert thunderstorms. Accompanied by lightning bolts and claps of thunder, huge sheets of rain would blanket the hot sand as far as the eye could see. The cooling water refreshed the earth and us.

Water produces marvelous changes in arid regions. For example, the pincushion cactus is completely dormant during the dry season. But after the first summer rains, cactuses burst into bloom, displaying delicate petals of pink, gold, and white.

Likewise, in the Holy Land after a rainstorm, dry ground can seemingly sprout vegetation overnight. Isaiah used rain's renewal to illustrate God's refreshing Word: "As the rain and the snow come down from heaven, and do not return to it without watering the earth and making it bud and flourish, so that it yields seed for the sower and bread for the eater, so is my word that goes out from my mouth; it will not return to me empty, but it will accomplish what I desire and achieve the purpose for which I sent it" (ISA. 55:10–11).

Scripture carries spiritual vitality. That's why it doesn't return void. Wherever it encounters an open heart, it brings refreshment, nourishment, and new life.

DENNIS FISHER

God's Word is like refreshing rain that waters crops and seed;
it brings new life to open hearts, and meets us in our need.

SPER

The Bible is to a thirsty soul what water is to a barren land.

When God Is Quiet

Read: 1 Kings 19:1–12

Then [Elijah] lay down under the bush and fell asleep. All at once an angel touched him and said, "Get up and eat." —v. 5

I love to take pictures of sunsets at Lake Michigan. Some are subtle shades of pastel. Others are bold strokes of bright color. Sometimes the sun sinks quietly behind the lake. Other times it goes down in what looks like a fiery explosion.

In pictures and in person, I prefer the latter. But both show the handiwork of God. When it comes to God's work in the world, my preferences are the same. I would rather see dramatic answers to prayer than ordinary provisions of daily bread. But both are the work of God.

Elijah may have had similar preferences. He had grown accustomed to being the center of God's grand displays of power. When he prayed, God showed up in dramatic ways—first in a miraculous defeat against the prophets of Baal and then in the end to a long and devastating drought (1 KINGS 18). But then Elijah felt afraid and started to run. God sent an angel to feed him to strengthen him for his journey. After 40 days he arrived in Horeb. God showed him that He was now communicating in a still small voice, not in flashy miracles (19:11–12).

If you're discouraged because God hasn't shown up in a blaze of glory, perhaps He's revealing himself with His quiet presence. *JULIE ACKERMAN LINK*

Lord, may we see you today in the small details of life in ways that we hadn't noticed before. Thank you for the gift of your quiet presence, wherever we may find it today.

God is in the small things as well as the great.

Pointing to God

Read: Deuteronomy 8:11–18

Remember your Creator . . . before the days of trouble come. –Ecclesiastes 12:1

"God bless our homeland, Ghana" is the first line of Ghana's national anthem. Other African anthems include: "O Uganda, may God uphold thee," "Lord, bless our nation" (South Africa), and "O God of creation, direct our noble cause" (Nigeria). Using the anthems as prayers, founding fathers called on God to bless their land and its people. Many national anthems in Africa and others from around the world point to God as Creator and Provider. Other lines of anthems call for reconciliation, transformation, and hope for a people often divided along ethnic, political, and social lines.

Yet today, many national leaders and citizens tend to forget God and do not live by these statements—especially when life is going well. But why wait until war, disease, storms, terrorist attacks, or election violence occurs before we remember to seek God? Moses warned the ancient Israelites not to forget God and not to stop following His ways when life was good (DEUT. 8:11). Ecclesiastes 12:1 urges us to "remember your Creator . . . before the days of trouble come."

Getting close to God while we are strong and healthy prepares us to lean on Him for support and hope when those difficult days in life come.

LAWRENCE DARMANI

Father, I always need you. Forgive me for thinking I am sufficient in myself. Help me to follow you and your ways whether life is easy or difficult. Thank you for caring for me.

Remembering our Creator can be our personal anthem.

A Wonderful Explosion

Read: John 13:31–35

As I have loved you, so you must love one another. —v. 34

In the book *Kisses from Katie,* Katie Davis recounts the joy of moving to Uganda and adopting several Ugandan girls. One day, one of her daughters asked, "Mommy, if I let Jesus come into my heart, will I explode?" At first, Katie said no. When Jesus enters our heart, it is a spiritual event.

However, after she thought more about the question, Katie explained that when we decide to give our lives and hearts to Jesus "we will explode with love, with compassion, with hurt for those who are hurting, and with joy for those who rejoice." In essence, knowing Christ results in a deep care for the people in our world.

The Bible challenges us to "rejoice with those who rejoice; mourn with those who mourn" (ROM. 12:15). We can consistently display this loving response because of the Holy Spirit's work in our hearts. When we receive Christ, the Holy Spirit comes to live inside us. The apostle Paul described it this way, "When you believed [in Christ,] you were marked in him with a seal, the promised Holy Spirit" (EPH. 1:13).

Caring for others—with God's supernatural assistance—shows the world that we are His followers (JOHN 13:35). It also reminds us of His love for us. Jesus said, "As I have loved you, so you must love one another" (v. 34).

JENNIFER BENSON SCHULDT

Dear Jesus, help me to experience your love more deeply so that I can share it with others. Empower me through your Holy Spirit so that I can glorify you.

Love given reflects love received.

When Others Won't Forgive

Read: Philippians 3:12–16

Forgetting what is behind . . . I press on toward the goal. –vv. 13–14

I was having lunch with two men who had opened their lives to Christ while they were in prison. The younger man had been discouraged by the fact that the family from whom he had stolen would not forgive him.

"My crime was violent," the older man said. "It continues to haunt and affect the family to this day. They have not forgiven me, . . . the pain is just too great. At first, I found myself paralyzed by this longing for their forgiveness." He continued his story: "Then one day I realized I was adding selfishness to my brokenness. It's a lot to expect that the family forgive me. I was focused on what I felt I needed to heal from my past. It took some time to realize that their forgiveness of me was a matter between them and God."

"How can you stand it?" the younger man asked.

The older man explained that God did for him what he didn't deserve and what others simply can't do: He died for our sins, and He keeps His promise to move our sins "as far as the east is from the west" (PS. 103:12) and "remembers [our] sins no more" (ISA. 43:25).

In the face of such great love, we honor Him by accepting His forgiveness as sufficient. We must forget what lies behind and keep pressing forward (PHIL. 3:13–14). *RANDY KILGORE*

Thank you, Father, for the work of Christ on the cross.
Help me to understand and accept what it means for me, and to be
a messenger of that forgiveness to those I meet along the way.

The work of Christ is sufficient for every sin.

Answer the Cry

Read: Isaiah 30:15–22

How gracious [the LORD] will be when you cry for help! —v. 19

When my grandchildren were young, my son took them to see the stage production of *The Lion King*. As the young lion, Simba, stood over his father, King Mufasa, who had been killed by his evil uncle, little Simba, afraid and alone, cried out, "Help, Help, Help!" At that moment, my 3-year-old grandson stood on his chair in the hushed theater and shouted, "Why doesn't somebody help him?!"

The Old Testament contains many accounts of God's people crying out for help. Although their trouble was often self-imposed due to their waywardness, God was still eager to come to their aid.

The prophet Isaiah had to deliver a lot of bad news, but in the midst of it he assured the people that "the LORD longs to be gracious to you; therefore he will rise up to show you compassion. . . . How gracious he will be when you cry for help!" (ISA. 30:18–19). Yet God often looked to His own people to be the answer to that cry for help (SEE ISA. 58:10).

Today, people all around us are in need of someone to take action to help them. It is a high privilege to become the hands of God as we respond on His behalf to cries for help. *JOE STOWELL*

Lord, remind me that you desire to show compassion
to those in need and that you often call on us to be
the instruments of that compassion. Give me an opportunity today
to show your love to at least one person in need.

Show that God cares by lending a helping hand.

Quiet Rest

Read: Mark 6:30–32; Psalm 4:7–8

In peace I will lie down and sleep, for you alone, LORD, make me dwell in safety. –Psalm 4:8

Some years ago my son Brian and I agreed to haul some equipment into an isolated Idaho backcountry ranch for a friend. There are no roads into the area, at least none that my truck could negotiate. So Ralph, the young ranch manager, arranged to meet us at road's end with a small wagon hitched to a pair of mules.

On the way into the ranch, Ralph and I started chatting and I learned that he lived on the property year-round. "What do you do in the winter?" I asked, knowing that winters in the high country were long and bitter and that the ranch had no electricity or telephone service, only a satellite radio. "How do you endure it?"

"Actually," he drawled, "I find it right peaceable."

In the midst of our pressure-filled days, we sometimes crave peace and quiet. There is too much noise in the air; there are too many people around. We want to "come aside . . . and rest a while" (MARK 6:31 NKJV). Can we find a place to do this?

Yes, there is such a place. When we take a few moments to reflect on God's love and mercy and cast our burdens on Him, we will find in that quiet God-filled space the peace that the world has taken away. *DAVID ROPER*

There is a place of quiet rest, near to the heart of God,
a place where all is joy and peace, near to the heart of God.
MCAFEE

Spending quiet time with God will bring quiet rest.

Strengthen My Hands

Read: Nehemiah 6:1–9, 15

Now strengthen my hands. —v. 9

Singapore's first Prime Minister, Lee Kuan Yew, is the man credited with making Singapore what it is today. During his leadership, Singapore grew to be rich and prosperous and one of the most developed nations in Asia. Asked if he ever felt like giving up when he faced criticism and challenges during his many years of public service, he replied, "This is a lifelong commitment."

Nehemiah, who led in the rebuilding of the wall of Jerusalem, refused to give up. He faced insults and intimidation from the enemies all around him as well as injustices from his own people (NEH. 4–5). His enemies even insinuated that he had a personal agenda (6:6–7). He sought help from God while taking every defensive step he could.

Despite the challenges, the wall was completed in 52 days (6:15). But Nehemiah's work was not complete. He encouraged the Israelites to study the Scriptures, to worship, and to keep God's law. After completing 12 years as governor (5:14), he returned to make sure his reforms were continuing (13:6). Nehemiah had a lifelong commitment to leading the people.

We all face challenges and difficulties in life. But as God helped Nehemiah, He will also strengthen our hands (6:9) for the rest of our lives in whatever tasks He gives to us. *C. P. Hia*

Dear Lord, sometimes it's easy to get discouraged
when faced with criticism or challenges.
Help me to persevere and grant me the strength to
be faithful to what you have called me to do.

Life's challenges are designed not to break us but to bend us toward God.

The Hand of God

Read: Psalm 63:1–8

I cling to you; your right hand upholds me. —v. 8

When NASA began using a new kind of space telescope to capture different spectrums of light, researchers were surprised at one of the photos. It shows what looks like fingers, a thumb, and an open palm showered with spectacular colors of blue, purple, green, and gold. Some have called it "The Hand of God."

The idea of God reaching out His hand to help us in our time of need is a central theme of Scripture. In Psalm 63 we read: "Because you are my help, I sing in the shadow of your wings. I cling to you; your right hand upholds me" (vv. 7–8). The psalmist felt God's divine help like a hand of support. Some Bible teachers believe that King David wrote this psalm in the wilderness of Judah during the terrible time of his son Absalom's rebellion. Absalom had conspired to dethrone his father, and David fled to the wilderness (2 SAM. 15–16). Even during this difficult time, God was present and David trusted in Him. He said, "Because your love is better than life, my lips will glorify you" (PS. 63:3).

Life can be painful at times, yet God offers His comforting hand in the midst of it. We are not beyond His reach. *DENNIS FISHER*

Beneath His watchful eye His saints securely dwell;
that hand which bears all nature up shall guard His children well.
DODDRIDGE

God bears the world's weight on His shoulder, yet holds His children in the palm of His hand.

Whose Will?

Read: Genesis 39:1–6, 20–23

"My Father, if it is possible, may this cup be taken from me. Yet not as I will, but as you will." —Matthew 26:39

"May all things happen according to your will" is a greeting frequently exchanged during Chinese New Year. As wonderful as that may sound, events turn out best when God's will plays out and not mine.

Given a choice, Joseph would not have wished to be a slave in Egypt (GEN. 39:1). But despite his captivity, he "prospered" because "the LORD was with [him]" (v. 2). The Lord even blessed his master's home "because of Joseph" (v. 5).

Joseph would never have chosen to go to prison in Egypt. But he did when falsely accused of sexual assault. However, for the second time we read: "the LORD was with him" (v. 21). There, he gained the trust of the warden (v. 22) so that the Lord "gave him success in whatever he did" (v. 23). His downward spiral into prison turned out to be the start of his rise to the top position in Egypt. Few people would choose to be promoted the way God promoted Joseph. But Joseph's God blesses, despite, and even through, adverse circumstances.

God had a purpose for bringing Joseph to Egypt, and He has a purpose for placing us where we are. Instead of wishing that all things happened according to our will, we could say, as our Savior did before going to the cross, "Not as I will, but as you will" (MATT. 26:39). *C. P. HIA*

Lord, it is far too easy to chase my own desires and passions. Forgive me for my selfish wants and pursuit of self-centered activities. Help me to place you first and to look for what you are doing and want to do in my life.

Patient waiting is often the highest way of doing God's will.

Our Source of Help

Read: Psalm 121

My help comes from the LORD, the Maker of heaven and earth. –v. 2

Twenty-year-old Lygon Stevens, an experienced mountaineer, had reached the summits of Mt. McKinley, Mt. Rainier, four Andean peaks in Ecuador, and 39 of Colorado's highest mountains. "I climb because I love the mountains," she said, "and I meet God there." In January 2008, Lygon died in an avalanche while climbing Little Bear Peak in southern Colorado with her brother Nicklis, who survived.

When her parents discovered her journals, they were deeply moved by the intimacy of her walk with Christ. "Always a shining light for Him," her mother said, "Lygon experienced a depth and honesty in her relationship with the Lord, which even seasoned veterans of faith long to have."

In Lygon's final journal entry, written from her tent 3 days before the avalanche, she said: "God is good, and He has a plan for our lives that is greater and more blessed than the lives we pick out for ourselves, and I am so thankful about that. Thank You, Lord, for bringing me this far and to this place. I leave the rest—my future—in those same hands and say thank You."

Lygon echoed these words from the psalmist: "My help comes from the LORD, the Maker of heaven and earth" (PS. 121:2). *DAVID MCCASLAND*

O God, our help in ages past, our hope for years to come.
Still be our guard while troubles last and our eternal home.
WATTS

We can trust our all-knowing God for the unknown future.

Sledding and Praying

Read: Mark 14:32–42

One of those days Jesus went out to a mountainside to pray, and spent the night praying to God. –Luke 6:12

When the snow flies in Michigan, I like to get my grandkids, grab our plastic sleds, and go slipping and sliding down our backyard. We zoom down the hill for about 10 seconds, and then climb back up for more.

When I travel to Alaska with a bunch of teenagers, we also go sledding. We are hauled by bus nearly to the top of a mountain. We jump on our sleds and, for the next 10 to 20 minutes (depending on levels of bravery), we slide at breakneck speeds down the mountain, holding on for dear life.

Ten seconds in my backyard or 10 minutes down an Alaskan mountain. They're both called sledding, but there is clearly a difference.

I've been thinking about this in regard to prayer. Sometimes we do the "10 seconds in the backyard" kind of praying—a quick, spur-of-the-moment prayer or a short thanks before eating. At other times, we're drawn to "down the mountain" praying—extended, intense times that require concentration and passion in our relationship with Him. Both have their place and are vital to our lives.

Jesus prayed often, and sometimes for a long time (Luke 6:12; Mark 14:32-42). Either way, let us bring the desires of our heart to the God of the backyards and the mountains of our lives. *DAVE BRANON*

Lord, please challenge us to pray constantly—both in short sessions and long. As we face the valleys, hills, and mountains of our lives, may we lift our hearts and minds to you in constant communication.

The heart of prayer is prayer from the heart.

A Closing Door

Read: 2 Cor. 5:18–6:2

Now is the time of God's favor, now is the day of salvation. —v. 2

Beep, beep, beep, beep. The warning sound and flashing lights alerted commuters that the train door was about to close. Yet a few tardy individuals still made a frenzied scramble across the platform and onto the train. The door closed on one of them. Thankfully, it rebounded and the passenger boarded the train safely. I wondered why people took such risks when the next train would arrive in a mere 4 minutes.

There is a far more important door that we must enter before it closes. It is the door of God's mercy. The apostle Paul tells us, "Now is the time of God's favor, now is the day of salvation" (2 COR. 6:2). Christ has come, died for our sins, and has risen from the grave. He has opened the way for us to be reconciled to God and has proclaimed for us the day of salvation.

Today is that day. But one day the door of mercy will close. To those who received and served Christ, He will say, "Come, you who are blessed by my Father; take your inheritance, the kingdom prepared for you" (MATT. 25:34). But those who don't know Him will be turned away (v. 46).

Our response to Jesus Christ determines our destiny. Today Jesus invites, "I am the gate; whoever enters through me will be saved" (JOHN 10:9).

POH FANG CHIA

Today Thy gate is open, and all who enter in shall find
a Father's welcome, and pardon for their sin.

ALLEN

There's no better day than today to enter into God's family.

Blended Together

Read: Ephesians 4:5–16

We are God's handiwork, created in Christ Jesus to do good works. –2:10

My wife, Janet, bought me a new Dreadnought D-35 guitar for my 65th birthday. Originally developed in the early 1900s, the Dreadnought style is larger than most guitars designed during that time, and it's known for its bold and loud tone. It was named after the large World War I British battleship the HMS *Dreadnought*. The back of the D-35 is unique. Because of the shortage of wide pieces of high quality rosewood, the craftsmen innovatively fit three smaller pieces of wood together, which resulted in a richer tone.

God's workmanship is a lot like that innovative guitar design. Jesus takes fragments and blends them together to bring Him praise. He recruited tax collectors, Jewish revolutionaries, fishermen, and others to be His followers. And down through the centuries Christ continues to call out people from varied walks of life. The apostle Paul tells us, "He makes the whole body fit together perfectly. As each part does its own special work, it helps the other parts grow, so that the whole body is healthy and growing and full of love" (EPH. 4:16 NLT).

In the Master's hand many kinds of people are fit together and are being built into something with great potential for praise to God and service for others.

DENNIS FISHER

Thank you, Lord, that you have placed us in your family—
that you are using us individually and together to bring you honor.
Help us to live in your power.

We can accomplish more together than we can alone.

For Our Health

Read: 1 Chronicles 16:7–14

Give praise to the LORD —v. 8

According to a prominent Duke University Medical Center researcher, "If thankfulness were a drug, it would be the world's best-selling product with [health benefits] for every major organ system."

For some, being thankful means simply living with a sense of gratitude—taking time to recognize and focus on the things we have, instead of the things we wish we had. The Bible takes the idea of thankfulness to a deeper level. The act of giving thanks causes us to recognize the One who provides our blessings (JAMES 1:17).

David knew that God was responsible for the safe delivery of the ark of the covenant in Jerusalem (1 CHRON. 15:26). As a result, he penned a song of gratitude that centered on God instead of simply expressing his delight in an important event. The ballad began: "Give praise to the LORD, proclaim his name; make known among the nations what he has done" (16:8). David's song went on to rejoice in God's greatness, highlighting God's salvation, creative power, and mercy (VV. 25–36).

Today we can be truly thankful by worshiping the Giver instead of the gifts we enjoy. Focusing on the good things in our lives may benefit our bodies, but directing our thanks to God benefits our souls.

JENNIFER BENSON SCHULDT

Gratitude is our natural response to God's grace.
Nothing so takes the heart out of a person as ingratitude.
Gratitude is not only the greatest of virtues, but the parent of all the others.
CICERO

True thanksgiving emphasizes the Giver rather than the gifts.

Chinese Proverbs

Read: 2 Timothy 2:1–6

Always give yourselves fully to the work of the Lord, because you know that your labor in the Lord is not in vain. –1 Corinthians 15:58

Chinese proverbs are common and often have stories behind them. The proverb "pulling up a crop to help it grow" is about an impatient man in the Song Dynasty. He was eager to see his rice seedlings grow quickly. So he thought of a solution. He would pull up each plant a few inches. After a day of tedious work, the man surveyed his paddy field. He was happy that his crop seemed to have "grown" taller. But his joy was short-lived. The next day, the plants had begun to wither because their roots were no longer deep.

In 2 Timothy 2:6, the apostle Paul compares the work of being a minister of the gospel to that of a farmer. He wrote to encourage Timothy that, like farming, making disciples can be continuous, hard labor. You plow, you sow, you wait, you pray. You desire to see the fruits of your labor quickly, but growth takes time. And as the Chinese proverb so aptly illustrates, any effort to hurry the process won't be helpful. Commentator William Hendriksen states: "If Timothy . . . exerts himself to the full in the performance of his God-given spiritual task, he . . . will see in the lives of others . . . the beginnings of those glorious fruits that are mentioned in Galatians 5:22, 23."

As we labor faithfully, we wait patiently on the Lord, who makes things grow (1 COR. 3:7).

POH FANG CHIA

Dear Lord of the harvest, help us to work faithfully as we wait patiently on you for the fruit. Encourage us when we are discouraged and strengthen us when we are weary. Help us to persevere, for you are faithful.

We sow the seed—God produces the harvest.

What Money Can't Buy

Read: Ephesians 1:3–14

In him we have redemption through his blood, the forgiveness of sins, in accordance with the riches of God's grace. –v. 7

"There are some things money can't buy—but these days, not many" according to Michael Sandel, author of *What Money Can't Buy*. A person can buy a prison-cell upgrade for $90 a night, the right to shoot an endangered black rhino for $250,000, and your doctor's cell phone number for $1,500. It seems that "almost everything is up for sale."

But one thing money can't buy is *redemption*—freedom from the stranglehold of sin. When the apostle Paul began writing about the rich nature of God's plan of salvation through Jesus, his heart erupted in praise: "In him we have redemption through his blood, the forgiveness of sins, in accordance with the riches of God's grace that he lavished on us" (EPH. 1:7–8).

Jesus's death on the cross was the high cost of delivering us from sin. And only He could pay that price because He was the perfect Son of God. The natural response to such free but costly grace is spontaneous praise from our hearts and commitment to the God who bought us through Jesus (1:13–14).

Praise to our loving God—He has come to set us free!

MARVIN WILLIAMS

What amazing love you have for us, heavenly Father!
That you gave your Son who willingly died in our place.
It seems too good to be true. Thank you!

Only Jesus's death could purchase our freedom.

Habits of a Healthy Mind

Read: Psalm 37:1–8

Trust in the LORD and do good. —v. 3

There is much said today about improving our health by developing habits of optimism, whether facing a difficult medical diagnosis or a pile of dirty laundry. Barbara Fredrickson, PhD, a psychology professor at the University of North Carolina, says we should try activities that build joy, gratitude, love, and other positive feelings. We know, however, that more is required than a general wish for good feelings. We need a strong conviction that there is a source of joy, peace, and love upon which we can depend.

Psalm 37:1–8 gives positive actions we can take as an antidote to pessimism and discouragement. Consider these mood boosters: Trust in the Lord, do good, dwell in the land, enjoy safe pasture (v. 3); delight in the Lord (v. 4); commit your way to the Lord; trust in Him (v. 5); be still before the Lord, wait patiently for Him, do not fret (v. 7); refrain from anger, turn from wrath (v. 8).

Because they are connected to the phrase "in the Lord," those directives are more than wishful thinking or unrealistic suggestions. It's because of Jesus, and in His strength, that they become possible.

Our one true source for optimism is the redemption that is in Jesus. He is our reason for hope! *DAVID MCCASLAND*

Lord, we can't manufacture hope, and even if we tried it wouldn't be real. Help us to find hope in you because of what Jesus has done for us. We know you are walking beside us.

When there's bad news, our hope is the good news of Jesus.

In Disguise

Read: Genesis 45:4–8

How abundant are the good things that you have stored up for those who fear you. —Psalm 31:19

In the weeks after my husband survived a heart attack, we often thanked God for sparing his life. I was asked many times during the next few months how I was doing. My answer was often a simple one: "Blessed. I feel blessed."

Blessings, however, come in different sizes and shapes. In fact, we don't always recognize them. Even when we are doing everything we think God wants us to do, we may still experience suffering. We are sometimes surprised that God does not answer the way we want or that His timing appears to be tardy.

We see this in Joseph's life. From a human perspective, we would think that God had forgotten all about him. For more than a decade, Joseph experienced suffering. He was tossed in a pit, sold into slavery, falsely accused, unjustly put in prison. Finally, however, God's faithfulness to him became evident to all as he was lifted up as a ruler of Egypt and saved many people from famine (GEN. 37–46). C. S. Lewis wrote: "When we lose one blessing, another is often most unexpectedly given in its place."

God had always had His hand of blessing on Joseph, as He does for all who trust Him. "Oh, how great is Your goodness" (PS. 31:19 NKJV).

CINDY HESS KASPER

Lord, you love us with an extravagant love, but so often we don't trust you in the crisis. Help us to learn and appreciate that you have everything we need—and so much more.

True happiness is knowing that God is good.

Birthday Celebration

Read: Psalm 71:5–18

From birth I have relied on you; . . . I will ever praise you. –v. 6

I used to love birthdays. I can still remember standing excitedly on our front porch waiting for my friends to show up for my 5th birthday party. I wasn't just excited about the balloons, the gifts, and the cake. I was happy that I was no longer only 4! I was growing up.

As I've gotten older, however, birthdays have sometimes been more discouraging than exciting. Last year when I celebrated a birthday that marked me by decades more than by years, my wife, Martie, cheered me up with the reminder that I should be grateful to be growing older. She pointed me to Psalm 71, where the psalmist talks about God's presence throughout his life. He remembers that God "brought me forth from my mother's womb" (71:6), and he proclaims with thankfulness, "God, you have taught me, and to this day I declare your marvelous deeds" (v. 17). And now, when the psalmist is older, he has the honor to proclaim "[God's] power to the next generation, [His] mighty acts to all who are to come" (v. 18). God had blessed the psalmist with His presence through every year of his life.

Birthdays now remind me of God's faithfulness. And they bring me closer to being in the presence of the One who has been with me all these years!

JOE STOWELL

Lord, remind me often that growing older means
I am growing nearer to you! Keep my heart filled with gratitude
for your many blessings, and keep my mind fixed on the joy of heaven.

Count your many blessings—birthday by birthday!

Who's the Boss?

Read: Romans 6:1–14

Sin shall no longer be your master, because you are not under the law, but under grace. –v. 14

As my wife was babysitting our two young grandsons, they began to argue over a toy. Suddenly, the younger (by 3 years) forcefully ordered his older brother, "Cameron, go to your room!" Shoulders slumped under the weight of the reprimand, the dejected older brother began to slink off to his room when my wife said, "Cameron, you don't have to go to your room. Nathan's not the boss of you!" That realization changed everything, and Cam, smiling, sat back down to play.

As followers of Christ, the reality of our brokenness and our inclination to sin can assume a false authority much like that younger brother. Sin noisily threatens to dominate our hearts and minds, and the joy drains from our relationship with the Savior.

But through the death and resurrection of Christ, that threat is an empty one. Sin has no authority over us. That is why Paul wrote, "Sin shall no longer be your master, because you are not under the law, but under grace" (ROM. 6:14).

While our brokenness is very real, Christ's grace enables us to live in a way that pleases God and expresses His transforming power to the world. Sin is no longer our boss. We now live in the grace and presence of Jesus. His dominion in our lives releases us from the bondage of sin. *BILL CROWDER*

Thank you for your grace, Lord, that cleanses us inside.
your grace is greater than all our sin. We know we can't live without it.
And we're grateful that we don't have to.

God pursues us in our restlessness, receives us in our sinfulness, holds us in our brokenness. SCOTTY SMITH

The Girl in the Yellow Coat

Read: Genesis 2:18–25

A man leaves his father and mother and is united to his wife, and they become one flesh. —v. 24

It was her yellow raincoat that caught my attention, and quickly I became increasingly interested in this cute freshman with long, brown hair. Soon I worked up my courage, interrupted Sue as she walked along reading a letter from a guy back home, and awkwardly asked her for a date. To my surprise, she said yes.

More than 4 decades later, Sue and I look back and laugh at our first uncomfortable meeting on that college campus—and marvel how God put a shy guy from Ohio together with a shy girl from Michigan. Through the years, we have faced innumerable crises together as we raised our family. We've negotiated parenting four kids, and we've struggled mightily with losing one of them. Problems big and small have tested our faith, yet we've stuck together. It took commitment from both of us and the grace of God. Today we rejoice in God's design, spelled out in Genesis 2:24—to leave our parents, to be unified as man and wife, and to become united as one flesh. We cherish this amazing plan that has given us such a wonderful life together.

God's design for marriage is beautiful. So we pray for married couples to sense how awesome it is to enjoy life together under the blessing of God's loving guidance.

DAVE BRANON

Lord, the first thing you organized during society's earliest days was marriage. Thank you for how you designed this amazing institution. Show me how to help strengthen others in their marriage relationship.

Marriage thrives in a climate of love, honor, and respect.

The Visitor

Read: Matthew 25:31–40

I needed clothes and you clothed me, I was sick and you looked after me, I was in prison and you came to visit me. —v. 36

A friend asked a newly retired man what he was doing now that he was no longer working full-time. "I describe myself as a visitor," the man replied. "I go see people in our church and community who are in the hospital or care facilities, living alone, or just need someone to talk and pray with them. And I enjoy doing it!" My friend was impressed by this man's clear sense of purpose and his care for others.

A few days before Jesus was crucified, He told His followers a story that emphasized the importance of visiting people in need. "The King will say to those on his right, '. . . I needed clothes and you clothed me, I was sick and you looked after me, I was in prison and you came to visit me'" (MATT. 25:34, 36). When asked, "When did we see you sick or in prison and go to visit you?" the King will answer, "Whatever you did for one of the least of these brothers and sisters of mine, you did for me" (vv. 39–40).

Our ministry of visiting has two beneficiaries—the person visited and Jesus himself. To go to a person with help and encouragement is direct service to our Lord.

Is there someone who would be encouraged by your visit today?

DAVID MCCASLAND

Lord Jesus, help me to see others with your eyes.
Show me what it means to demonstrate your love to those around me.
Thank you for the love you give to me that I can share.

Compassion is understanding the troubles of others, coupled with an urgent desire to help.

Back from the Dead

Read: Ephesians 2:1–10

[God] made us alive with Christ even when we were dead. —v. 5

Can a man be officially alive after being declared legally dead? That question became international news when a man from Ohio showed up in good health after being reported missing more than 25 years earlier. At the time of his disappearance he had been unemployed, addicted, and hopelessly behind in child support payments. So he decided to go into hiding. On his return, however, he discovered how hard it is to come back from the dead. When the man went to court to reverse the ruling that had declared him legally dead, the judge turned down his request, citing a 3-year time limit for changing a death ruling.

That unusual request of a human court turns out to be a common experience for God. Paul's letter to the Ephesians tells us that though we were spiritually dead, God "made us alive with Christ" (EPH. 2:1, 5). Yet declaring and making us spiritually alive was a deeply painful matter for God. Our sin and its consequent spiritual death required the suffering, death, and resurrection of God's Son (vv. 4–7).

It's one thing to show evidence of physical life. Our challenge is to show evidence of spiritual life. Having been declared alive in Christ, we are called to live in gratitude for the immeasurable mercy and life given to us.

MART DEHAAN

Father in heaven, our hearts are full of gratitude for the way you reached out to us when we were dead in our sins. May we live joyfully and with unending appreciation for what you did to give us life.

Jesus died that we might live.

The Well-Watered Life

Read: Jeremiah 17:1–8

They will be like a tree planted by the water . . . ; its leaves are always green. —v. 8

I have a friend who lives on a ranch in the wide-open spaces of Montana. The road to his home is a long trail that winds through the parched and barren landscape of the wilderness. As you drive toward his home, you can't help but notice the contrasting strip of green trees and vibrant vegetation meandering through the ranch. One of the finest trout rivers in North America cuts through the property, and anything that grows near its banks gets the benefit of an unending source of vital water.

This is the picture Jeremiah paints when he says that those who trust in the Lord are "like a tree planted by the water that sends out its roots by the stream" (JER. 17:8). Many may choose the wilting heat and choking drought of life apart from God, but those who trust in God will be vibrant and fruitful. Depending on Him is like putting our roots into the refreshing water of His goodness. We are strengthened with the confidence that His steadfast love for us will never fail.

God will ultimately make all things right. Trusting that He will turn our pain to gain and use suffering to mature us empowers us to become fruit-bearers in a dry and thirsty land. *JOE STOWELL*

Lord, thank you for not leaving me alone in the withering heat of life. I will put the roots of my trust into the river of your unfailing promises and steadfast love!

Put your roots down by the river of God's goodness.

The Word Among Us

Read: Psalm 119:17–24

Your statutes are my delight; they are my counselors. —v. 24

The Word of God comes to us in many forms. Bible-centered preaching, Scripture reading, songs, study groups, and devotional articles bring to us the truths of God from Scripture. But we can't overlook personal reading and studying either.

My heart has recently been touched by a careful, paragraph-by-paragraph study of Deuteronomy alongside the Sermon on the Mount in Matthew 5–7. Both passages contain codes of belief: The Ten Commandments (DEUT. 5:6–21) and the Beatitudes (MATT. 5:3–12). Deuteronomy shows us the old covenant—the law God wanted His people to follow. In Matthew, Jesus shows us how He has come to fulfill that law and establish the principles of the new covenant, which frees us from the burden of the law.

The Holy Spirit comes alongside the Word of God to teach, empower, instruct, convict, and purify us. The result is understanding, repentance, renewal, and growth in Jesus. Theologian Philip Jacob Spener wrote: "The more at home the Word of God is among us, the more we will bring about faith and its fruits." Let's pray with the psalmist: "Open my eyes that I may see wonderful things in your law" so that we might live it out in our lives (PS. 119:18).

DAVE EGNER

"Heavenly Father, we bow in your presence.
Let your Word be our rule and guide, your Spirit our teacher,
and your greater glory be our supreme concern,
through Jesus Christ our Lord. Amen."

JOHN R. W. STOTT

When the Word of God is within us, it flows out from our life.

A Matter of Love

Read: Mark 12:28–34

Love the Lord your God with all your heart and with all your soul and with all your strength. —Deuteronomy 6:5

"Where intellect and emotion clash, the heart often has the greater wisdom" wrote the authors of *A General Theory of Love*. In the past, they say, people believed that the mind should rule the heart, but science has now discovered the opposite to be true. "Who we are and who we become depends, in part, on whom we love."

Those familiar with Scripture recognize this as an ancient truth, not a new discovery. The most important commandment God gave to His people gives the heart the prominent place. "Love the Lord your God with all your heart and with all your soul and with all your strength" (Deut. 6:5). Not until the gospels of Mark and Luke do we learn that Jesus added the word mind (Mark 12:30; Luke 10:27). So, what scientists are just now discovering, the Bible taught all along.

Those of us who follow Christ also know the importance of whom we love. When we obey the greatest commandment and make God the object of our love, we can be assured of having a purpose that transcends anything we could imagine or our strength could achieve. When our desire for God dominates our hearts, our minds will stay focused on ways to serve Him, and our actions will further His kingdom on earth and in heaven.

Julie Ackerman Link

Lord, we long to make you the supreme desire of our heart. As you taught your disciples to pray, so too we ask you to teach us how to love. Guide us today.

Count as lost each day you have not used in loving God. Brother Lawrence

Bring the Boy to Me

Read: Mark 9:14–27

Jesus replied, ". . . Bring the boy to me." –v. 19

"I don't believe in God and I won't go," Mark said.

Amy struggled to swallow the lump in her throat. Her son had changed from a happy boy to a surly and uncooperative young man. Life was a battleground, and Sunday had become a day to dread, as Mark refused to go to church with the family. Finally his despairing parents consulted a counselor, who said: "Mark must make his own faith journey. You can't force him into the kingdom. Give God space to work. Keep praying, and wait."

Amy waited—and prayed. One morning the words of Jesus that she had read echoed through her mind. Jesus's disciples had failed to help a demon-possessed boy, but Jesus had the answer: "Bring the boy to me" (MARK 9:19). The sun shone through the window at Amy's side, making a pool of light on the floor. If Jesus could heal in such an extreme situation, then surely He could also help her son. She pictured herself and Mark standing in that light with Jesus. Then she mentally stepped back, leaving her son alone with the One who loved him even more than she did.

Every day Amy silently handed Mark to God, clinging to the assurance that He knew Mark's needs, and would in His time and in His way, work in his life.

MARION STROUD

Father, I lift my beloved to you, knowing that you love him even more than I do and you understand just what to do to meet his need. I commit him to your care.

Prayer is the voice of faith trusting that God knows and cares.

Taming the Untamable

Read: James 3:1–12

No human being can tame the tongue. —v. 8

From Vietnamese pot-bellied pigs to Siberian foxes, humans have learned to tame wild animals. People enjoy teaching monkeys to "act" in commercials or training deer to eat out of their hands. As the apostle James put it, "All kinds of animals, birds, reptiles and sea creatures are being tamed and have been tamed by mankind" (3:7).

But there is something we cannot tame. All of us have trouble getting a little thing called the tongue under control. "No human being can tame the tongue," James tells us (v. 8).

Why? Because while our words may be on the tip of our tongue, they originate from deep within us. "The mouth speaks what the heart is full of" (MATT. 12:34). And thus the tongue can be used for both good and evil (JAMES 3:9). Or, as scholar Peter Davids put it, "On the one hand, [the tongue] is very religious, but, on the other, it can be most profane."

If we cannot tame this unruly tongue of ours, is it destined to be a daily problem for us, always prone to speak evil? (v. 10). By God's grace, no. We are not left to our own devices. The Lord will "set a guard over my mouth"; He will "keep watch over the door of my lips" (PS. 141:3). He can tame the untamable.

DAVE BRANON

Lord, my mouth sometimes speaks words that don't honor you.
Thank you that by your Spirit my untamed tongue can be
brought under divine control. Please guard my mouth today.

To rule your tongue, let Christ rule in your heart.

Building a Bridge

Read: 1 Thessalonians 1:1–10

Your faith in God has become known everywhere. Therefore we do not need to say anything about it. —v. 8

James Michener's *Centennial* is a fictional account of the history and settlement of the American West. Through the eyes of a French-Canadian trader named Pasquinel, Michener converges the stories of the Arapaho of the Great Plains and the European-based community of St. Louis. As this rugged adventurer moves between the growing clutter of the city and the wide-open spaces of the plains, he becomes a bridge between two drastically different worlds.

Followers of Christ also have the opportunity to build bridges between two very different worlds—those who know and follow Jesus and those who do not know Him. Early Christians in Thessalonica had been building bridges to their idol-worshiping culture, so Paul said of them, "The Lord's message rang out from you not only in Macedonia and Achaia—your faith in God has become known everywhere" (1 THESS. 1:8). The bridge they were building had two components: "the Lord's message" and the example of their faith. It was clear to everyone that they had "turned to God from idols to serve the living and true God" (v. 9).

As God declares himself to those around us by His Word and through our lives, we can become a bridge to those who do not yet know the love of Christ.

BILL CROWDER

Father, help us live in such a way that others will want to know about your Son. May we not merely try to do what's "right" but instead live as people forgiven and loved by you.

Live the gospel, and others will listen.

Mirror, Mirror

Read: James 1:19–27

Whoever looks intently into the perfect law . . . and continues in it . . . will be blessed in what they do. —v. 25

How often do you see your reflection in a mirror? Some studies say that the average person looks in a mirror 8 to 10 times a day. Other surveys say it could be as many as 60 to 70 times a day, if glancing at our reflection in store windows and smart phone screens is included.

Why do we look so often? Most experts agree that it's to check our appearance, especially before meetings or social gatherings. If something is amiss, we want to fix it. Why look if we don't plan to change what's wrong?

The apostle James said that reading or hearing God's Word without acting on it is like looking in a mirror and forgetting what we've seen (1:22–24). But the better alternative is to look closely and act on what we see. James said, "Whoever looks intently into the perfect law that gives freedom, and continues in it—not forgetting what they have heard, but doing it—they will be blessed in what they do" (v. 25).

If we hear God's Word without taking action, we fool only ourselves (v. 22). But when we examine ourselves in light of God's Word and obey His instructions, God liberates us from all that keeps us from looking more and more like Him each day. *DAVID MCCASLAND*

Thank you, Lord, for the Bible, your Word to us.
Give us wisdom and guidance as we read its pages.
Make us sensitive to your voice and give us hearts to obey.

The Bible is a mirror that lets us see ourselves as God sees us.

Battling Distractions

Read: Luke 10:38–42

Mary has chosen what is better, and it will not be taken away from her. —v. 42

Every day I drive the same highway to and from the office, and every day I see an alarming number of distracted drivers. Usually they're talking on the phone or texting, but I have also seen people reading the newspaper, putting on makeup, and eating a bowl of cereal while trying to maneuver a car at 70+ miles per hour! In some circumstances, distractions are fleeting and harmless. In a moving vehicle, they can kill.

Sometimes distractions can be a problem in our relationship with God. In fact, that was the concern Jesus had for His friend Martha. She "was distracted by all the preparations that had to be made" for a meal (LUKE 10:40). When she complained about her sister Mary's lack of help (apparently due to her devotion to Christ and His teaching), Jesus told her, "Martha, Martha, . . . you are worried and upset about many things, but few things are needed—or indeed only one. Mary has chosen what is better, and it will not be taken away from her" (vv. 41–42).

Martha's distractions were well-intentioned. But she was missing the opportunity to listen to Jesus and enjoy His presence. He is deserving of our deepest devotion, and He alone can fully enable us to overcome any of life's distractions.

BILL CROWDER

Lord, I want a heart like Mary's—that takes time to sit at your feet to learn from you and be close to you. And I want a heart like Martha's—that takes time to serve you, the One I love.

If you want to be miserable, look within; distracted, look around; peaceful, look up.

Weighed Down

Read: Hebrews 12:1–5

Let us throw off everything that hinders and the sin that so easily entangles. And let us run with perseverance the race marked out for us. —v. 1

August 10, 1628, was a dark day in naval history. On that day the royal warship *Vasa* set out on her maiden voyage. After taking 2 years to build, being lavishly decorated and holding 64 cannons, the pride of the Swedish navy sank only one mile out to sea. What went wrong? The excessive load was too heavy to make her seaworthy. Excess weight pulled the *Vasa* to the bottom of the ocean.

The Christian life can also be weighed down by excess baggage. Encouraging us in our spiritual journey, the book of Hebrews says: "Let us throw off everything that hinders and the sin that so easily entangles. And let us run with perseverance the race marked out for us, fixing our eyes on Jesus, the pioneer and perfecter of faith" (12:1–2).

Like the lavishly decorated ship, we may project to others an impressive exterior. But if on the inside we are weighed down with sin, our perseverance can be impaired. There is a remedy, however. By relying on God's guidance and the empowering of the Holy Spirit, our load can be lightened and our perseverance buoyant.

Forgiveness and grace are always available to the spiritual traveler.

DENNIS FISHER

Father in heaven, too often I try to mask the burden and weight of sin in my life with the outward activities of the Christian life. Forgive me. Help me to set aside the things that keep me from running a good race.

Perseverance is as much about a strong won't as a strong will.

Approaching God

Read: Isaiah 6:1–8

Holy, holy, holy is the LORD Almighty; the whole earth is full of his glory. —v. 3

It used to bother me that the closer I drew to God in my walk with Him, the more sinful I felt. Then a phenomenon I observed in my room enlightened me. A tiny gap in the curtain covering my window threw a ray of light into the room. As I looked, I saw particles of dirt drifting in the beam. Without the ray of light, the room seemed clean, but the light revealed the dirty particles.

What I observed shed light on my spiritual life. The closer I approach the Lord of light, the clearer I see myself. When the light of Christ shines in the darkness of our lives, it exposes our sin—not to discourage us, but to humble us to trust in Him. We can't depend on our own righteousness, since we are sinners and fall short of God's standards (ROM. 3:23). When we are proud, the light reveals our heart and we cry as Isaiah did, "Woe to me! . . . For I am a man of unclean lips, . . . and my eyes have seen the King, the LORD Almighty" (ISA. 6:5).

God is absolutely perfect in every way. Approaching Him calls for humility and childlike trust, not self-importance and pride. For it is by grace that He draws us to himself. It is good for us that we feel unworthy as we draw closer to God, for it humbles us to rely on Him alone.

LAWRENCE DARMANI

Holy, Holy, Holy! Though the darkness hide Thee,
though the eyes of sinful man Thy glory may not see.
Only Thou art holy—there is none beside Thee,
perfect in power, in love and purity.

HEBER

There is no room for pride when we walk with God.

Ask the Author

Read: 1 Corinthians 2:9–16

We have the mind of Christ. —v. 16

Over the years I've been part of various book groups. Typically, several friends read a book and then we get together to discuss the ideas the author has put forward. Inevitably, one person will raise a question that none of us can answer. And then someone will say, "If only we could ask the author." A popular new trend in New York City is making that possible. Some authors, for a hefty fee, are making themselves available to meet with book clubs.

How different it is for those of us who gather to study the Bible. Jesus meets with us whenever we get together. No fees. No scheduling conflicts. No travel expenses. Furthermore, we have the Holy Spirit to guide our understanding. One of the last promises Jesus made to His disciples was that God would send the Holy Spirit to teach them (JOHN 14:26).

The Author of the Bible is not limited by time or space. He can meet with us at any time and any place. So whenever we have a question, we can ask with the assurance that He will answer—though perhaps not according to our timetable.

God wants us to have the mind of the Author (1 COR. 2:16) so that through the teaching of the Spirit we will comprehend the greatness of the gift He has freely given us (v. 12).

JULIE ACKERMAN LINK

Lord, thank you that you are meeting with me right now. I want to be taught by you.
I don't want just to have more knowledge about you;
I want to know you in the depths of my heart.

When you open your Bible, ask the Author to open your mind and heart.

The Unseen World

Read: Numbers 22:21–31

The angel of the LORD [was] standing in the road. —v. 23

Did you know that the microbes on just one of your hands outnumber all of the people on the earth? Or that millions of microbes could fit into the eye of a needle? These one-celled, living organisms are too small for us to see without a microscope, yet they live in the air, soil, water, and even in our bodies. We constantly interact with them, even though their world is completely beyond our senses.

The realities of the spiritual world are also often not visible to us humans, as the prophet Balaam discovered. He was trudging along the road with his two servants when his donkey "saw the angel of the LORD standing in the road with a drawn sword in his hand" (NUM. 22:23). To avoid the angel, the animal walked into a field, crushed Balaam's foot against a wall, and lay down with Balaam still on her back. Balaam was angry and struck the donkey. He didn't realize something supernatural was going on—until God opened his eyes (v. 31).

The Bible tells us that a spiritual world does exist, and we may sometimes encounter realities from that realm—both good and bad (HEB. 13:2; EPH. 6:12). Because of this, we are encouraged to be watchful, prayerful, and prepared. Just as God rules the world we see, He also rules the unseen world. *JENNIFER BENSON SCHULDT*

Heavenly Father, help us to be strong in you and in the power of your might. Open our eyes so that we may see the spiritual realities you have for us.

All that is seen and unseen is under God's sovereign power.

Longing for Rescue

Read: Matthew 1:18–25

[Mary] will give birth to a son, and you are to give him the name Jesus, because he will save his people from their sins. —v. 21

The movie *Man of Steel,* released in 2013, is a fresh imagining of the Superman story. Filled with breathtaking special effects and nonstop action, it drew crowds to movie theaters around the world. Some said that the film's appeal was rooted in its amazing technology. Others pointed to the enduring appeal of the "Superman mythology."

Amy Adams, the actress who plays Lois Lane in the movie, has a different view of Superman's appeal. She says it is about a basic human longing: "Who doesn't want to believe that there's one person who could come and save us from ourselves?"

That's a great question. And the answer is that someone has *already* come to save us from ourselves, and that someone is Jesus. Several announcements were made regarding the birth of Jesus. One of them was from the angel Gabriel to Joseph: "[Mary] will give birth to a son, and you are to give him the name Jesus, because he will save his people from their sins" (MATT. 1:21).

Jesus came—He did so to save us from our sin and from ourselves. His name means "the Lord saves"—and our salvation was His mission. The longing for rescue that fills the human heart ultimately is met by Jesus.

BILL CROWDER

Shout salvation full and free, highest hills and deepest caves;
this our song of victory—Jesus saves! Jesus saves!
OWENS

Jesus's name and mission are the same—He came to save us.

His Choice

Read: 2 Thess. 2:13–17

God from the beginning chose you for salvation. —v. 13 NKJV

When our children were small, I often prayed with them after we tucked them into bed. But before I prayed, I sometimes would sit on the edge of the bed and talk with them. I remember telling our daughter Libby, "If I could line up all the 4-year-old girls in the world, I would walk down the line looking for you. After going through the entire line, I would choose you to be my daughter." That always put a big smile on Libby's face because she knew she was special.

If that was a smile-worthy moment for her, think of the grace-filled fact that the Creator-God of the universe "from the beginning chose you for salvation" (2 THESS. 2:13 NKJV). Before time began, He desired to make you His own. This is why Scripture often uses the picture of adoption to communicate the amazing reality that, through no merit or worthiness of our own, we have been chosen by Him.

This is stunning news! We are "loved by the Lord" (v. 13) and enjoy the benefits of being part of His family. This glorious truth should fill our lives with humility and gratitude. "May our Lord Jesus Christ himself and God our Father, who loved us . . . strengthen you in every good deed and word" (vv. 16–17).

JOE STOWELL

I will be forever grateful that I am your child, Father, and that you love me! Teach me to remember all the benefits of belonging to you, and may I serve you faithfully as part of your family.

It's God's choice to love you and to make you part of His family.

Changed Perspective

Read: Acts 17:16–23

While Paul was waiting for them in Athens, he was greatly distressed to see that the city was full of idols. —v. 16

As an early riser, my wife enjoys the quiet moments before the house wakes up and uses it to read the Bible and pray. Recently she settled into her favorite chair, only to be confronted by a rather messy couch left there by "someone" watching a football game the night before. The mess distracted her at first, and her frustration with me interrupted the warmth of the moment.

Then a thought hit her, and she moved to the couch. From there, she could look out our front windows to the sun rising over the Atlantic Ocean. The beauty of the scene God painted that morning changed her perspective.

As she told me the story, we both recognized the lesson of the morning. While we can't always control the things of life that impact our day, we do have a choice. We can continue to brood over the "mess," or we can change our perspective. When Paul was in Athens, "he was greatly distressed to see that the city was full of idols" (ACTS 17:16). But when he changed his perspective, he used their interest in religion as an opportunity to proclaim the true God, Jesus Christ (vv. 22–23).

As my wife left for work, it was time for someone else to change his perspective—for me to let the Lord help me to see my messes through her eyes and His.

RANDY KILGORE

Dear Lord, grant us the wisdom to change our perspective rather than linger over messes. Help us to see—and fix—the "messes" we make for others.

Wisdom is seeing things from God's perspective.

A Consistent Life

Read: Daniel 6:1–10

[Daniel] got down on his knees and prayed, giving thanks to his God, just as he had done before. —v. 10

While studying the book of Daniel, I was struck by how easily he could have avoided being thrown into the den of lions. Daniel's jealous rivals in the government of Babylon laid a trap based on his consistent practice of daily prayer to God (DAN. 6:1–9). Daniel was fully aware of their plot and could have decided to pray privately for a month until things settled down. But that was not the kind of person he was.

"Now when Daniel learned that the decree had been published, he went home to his upstairs room where the windows opened toward Jerusalem. Three times a day he got down on his knees and prayed, giving thanks to his God, just as he had done before" (v. 10). Daniel did not panic, nor bargain with God. Instead, he continued "just as he had done before" (v. 10). He was not intimidated by the pressure of persecution.

The lesson for me was the power of Daniel's life of consistent devotion to the Lord. His strength came from God, whom Daniel wanted to please every day. When a crisis came, Daniel didn't need to change his daily practice to meet it. He simply stayed committed to his God.

DAVID MCCASLAND

Father, I want to stand for you when persecution comes as Daniel did.
Give me that same bold commitment to pray
and not to be ashamed of knowing you.
Help me to live my faith publicly.

God empowers us to stand for Him as we bow to pray.

Catching up with Us

Read: Psalm 32:1–5

When I kept silent, my bones wasted away through my groaning. —v. 3

A pastor told this story on himself in his local newspaper. He was chatting with an older man to whom he had just been introduced. "So, you used to work for a utility company," the pastor said, naming the organization. "Sure did," the man responded. The pastor remarked that when he was a kid the cables from that company ran across his parents' property. "Where did you live?" the man asked. When the pastor told him, the man said, "I remember that property. I had a tough time keeping the cable warning signs up. Kids were always shooting them down." When the pastor's face flushed with embarrassment, the man said, "You were one of the shooters, weren't you?" And indeed he was.

The pastor labeled his confessional story: "Be sure your signs will find you out," a clever play on Moses's words in Numbers 32:23: "Be sure that your sin will find you out."

Old wrongs have a way of catching up with us. And old sins that have not been dealt with can lead to serious consequences. As David laments in Psalm 32: "When I kept silent, my bones wasted away" (v. 3). But confessing our wrong restores our fellowship with the Lord: "I acknowledged my sin to you . . . and you forgave the guilt of my sin" (v. 5). Through confession, we can enjoy God's forgiveness. *DAVE BRANON*

Dear Lord, it's time to come clean with you.
I've held on to __________ for too long. Thank you that this sin
is under the blood of Christ. Restore me to fellowship with you.

Christians can erase from their memory what God has erased from the record.

Learn the Cost

Read: 1 Peter 1:17–21

You were bought at a price. –1 Corinthians 6:20

We gave our 2-year-old son a pair of new boots recently. He was so happy that he didn't take them off until it was bedtime. But the next day he forgot all about the boots and put on his old sneakers. My husband said, "I wish he knew how much things cost."

The boots were expensive, but a young child doesn't know about working hours, salaries, and taxes. A child receives the gifts with open arms, but we know that he can't be expected to fully appreciate the sacrifices his parents make to give him new things.

Sometimes I behave like a child. With open arms I receive God's gifts through His many mercies, but am I thankful? Do I consider the price that was paid so I can live a full life?

The cost was expensive—more than "perishable things such as silver or gold." As we read in 1 Peter, it required "the precious blood of Christ, a lamb without blemish or defect" (1:18–19). Jesus gave His life, a high price to pay, to make us part of His family. And God raised Him from the dead (v. 21).

When we understand the cost of our salvation, we learn to be truly thankful. *KEILA OCHOA*

Lord, help me to understand, to take in what it meant for you, the Holy One, to bear my sin. Remind me to give you thanks for salvation and for all the ways you show me your love throughout my day today.

Salvation is infinitely costly, but absolutely free.

A Deadly Weapon

Read: Nehemiah 4:1–10

Those who hope in the Lord will renew their strength. . . . They will run and not grow weary, they will walk and not be faint. —Isaiah 40:31

Boxing legend Muhammad Ali used several ring tactics to defeat his opponents; one tactic was taunting. In his fight with George Foreman in 1974, Ali taunted Foreman, "Hit harder! Show me something, George. That don't hurt. I thought you were supposed to be bad." Fuming, Foreman punched away furiously, wasting his energy and weakening his confidence.

It's an old tactic. By referring to Nehemiah's efforts at rebuilding the broken wall of Jerusalem as nothing more than a fox's playground (NEH. 4:3), Tobiah intended to weaken the workers with poisonous words of discouragement. Goliath tried it on David by despising the boy's simple weapons of a sling and stones (1 SAM. 17:41–44).

A discouraging remark can be a deadly weapon. Nehemiah refused to surrender to Tobiah's discouragements, just as David rejected Goliath's diabolical teasing. Focusing on God and His help rather than on their discouraging situations, David and Nehemiah both achieved victory.

Taunting can come from anybody, including those who are close to us. Responding to them negatively only saps our energy. But God encourages us through His promises: He will never forsake us (PS. 9:10; HEB. 13:5), and He invites us to rely on His help (HEB. 4:16).

LAWRENCE DARMANI

Lord, it's easy to let discouragement sap my energy and joy.
Help me to reject all agents of discouragement in my life
and to trust in you for comfort and strength.

If you're in a tunnel of discouragement, keep walking toward the Light.

A Season for Everything

Read: Ecclesiastes 3:1–13

There is a time for everything . . . a season for every activity. –v. 1

If you're like me, you've struggled with having to say no to taking on a new responsibility—especially if it's for a good cause and directly related to helping others. We may have sound reasons for carefully selecting our priorities. Yet sometimes, by not agreeing to do more, we may feel guilty or we may think that somehow we have failed in our walk of faith.

But according to Ecclesiastes 3:1-8, wisdom recognizes that everything in life has its own season—in human activities as in the realm of nature. "There is a time for everything, and a season for every activity under the heavens" (v. 1).

Perhaps you are getting married or becoming a parent for the first time. Maybe you are leaving school and entering the workforce, or moving from fulltime work to retirement. As we move from season to season, our priorities change. We may need to put aside what we did in the past and funnel our energy into something else.

When life brings changes in our circumstances and obligations, we must responsibly and wisely discern what kind of commitments we should make, seeking in whatever we do to "do it all for the glory of God" (1 COR. 10:31). Proverbs 3:6 promises that as we acknowledge Him in all our ways, He will guide us in the way we should go. *POH FANG CHIA*

Heavenly Father, give me your wisdom to know what priorities I need to have at this season of my life. Guide me in all that I do. I only want to bring you the honor you deserve with the way I live.

Commitment to Christ is a daily calling that challenges us.

House-Hunting Ants

Read: Numbers 13:25–14:9

Lord, you have been our dwelling place throughout all generations. —Psalm 90:1

According to researchers from the University of Bristol, the European rock ant may be better than we are at staying on top of the housing market. The researchers found that the ant colonies use scout ants to continually monitor their colonies' living conditions. Using social skills complex enough to stun the scientists, the rock ants work together to find the right living space, darkness, and security needed to give the queen mother and her larvae the best available housing.

In the days of Moses, the families of Israel were looking for a new home. The slave yards of Egypt had been brutal. The wilderness of Sinai was no place to settle down. But there was a problem. According to Israelite scouts, the homeland to which God was leading them was already occupied—by walled cities and giants who made the scouts feel like grasshoppers in their own eyes (NUM. 13:28, 33).

Sometimes it may be helpful to compare ourselves to insects. House-hunting rock ants instinctively follow the ways of their Creator. But we often let our fears keep us from following and trusting God. When we rest in the assurance of His presence and love, we can say, "Lord, you have been our dwelling place throughout all generations." *MART DEHAAN*

Father in heaven, please help us to see that today there is no better place to live than in your presence and love. Help us learn to settle in and be comfortable with our place in you.

Finding ourselves at home in God is a good place to be.

Start with Me

Read: 1 Corinthians 13:4–13

[Do not look] to your own interests, but each of you to the interests of others. —Philippians 2:4

I call them Mell Notes—little comments my daughter Melissa made in her Bible to help her apply a passage to her life.

In Matthew 7, for instance, she had drawn a box around verses 1 and 2 that talk about not judging others because, when you do, "with the measure you use, it will be measured to you." Next to it she wrote this Mell Note: "Look at what you are doing before you look at others."

Melissa was an "others-oriented" teen. She lived the words of Philippians 2:4. Her classmate Matt, who knew her from church nursery through her final days in the eleventh grade when she died in a car accident, said of Melissa at her memorial service: "I don't think I ever saw you without a smile or something that brightened up people's days." Her friend Tara said this: "Thanks for being my friend, even when no one else was as nice and cheerful as you."

In a day in which harsh judgment of others seems to be the rule, it's good to remember that love starts with us. The words of Paul come to mind: "Now these three remain: faith, hope and love. But the greatest of these is love" (1 COR. 13:13).

What a difference we'll make if, when we look at others, we say, "Love starts with me." And wouldn't that be a great reflection of God's love for us? *DAVE BRANON*

Lord, thank you for the great love you lavished on us when you sent your Son to die and be resurrected so that we could be with you eternally. In response, help us to love others. Lord, we want to be like you.

Embracing God's love for us is the key to loving others.

Solving the Mystery

Read: Romans 5:1–11

But God demonstrates his own love for us in this: While we were still sinners, Christ died for us. —v. 8

One of the most popular tourist attractions in England is the giant stone pillars of Stonehenge. These massive pieces of granite are also a great source of mystery. Every year, people travel to Stonehenge with questions such as: Why were they erected? Who accomplished this extraordinary engineering marvel? And perhaps we wonder most of all how they did it. But visitors leave having received no answers from the silent stones. The mystery remains.

The Scriptures speak of a greater mystery—the fact that God came to live among us as a man. Paul wrote in 1 Timothy 3:16, "The mystery from which true godliness springs is great: He appeared in the flesh, was vindicated by the Spirit, was seen by angels, was preached among the nations, was believed on in the world, was taken up in glory."

This brief overview of the life of Christ—the mystery of godliness—is remarkable. What prompted the Creator of the universe to come and live and die for His creation, however, is not a mystery. "But God demonstrates his own love for us in this: While we were still sinners, Christ died for us" (ROM. 5:8). God's great love for us is at the root of the mystery of godliness, and the cross has made it plain for all to see. *BILL CROWDER*

Lord, we may not understand everything you have done for us, or how you have done it. But we know you love us and sent Jesus to die for us, and that is all we need to know.

How Christ became a human being may be a mystery, but God's love isn't.

The Power to Survive

Read: 2 Corinthians 4:7–12

We are hard pressed on every side, but not crushed. —v. 8

When I was growing up, I had an inflatable plastic punching dummy. It was about as tall as I was and had a smiling face painted on it. My challenge was to hit it hard enough to make it stay down. But no matter how hard I tried, it always bounced right back up again. The secret? There was a lead weight in the bottom that always kept it upright. Sailboats operate by the same principle. The lead weights in their keels provide the ballast to keep them balanced and upright in strong winds.

It's like that in the life of a believer in Christ. Our power to survive challenges resides not in us but with God, who dwells within us. We're not exempt from the punches that life throws at us nor from the storms that inevitably threaten our stability. But with full confidence in His power to sustain us, we can say with Paul, "We are hard pressed on every side, but not crushed; perplexed, but not in despair; persecuted, but not abandoned; struck down, but not destroyed" (2 COR. 4:8–9).

Join the many travelers through life who through deep waters of pain and suffering embrace with unshakable confidence the truth that God's grace is sufficient and that in our weakness He is made strong (12:9). It will be the ballast to your soul.

JOE STOWELL

Lord, give me the grace to trust in your power to ultimately prevail in the midst of the challenges of life. May my trust in you be rewarded by the power of your overcoming strength.

The power of God within you is greater than the pressure of troubles around you.

Pursuing Holiness

Read: Romans 6:14–23

Make every effort to live in peace with everyone and to be holy. —Hebrews 12:14

We often see surveys that ask people if they are happy, satisfied with their work, or enjoying life. But I've never seen an opinion poll that asked, "Are you holy?" How would you answer that question?

One Bible dictionary defines holiness as "separation to God and conduct fitting for those separated." Author Frederick Buechner said that when writing about a person's character, "nothing is harder to make real than holiness." He adds that "holiness is not a human quality at all, like virtue. Holiness is . . . not something that people do, but something that God does in them."

Romans 6 presents the stunning gift that God gives us through faith in Christ: "We were therefore buried with him through baptism into death in order that, just as Christ was raised from the dead through the glory of the Father, we too may live a new life" (v. 4). The pursuit of holiness occurs daily as we yield ourselves in obedience to the Lord instead of following our old ways of self-gratification. "Now you are free from the power of sin and have become slaves of God. Now you do those things that lead to holiness and result in eternal life" (v. 22 NLT).

Are you becoming more holy? By God's grace and power, the answer can be a resounding "Yes! More and more each day." *DAVID MCCASLAND*

What were Jesus's characteristics?
In what ways can I cooperate with Him to make those qualities
become more a part of my life?

The choice to pursue holiness is a matter of life or death.

Cat Gate

Read: John 10:1–10

I am the gate; whoever enters through me will be saved. They will come in and go out, and find pasture. —v. 9

My husband, Jay, and I have a new family member—a 2-month-old tabby cat named Jasper. To keep our new kitten safe, we've had to break some old habits, like leaving doors open. But one thing remains a challenge: the open stairway. Cats like to climb. Even as kittens, they know that the world looks better when you're looking down on it. So whenever I have Jasper downstairs with me, she is determined to go upstairs. Trying to keep her confined to a safe place near me has tested my ingenuity. Gates that work with children and dogs do not work with cats.

My cat gate dilemma brings to mind the metaphor Jesus used to describe himself: "I am the gate for the sheep," He said (JOHN 10:7). Middle Eastern sheepfolds were enclosures with an opening for the sheep to go in and out. At night, when the sheep were safely inside, the shepherd would lie in the opening so that neither sheep nor predators could get past him.

Although I want to keep Jasper safe, I am not willing to make myself the gate. I have other things to do. But that's what Jesus Christ does for us. He places himself between us and our enemy, the devil, to protect us from spiritual harm. *JULIE ACKERMAN LINK*

Thank you, Jesus, for being my gate. Through you I have salvation
and by your power I am safe from spiritual harm.
Surround me with your protection. I trust in you.

The closer to the Shepherd, the farther from the wolf.

Unexpected Encounter

Read: Ruth 2:11–20

May the LORD repay you . . . . May you be richly rewarded by the LORD, the God of Israel. —v. 12

Drew, young and enthusiastic, was leading the singing for the first time in a large church. Lois, a longtime attender, wanted to encourage him, but she thought it would be too difficult to get to the front of the church before he left. But then she saw a way to snake through the crowd. Lois told Drew, "I appreciate your enthusiasm in worship. Keep serving Him!"

As Lois walked away, she ran into Sharon, whom she hadn't seen in months. After a short conversation, Sharon said, "Thank you for what you do for the Lord. Keep serving Him!" Because Lois had gone out of her way to give encouragement, she was now in the right place to receive unexpected encouragement.

After Ruth and her mother-in-law, Naomi, left Moab and returned to Israel, they received an unexpected blessing. They were both widows with no one to provide for them, so Ruth went to glean grain from a field (RUTH 2:2–3). The field happened to be owned by Boaz, a distant relative of Naomi's. He noticed Ruth, provided for her needs, and later became her husband (2:20; 4:13). Ruth received a blessing because she was in the right place at the right time (2:11–23).

Sometimes God uses unexpected encounters to bring unexpected blessings.

ANNE CETAS

Dear Lord, help me to go out of my way to encourage others—whether or not I receive anything in return. My heart's desire is to help others along the way to know you. May I be your hands and feet.

When it comes to helping others, always be ready.

Texting God

Read: Colossians 1:3–12

For this reason, since the day we heard about you, we have not stopped praying for you. —v. 9

An article in *The Washington Post* told about a 15-year-old girl who sent and received 6,473 cell phone text messages in a single month. She says about her constant communication with friends, "I would die without it." And she is not alone. Researchers say that US teens with cell phones average more than 2,200 text messages a month.

To me, this ongoing digital conversation offers a remarkable illustration of what prayer could and should be like for every follower of Christ. Paul seemed to be constantly in an attitude of prayer for others: "We have not stopped praying for you" (COL. 1:9). "Pray in the Spirit on all occasions with all kinds of prayers and requests" (EPH. 6:18). "Pray continually" (1 THESS. 5:17). But how can we possibly do that?

Missionary Frank Laubach described his habit of "shooting" prayers at people as he encountered them during the course of each day. In a sense, he was "texting" God on their behalf, staying in constant communication with the Father. Laubach believed that prayer is the mightiest force in the world, and said: "My part is to live in this hour in continuous inner conversation with God and in perfect responsiveness to His will."

Pray continually. Perhaps what Paul urged us to do *can* be done.

DAVID MCCASLAND

Father, give me a desire to pray to you regularly.
May I turn to you before I do anything else.

Prayer should be as natural as breathing.

Hand Me the Binoculars!

Read: Psalm 19:1–6

The heavens declare the glory of God; the skies proclaim the work of his hands. —v. 1

When I was in elementary school my friend Kent and I would often spend time looking at the night sky with a pair of German-made binoculars. We marveled at the stars in the sky and the mountains on the moon. All throughout the evening we took turns saying, "Hand me the binocs!"

Centuries earlier a Jewish shepherd boy looked up at the night sky and also marveled. He did not have a pair of binoculars or a telescope to aid him. But he had something even more important—a personal relationship with the living God. I imagine the sheep quietly bleating in the background as David gazed skyward. Later he would write the inspired text: "The heavens declare the glory of God; the skies proclaim the work of his hands. Day after day they pour forth speech; night after night they reveal knowledge" (PS. 19:1–2).

In our busy schedules, we can so easily forget to stand in awe of the heavenly beauty our Creator has prepared for our enjoyment and His glory. When we set aside time to look at the night sky and marvel at what is there, we gain a deeper understanding of God and His eternal power and glory.

DENNIS FISHER

We believe that this is your world, Lord. We marvel at you and your creativity when we look at the sky and the world around us. You, and what you have done, are amazing! We stand in awe of you.

In the wonders of God's creation, we see His majesty and His character.

Giving Up Our Mirrors

Read: Philippians 2:1–5

They made the bronze basin and its bronze stand from the mirrors of the women who served. —Exodus 38:8

When Moses gathered the children of Israel together to begin work on the tabernacle (EX. 35–39), he called on Bezalel, a gifted artisan, to help make the furnishings. We're told that certain women were asked to give their precious bronze mirrors to make the bronze basin he was constructing (38:8). They gave them up to help prepare a place where God's presence would reside.

Give up our mirrors? For most of us, that would be hard to do. That's not something we're asked to do, but it makes me think about how too much scrutiny and self-examination can be disconcerting. It can make us think too much about ourselves and not enough about others.

When we can forget about our own faces quickly and remember that God loves us as we are—in all our imperfections—then we can begin to "look out not only for [our] own interests, but also for the interests of others" (PHIL. 2:4 NKJV).

Augustine said that we get lost in loving ourselves but found in loving others. Put another way, the secret of happiness is not getting our face right but giving our hearts away, giving our lives away, giving our selves away, in love.

DAVID ROPER

Father, may I think more of others today than I think of myself. May I lose my thoughts about myself in my thoughts of other people and their needs.

A heart that is focused on others will not be consumed with self.

The Go-Between

Read: Exodus 20:18–26

The people remained at a distance, while Moses approached . . . where God was. —v. 21

Imagine standing at the bottom of a mountain, elbow-to-elbow with everyone in your community. Thunder and lightning flash; you hear an earsplitting trumpet blast. Amid flames, God descends on the mountaintop. The summit is enveloped in smoke; the entire mountain begins to shake, and so do you (EX. 19:16–20).

When the Israelites had this terrifying experience near Mount Sinai, they begged Moses, "Speak to us yourself and we will listen. But do not have God speak to us or we will die" (20:19). The Israelites were asking Moses to mediate between them and the Almighty. "So the people remained at a distance, while Moses approached the thick darkness where God was" (v. 21). After meeting with God, Moses brought God's messages back down the mountain to the people below.

Today, we worship the same God who displayed His staggering greatness on Mount Sinai. Because God is perfectly holy and we are desperately sinful, we cannot relate to Him. Left to ourselves we too would (and should) shake in terror. But Jesus made it possible for us to know God when He took our sins on himself, died, and rose again (1 COR. 15:3–4). Even now, Jesus is the go-between for us to a holy and perfect God (ROM. 8:34; 1 TIM. 2:5).

JENNIFER BENSON SCHULDT

Dear Jesus, thank you for laying down your life so that I could know God. I worship you as the only one who bridges the gap between God and me.

Jesus bridges the gap between God and us.

God Is Listening

Read: Psalm 5

In the morning, LORD, you hear my voice; in the morning I lay my requests before you and wait expectantly. —v. 3

The day before Billy Graham's interview in 1982 on *The Today Show*, his director of public relations, Larry Ross, requested a private room for Graham to pray in before the interview. But when Mr. Graham arrived at the studio, his assistant informed Ross that Mr. Graham didn't need the room. He said, "Mr. Graham started praying when he got up this morning, he prayed while eating breakfast, he prayed on the way over in the car, and he'll probably be praying all the way through the interview." Ross later said, "That was a great lesson for me to learn as a young man."

Prayerfulness is not an event; it is a way of being in relationship with God. This kind of intimate relationship is developed when God's people view prayerfulness as a way of life. The Psalms encourage us to begin each day by lifting our voice to the Lord (PS. 5:3); to fill our day with conversations with God (55:17); and in the face of accusations and slander, to give ourselves totally to prayer (109:4). We develop prayer as a way of life because we desire to be with God (42:1–4; 84:1–2; 130:5–6).

Prayer is our way of connecting with God in all life's circumstances. God is always listening. We can talk to Him any time throughout the day.

MARVIN WILLIAMS

What is one major obstacle to developing your prayer life? What changes do you sense God wants to make in your heart so that you see prayer as a way of life?

In prayer, God hears more than your words—He listens to your heart.

A Good Name

Read: Proverbs 10:2–15

A good name is more desirable than great riches. —Proverbs 22:1

Charles Ponzi's name will be forever associated with the financial fraud scheme he elevated to a way of life. After some minor financial crimes and brief times in jail, in early 1920 he began offering investors a 50 percent return on their money in 45 days and a 100 percent return in 90 days. Although it seemed too good to be true, the money poured in. Ponzi used money from new investors to pay prior investors and fund his lavish lifestyle. By the time his fraud was discovered in August 1920, investors had lost 20 million dollars and five banks had failed. Ponzi spent 3 years in prison, was later deported to Italy, and died penniless in 1949 at the age of 66.

The Old Testament book of Proverbs frequently contrasts the reputations of wise and foolish people: "The name of the righteous is used in blessings, but the name of the wicked will rot. . . . Whoever walks in integrity walks securely, but whoever takes crooked paths will be found out" (PROV. 10:7, 9). Solomon sums it up by saying, "A good name is more desirable than great riches; to be esteemed is better than silver or gold" (22:1).

We seek a good name, not to honor ourselves but to glorify Christ our Lord whose name is above all names. *DAVID MCCASLAND*

Lord, you know what is best, and you desire to lead us in paths that are right and good. Give us the courage to trust and to follow you in the way of right living for your name's sake.

A good name honors our great God.

Unwelcome Visitors

Read: James 1:2–12

Consider it pure joy . . . whenever you face trials . . . , because you know that the testing of your faith produces perseverance. —vv. 2–3

Recently my wife, Marlene, and I received a panicky phone call from our son and his wife. The night before, they had found two bats in their house. I know bats are an important part of the ecosystem, but they are not my favorite among God's creatures, especially when they are flying around inside.

Yet Marlene and I were thankful we could go over to our kids' house and help. We helped them to plug the holes that might have been used by these unwelcome visitors to enter their house.

Another unwelcome visitor that often intrudes into our lives is suffering. When trials come, we can easily panic or lose heart. But these difficult circumstances can become the instruments our loving heavenly Father uses to make us more like Christ. That's why James wrote, "Consider it pure joy, my brothers and sisters, whenever you face trials of many kinds, because you know that the testing of your faith produces perseverance. Let perseverance finish its work" (JAMES 1:2–4).

We are not expected to enjoy trials or to celebrate suffering. But when these unwelcome visitors arrive, we can look for God's hand in them and trust that He can use them to make us more like His Son. *BILL CROWDER*

Thank you, Father, that you give to us each day what you know is best.
We're thankful that we can trust your heart, which is kind beyond all measure.

Trials may visit us, but our God is always with us.

Dangerous Shortcuts

Read: Matthew 4:1–10

Man shall not live on bread alone, but on every word that comes from the mouth of God. —v. 4

During recent elections in my country, one struggling mom I know exchanged her vote for a bag of diapers. We had discussed the benefits of each candidate, so her choice disappointed me. "But what about your convictions?" I asked. She remained silent. Six months after her candidate won, taxes went even higher. Everything is now more expensive than before . . . even diapers!

In countries around the world, political corruption is not new. Spiritual corruption is not new either. Satan tried to lure Jesus into "selling" His convictions (MATT. 4:1–10). The tempter came to Him when He was tired and hungry. He offered Him immediate satisfaction, fresh bread in seconds, a miraculous delivery, the kingdoms of the world and their glory.

But Jesus knew better. He knew that shortcuts were dangerous enemies. They may offer a road free from suffering, but in the end the pain they carry is much worse than anything we can imagine. "It is written," Jesus said three times during His temptation (VV. 4, 7, 10). He held firm to what He knew was true from God and His Word.

When we are tempted, God can help us too. We can depend on Him and the truth of His Word to help us avoid dangerous shortcuts. *KEILA OCHOA*

What shortcuts to satisfaction do I tend to be tempted by?
What could I do to prepare myself?

God's road is not easy, but it leads to eternal satisfaction.

A Place to Be

Read: Nehemiah 1:4–11

I am going . . . to prepare a place for you. —John 14:2

A thousand strands of time, events, and people weave into a tapestry we call *place*. More than just a house, place is where meaning, belonging, and safety come together under the covering of our best efforts at unconditional love. Place beckons us with memories buried deep in our souls. Even when our place isn't perfect, its hold on us is dramatic, magnetic.

The Bible speaks frequently of place. We see an example in Nehemiah's longing for a restored Jerusalem (NEH. 1:3–4; 2:2). It's no surprise, then, that Jesus would speak of place when He wants to comfort us. "Do not let your hearts be troubled," He began. Then He added: "I am going . . . to prepare a place for you" (JOHN 14:1–2).

For those who have fond memories of earthly places, this promise links us to something we can easily understand and look forward to. And for those whose places have been anything but comforting and safe, Jesus promises that one day they will hear the sweet song place sings, for they will inhabit it with Him.

Whatever the struggle, whatever the faltering on your faith journey, remember this: There's a place in heaven already waiting, fitted just for you. Jesus wouldn't have said so if it weren't true. *RANDY KILGORE*

Jesus, I can't wait to live in the home you have prepared for me.
Thank you that no matter what my earthly place holds, comfort or pain,
my home with you will be so much better.

May the memory of our earthly place point us with hope to our heavenly place.

A Gift of Hope

Read: Judges 13:1–7

He will take the lead in delivering Israel from the hands of the Philistines. —v. 5

When a powerful typhoon swept through the city of Tacloban, Philippines, in 2013, an estimated 10,000 people died, and many who survived found themselves homeless and jobless. Necessities became scarce. Three months later, while the town was still struggling to dig itself out from the destruction, a baby was born on a roadside near Tacloban amid torrents of rain and strong wind. Although the weather brought back painful memories, residents worked together to find a midwife and transport the mother and newborn to a clinic. The baby survived, thrived, and became a symbol of hope during a time of despair.

Forty years of Philistine oppression marked a grim period in Israel's national history. During this time, an angel informed an Israelite woman that she would give birth to a special son (JUDG. 13:3). According to the angel, the baby would be a Nazirite—a man set apart to God—and would "take the lead in delivering Israel from the hands of the Philistines" (v. 5). The infant, Samson, was a gift of hope born in a troubled time.

Trouble is unavoidable, yet Jesus has the power to rescue us from despair. Christ was born "to shine on those living in darkness and in the shadow of death, to guide our feet into the path of peace" (LUKE 1:76–79).

JENNIFER BENSON SCHULDT

Lord, help me to see beyond my circumstances and put my hope in you. All authority and power are yours. Remind me of your goodness, and let me rest in your love.

Jesus is the hope that calms life's storms.

Justice and Mercy Combined

Read: Nahum 1:1–9

The LORD is good, a refuge in times of trouble. —v. 7

When a defendant stands before a judge, he or she is at the mercy of the court. If the defendant is innocent, the court should be a refuge. But if the defendant is guilty, we expect the court to exact punishment.

In Nahum, we see God as both a refuge and a judge. It says, "The LORD is good, a refuge in times of trouble" (1:7). But it also says, "He will make an end of Nineveh; he will pursue his foes into the realm of darkness" (v. 8). Over 100 years earlier, Nineveh had repented after Jonah preached God's forgiveness, and the land was safe (JONAH 3:10). But during Nahum's day, Nineveh was plotting "evil against the LORD" (NAH. 1:11). In chapter 3, Nahum details Nineveh's destruction.

Many people know only one side of God's dealings with the human race but not the other. They think that He is holy and wants only to punish us, or that He is merciful and wants only to show kindness. In truth, He is judge and refuge. Peter writes that Jesus "entrusted himself to him who judges justly" (1 PETER 2:23). As a result, He "bore our sins in his body on the cross, so that we might die to sins and live for righteousness" (v. 24).

The whole truth about God is good news! He is judge, but because of Jesus, we can go to Him as our refuge. *DAVE BRANON*

Lord, never let us underestimate you by seeing only one side of your role in our lives. Help us to enjoy your love and kindness while recognizing how much you hate sin.

God's justice and mercy intersect at the cross.

The Family of Faith

Read: 1 Thessalonians 2:6–14

We loved you so much. —v. 8

During the 1980s, a singles' class at our church became a close-knit family for many people who had lost a spouse through divorce or death. When someone needed to move, class members packed boxes, carried furniture, and provided food. Birthdays and holidays were no longer solitary events as faith and friendship merged into an ongoing relationship of encouragement. Many of those bonds forged during adversity three decades ago continue to flourish and sustain individuals and families today.

Paul's letter to the followers of Jesus in Thessalonica paints a picture of life-giving relationships in God's family. "Just as a nursing mother cares for her children, so we cared for you" (1 THESS. 2:7). "Surely you remember, brothers and sisters, our toil and hardship; we worked . . . not to be a burden to anyone" (v. 9). "We dealt with each of you as a father deals with his own children" (v. 11). Like mothers, fathers, brothers, and sisters, Paul and his associates shared the gospel and their lives with these fellow believers whom they "loved . . . so much" (v. 8).

In God's family of faith, He provides mothers, fathers, sisters, and brothers for us. The Lord gives His joy as we share our lives together in His grace and love.

DAVID MCCASLAND

Father, you've called us to serve one another. Give me a heart willing to accept the care of others. May I ask for help when I am in need and respond with a heart of grace to others when they ask me for help.

God loves you and me; let's love one another.

March 23

Son Reflector

Read: John 1:1–9

He came as a witness to testify concerning that light. —v. 7

The cozy little village of Rjukan, Norway, is a delightful place to live—except during the dark days of winter. Located in a valley at the foot of the towering Gaustatoppen Mountain, the town receives no direct sunlight for nearly half of the year. Residents had long considered the idea of placing mirrors at the top of the mountain to reflect the sun. But the concept was not feasible until recently. In 2005, a local artist began "The Mirror Project" to bring together people who could turn the idea into reality. Eight years later, in October 2013, the mirrors went into action. Residents crowded into the town square to soak up the reflected sunlight.

In a spiritual sense, much of the world is like the village of Rjukan—mountains of troubles keep the light of Jesus from getting through. But God strategically places His children to act as reflectors. One such person was John the Baptist, who came "to testify concerning that light"—Jesus—who gives light to "those living in darkness and in the shadow of death" (JOHN 1:7; LUKE 1:79).

Just as sunlight is essential for emotional and physical health, so exposure to the light of Jesus is essential for spiritual health. Thankfully, every believer is in a position to reflect His light into the world's dark places.

JULIE ACKERMAN LINK

Dear Father, help me to reflect your light into the world around me today.
May all that I say and do bear witness of your light and truth.
May others see how wonderful you are.

A world in darkness needs the light of Jesus.

MARCH 24

Simply Trusting

Read: Psalm 56

When I am afraid, I put my trust in you. –v. 3

When our children were young, taking them to the doctor's office was an interesting experience. The waiting room was filled with toys they could play with and children's magazines I would read to them. So getting that far with them was no problem. But as soon as I picked them up to carry them into the appointment, everything changed. Suddenly the fun turned into fear as the nurse approached with the needle for the needed shot. The closer she got, the tighter they hugged my neck. They would cling to me for comfort, probably hoping for rescue, not knowing that it was for their own good.

Sometimes in this fallen world we move from times of peace and tranquility into the painful realm of trouble. At that point, the question is, "How will I respond?" We can be fearful and wonder why God allowed this to happen to us, or we can trust that in the midst of this trouble He is doing something that in the end is for our best, even if it hurts. We would do well to remember the words of the psalmist who wrote, "When I am afraid, I put my trust in you" (PS. 56:3).

Like my children, the tougher it gets, the tighter we should hug His neck. Trust Him. His love never fails! *JOE STOWELL*

Come quickly, Lord, to help me. Teach me to trust you in times of trouble. Remind me of your presence and of the fact that you hold me in your loving arms.

Cling to your heavenly Father; He is your only hope.

God's Clocks

Read: Luke 2:36–40

She . . . spoke about the child to all who were looking forward to the redemption of Jerusalem. —v. 38

I visit two elderly women from time to time. One has no financial worries, is fit for her age, and lives in her own home. But she can always find something negative to say. The other is crippled with arthritis and rather forgetful. She lives in simple accommodations, and keeps a reminder pad so she won't forget her appointments. But to every visitor to her tiny apartment, her first comment is always the same: "God is so good to me." Handing her the reminder pad on my last visit, I noticed that she had written the day before "Out to lunch tomorrow! Wonderful! Another happy day."

Anna was a prophetess at the time of Jesus's birth, and her circumstances were hard (LUKE 2:36–37). Widowed early and possibly childless, she may have felt purposeless and destitute. But her focus was on God and serving Him. She was yearning for the Messiah, but in the meantime she was busy about God's business—praying, fasting, and teaching others all that she had learned from Him.

Finally the day arrived when she—now in her eighties—saw the infant Messiah in his young mother's arms. All her patient waiting was worthwhile. Her heart sang with joy as she praised God and then passed the glad news on to others. *MARION STROUD*

Lord, I don't want to be a complainer anymore. I want to be a person who overflows with thankfulness for others and for you. May I accept whatever you give me in your time. Show me how to start today.

It's hard to see both God's plan and our part. But their intersection is the best place to be.

The Definite Choice

Read: Joshua 24:15–24

We will serve the LORD. —v. 21

Coming from someone who used to value ancestral gods, my 90-year-old father's statement near the end of his life was remarkable: "When I die," he spoke laboriously, "nobody should do anything other than what the church will do. No soothsaying, no ancestral sacrifices, no rituals. As my life is in the hands of Jesus Christ, so shall my death be!"

My father chose the path of Christ in his old age when he invited Jesus into his life as Savior. His contemporaries mocked him: "An old man like you shouldn't be going to church!" But my father's choice to follow and worship the true God was definite, like the people Joshua addressed.

"Choose for yourselves this day whom you will serve," Joshua challenged them. "But as for me and my household, we will serve the LORD" (JOSH. 24:15). Their response was resolute—they chose to worship the Lord. Even after Joshua warned them to count the cost (vv. 19–20), they still resolved to follow the Lord, recalling His deliverance, provision, and protection (vv. 16–17, 21).

Such a confident choice, however, calls for equally confident actions, as Joshua strongly reminded them: "Throw away the foreign gods . . . and yield your hearts to the LORD" (v. 23). Have you made a choice to live for God?

LAWRENCE DARMANI

Teach me all it means, Lord, to choose you. I want my words, actions, and attitudes to show the love for you that I have in my heart. you are worthy of far more than I could ever do.

A definite choice demands definite actions.

Foley Artists

Read: John 16:7–15

Satan himself masquerades as an angel of light. –2 Corinthians 11:14

Crunch. Crunch. Whoosh! In the early days of film, Foley artists created sounds to support the story's action. Squeezing a leather pouch filled with cornstarch made the sound of snow crunching, shaking a pair of gloves sounded like bird wings flapping, and waving a thin stick made a whoosh sound. To make movies as realistic as possible, these artists used creative techniques to replicate sounds.

Like sounds, messages can be replicated. One of Satan's most frequently used techniques is that of replicating messages in spiritually dangerous ways. Paul warns in 2 Corinthians 11:13-14, "For such people are false apostles, deceitful workers, masquerading as apostles of Christ. And no wonder, for Satan himself masquerades as an angel of light." Paul is warning us about false teachers who turn our attention away from Jesus Christ and the message of His grace.

Jesus said that one purpose of the Holy Spirit living in us is that "when he, the Spirit of truth, comes, he will guide you into all the truth" (JOHN 16:13). With the help and guidance of the Spirit, we can find the safety of truth in a world of counterfeit messages. *BILL CROWDER*

We need you, Holy Spirit, to help us discern truth from error.
We can be easily deceived by others or even by our own hearts.
May we be open to learn from you and not be led astray.

The Holy Spirit is our ever-present Teacher.

Trail Trees

Read: Isaiah 53:4–12

They pierce my hands and my feet. . . . They divide my clothes among them and cast lots for my garment. –Psalm 22:16–18

In recent years, my daughter has become fascinated with the history of the indigenous people in northern Michigan where she lives. One summer afternoon when I was visiting, she showed me a road that had a sign designating "Trail Trees." She explained to me that it's believed that long ago the Native Americans bent young trees to point the way to specific destinations and that they continued to grow in an unusual shape.

The Old Testament serves a similar purpose. Many commands and teachings of the Bible direct our hearts to the way the Lord wants us to live. The Ten Commandments are great examples of that. But in addition, the prophets of the Old Testament pointed the way to a coming Messiah. Thousands of years before Jesus came, they spoke of Bethlehem—Jesus's birthplace (SEE MICAH 5:2 AND MATT. 2:1–6). They described Jesus's death on the cross in striking detail (SEE PS. 22:14–18 AND JOHN 19:23–24). And Isaiah 53:1-12 points to the sacrifice Jesus would make as the Lord "laid on him the iniquity of us all" (v. 6; SEE LUKE 23:33).

Millennia ago, God's Old Testament servants pointed to God's Son—Jesus—the One who "took up our pain and bore our suffering" (ISA. 53:4). He is the way to life.

CINDY HESS KASPER

Thank you for the simple message of salvation.
Jesus, you are the way, the truth, and the life.
Thank you for giving your life for me. I love you.

Jesus sacrificed His life for ours.

The Mud Puddle

Read: Psalm 119:1–8

Blessed are those who keep His statutes and seek him with all their heart! —v. 2

My friend Ed was telling me a story about his little son. He was standing in a mud puddle, so Ed told him to get out. But instead, his son began running through the puddle. "No *running* through it either," he said. So the boy began walking through the water. When Ed told him, "No *walking*!" the boy stood with just his toes in the water, looking defiantly at his dad. The child knew what his father wanted, but he didn't want to do it.

Sometimes I'm like that stubborn little boy. I know that what I'm doing isn't pleasing to the Lord, but I do it anyway. God told the children of Israel to "fully obey the LORD your God" (DEUT. 28:1), but they failed repeatedly. The psalmist acknowledged his struggle in Psalm 119, "Oh, that my ways were steadfast in obeying your decrees!" (v. 5).

Jealousy, hatred, rebellion—they occur all too often. But God provided for our redemption through the sacrifice of His Son, the Lord Jesus Christ. The Holy Spirit helps us when we are tempted (1 COR. 10:13); and when we confess our wrongdoing, God promises to forgive us (1 JOHN 1:9).

If you are like me and keep running back into the mud puddles of life, don't give up. God will help you to resist temptation, and He will never stop loving you!

DAVE EGNER

Dear Lord, help me when I'm tempted. Bring the promises of the Bible to mind and strengthen me by your Holy Spirit to say no to temptation. Let all my words and deeds bring honor to your name.

To master temptation, let Christ master you.

Sharing a Burger

Read: James 2:14–17

Do not forget to do good and to share with others, for with such sacrifices God is pleased. —Hebrews 13:16

Lee Geysbeek of Compassion International told about a woman who had the opportunity to travel to a distant land to visit the child she sponsored. She decided to take the child, who was living in abject poverty, to a restaurant.

The boy ordered a hamburger, and the sponsor ordered a salad. When the food came to the table, the boy, who assuredly had never had such a meal in his life, surveyed the scene. He looked at his huge hamburger and over at his sponsor's small salad. Then he took his knife and cut the burger in half, offered it to his sponsor, rubbed his tummy, and asked, "Hungry?"

A child who had next to nothing his whole life was willing to share half of what he had with someone he thought might need more. This child can be a good reminder the next time we meet someone in physical, emotional, or spiritual need. As followers of Jesus, our faith in Him should be mirrored through our actions (JAMES 2:17).

We encounter people in need every day. Some around the globe, some simply around the corner. Some in need of a warm meal, others a kind word. What a difference followers of Christ, who have experienced His love, could make by doing good and sharing (HEB. 13:16). *DAVE BRANON*

Today, Lord, help me see beyond my own problems to the needs of others. Guide my hand to give instead of get, to offer instead of ask, and to bless instead of seeking blessings. May your name be honored.

To be doing good is man's most glorious task. SOPHOCLES

When We're Let Down

Read: 1 Samuel 17:33–50

It is not by sword and spear that the LORD saves; for the battle is the LORD's, and he will give all of you into our hands. –v. 47

On August 4, 1991, the MTS *Oceanos* cruise ship ran into a terrible storm off the coast of South Africa. When the ship began to sink, the captain decided to abandon ship and left with his officers, failing to notify those onboard of any problem. Passenger Moss Hills, a British musician, noticed that something was wrong and sent out a Mayday signal to the South African coast guard. Then, taking matters into their own hands, Moss, his wife Tracy, and other entertainers on board helped organize the evacuation of all passengers by assisting them as they were lifted into helicopters.

Sometimes those we look to for leadership can let us down. When King Saul and his officers faced the belligerent insults of the Philistine giant Goliath, they responded with fear and timidity (1 SAM. 17:11). But a young musician and shepherd boy named David had faith in God that transformed his perspective on this threat. David said to Goliath, "You come against me with sword and spear . . . , but I come against you in the name of the LORD Almighty" (v. 45). David defeated the enemy and turned the tide of battle (v. 50). He did not look to earthly leaders for his strength but to the living God.

When others let us down, God may be calling us to provide leadership in His strength and for His honor. *DENNIS FISHER*

Dear Lord, I don't have the power on my own to lead others through a difficult situation. But you are all-powerful. Give me the courage to help others as I rely on your strength that cannot fail.

Only as we follow Christ can we lead others in the right direction.

That Is Mine!

Read: Ezekiel 29:1–9

I am the Lord; that is my name! —Isaiah 42:8

The Nile of Africa, which spans 6,650 kilometers (more than 4,100 miles) and flows northward across several northeastern African countries, is the world's longest river. Over the centuries, the Nile has provided sustenance and livelihood for millions of citizens in the countries it passes through. Currently, Ethiopia is building what will become Africa's largest hydro-power dam on the Nile. It will be a great resource for the area.

Pharaoh, the king of Egypt, claimed to be the Nile's owner and originator. He and all Egypt boasted, "The Nile belongs to me; I made it for myself" (Ezek. 29:3, 9). They failed to acknowledge that God alone provides natural resources. As a result, God promised to punish the nation (vv. 8–9).

We are to care for God's creation, and not forget that everything we have comes from the Lord. Romans 11:36 says, "For from him and through him and for him are all things. To him be the glory forever!" He is the One who also endows humanity with the ability to manufacture and invent man-made resources. Whenever we talk about a good thing that has come to us or that we have accomplished, we need to remember what God says in Isaiah 42:8, "I am the Lord; that is my name! I will not yield my glory to another."

Lawrence Darmani

Praise the Lord God, the God of Israel, who alone does such wonderful things. Praise your glorious name forever! Let the whole earth be filled with your glory.

To God be the glory—great things He has done!

Pray First

Read: 1 Samuel 23:1–5

[David] inquired of the Lord. –v. 2

When my husband and I supervise our son's piano practice sessions, we begin by asking God to help us. We pray first because neither my husband nor I know how to play the instrument. Together, all three of us are coming to understand musical mysteries such as the meaning of "staccato" and "legato" and when to use the piano's black keys.

Prayer becomes a priority when we realize that we need God's help. David needed God's assistance in a dangerous situation as he considered fighting the Philistines in the city of Keilah. Before engaging in battle, "[David] inquired of the Lord, saying, 'Shall I go and attack these Philistines?'" (1 Sam. 23:2). God gave His approval. However, David's men admitted that the enemy forces intimidated them. Before a single sword was lifted against the Philistines, David prayed again. God promised him the victory he later claimed (v. 4).

Does prayer guide our lives, or is it our last resort when trouble strikes? We sometimes fall into the habit of making plans and then asking God to bless them, or praying only in moments of desperation. God does want us to turn to Him in moments of need. But He also wants us to remember that we need Him all the time (Prov. 3:5–6).

Jennifer Benson Schuldt

Dear God, please guide me as I walk through this life.
Help me not to act only by my own wisdom, but to seek your will
in every situation.

God wants us to pray before we do anything at all.

Don't Worry!

Read: 1 Peter 5:1–11

Casting all your care upon Him, for He cares for you. —v. 7 NKJV

George Burns, American actor and humorist, said, "If you ask, 'What is the single most important key to longevity?' I would have to say it is avoiding worry, stress, and tension. And if you didn't ask me, I'd still have to say it." Burns, who lived to be 100, enjoyed making people laugh, and apparently followed his own advice.

But how can we keep from worrying when our lives are so uncertain, so filled with problems and needs? The apostle Peter offered this encouragement to the followers of Jesus who had been forcibly scattered across Asia during the first century: "Humble yourselves, therefore, under God's mighty hand, that he may lift you up in due time. Cast all your anxiety on him because he cares for you" (1 PETER 5:6–7).

Peter's instructions were not given to help us avoid suffering (v. 9), but so we can find peace and power to stand victorious against the attacks of Satan (vv. 8–10). Instead of being consumed by anxiety and worry, we are set free to enjoy God's love for us and express it to each other.

Our goal should not be to see how many years we can live but instead to live fully in loving service to the Lord for all the years we are given.

DAVID MCCASLAND

Lord, I admit that I take things into my own hands and worry.
That weighs my spirit down and sometimes robs my nights of rest.
Lift the heaviness from my heart as I lean into you.

God is my Father, I will never think of anything that He will forget, so why should I worry? OSWALD CHAMBERS

Too Much for Me

Read: Matthew 26:36–46

My Father, if it is possible, may this cup be taken from me. —v. 39

"God never gives us more than we can handle," someone said to a father whose 5-year-old son had just lost his battle with cancer. These words, which were intended to encourage him, instead depressed him and caused him to wonder why he wasn't "handling" the loss of his boy at all. The pain was so much to bear that he could hardly even breathe. He knew his grief was too much for him and that he desperately needed God to hold him tight.

The verse that some use to support the statement "God never gives us more than we can handle" is 1 Corinthians 10:13, "When you are tempted, he will also provide a way out so that you can endure it." But the context of these words is temptation, not suffering. We can choose the way out of temptation that God provides, but we can't choose a way out of suffering.

Jesus himself wanted a way out of His upcoming suffering when He prayed, "My soul is overwhelmed with sorrow to the point of death. . . . My Father, if it is possible, may this cup be taken from me" (MATT. 26:38–39). Yet He willingly went through this for our salvation.

When life seems too much to bear, that's when we throw ourselves on God's mercy, and He holds on to us. *ANNE CETAS*

Father, I feel vulnerable and weak. I know you are my refuge and strength, my help in trouble. I call upon your name, Lord. Hold on to me.

With God behind you and His arms beneath you, you can face whatever lies ahead.

The Best Fishing Holes

Read: Revelation 22:1–5

[Paul] was caught up to paradise and heard inexpressible things.
—2 Corinthians 12:4

My friend Gus passed away a few months ago. Gus was a fellow trout fisherman. Weekends usually found him in his little boat on a nearby lake, casting for fish. I got a letter from his daughter Heidi the other day. She told me she's been talking about heaven with her grandkids since Gus went to his home in heaven. Her 6-year-old grandson, who also loves to fish, explained what heaven is like and what Great-Grandpa Gus is doing: "It's really beautiful," he mused, "and Jesus is showing Grandpa Gus where the best fishing holes are."

When Paul reported his God-given vision of heaven, words failed him. He said, "I was caught up to paradise and heard things so astounding that they cannot be expressed in words" (2 COR. 12:4 NLT). Words cannot convey the facts of heaven—perhaps because we humans are unable to comprehend them.

While we might gain some comfort from knowing more details about heaven, it is not the knowledge of heaven that assures us; it is our knowledge of God himself. Because I know Him and I know how good He is, I can leave this life and everything in it with utter confidence that heaven will be beautiful and Jesus will show me "where the best fishing holes are"—because that's the kind of God He is! *DAVID ROPER*

Let us beg and pray Him day by day to reveal Himself to our souls more fully, to quicken our sense, to give us sight and hearing, taste and touch of the world to come.
JOHN HENRY NEWMAN

Nothing on earth compares to being with Christ in heaven.

Pascal's Prayer

Read: Philippians 4:4–13

So whether you eat or drink or whatever you do, do it all for the glory of God. —1 Corinthians 10:31

Blaise Pascal, the brilliant seventeenth-century intellectual, made significant contributions in the fields of science and mathematics. He established the groundwork for the development of mechanical calculators and modern hydraulic operations.

As a young man, Pascal had a profound encounter with Jesus Christ. This life-changing experience motivated him to refocus his study from science and math to theology.

Pascal wrote a remarkable prayer that can help each believer in facing the tasks of life. He prayed: "Lord, help me to do great things as though they were little, since I do them with Your power; and little things as though they were great, since I do them in Your name."

Pascal's supplication is profoundly scriptural. Paul said, "I can do all this through him who gives me strength" (PHIL. 4:13) and admonishes us: "Whatever you do, do it all for the glory of God" (1 COR. 10:31). Pascal echoes these admonitions to depend on God for His power and to view every act as important, since it will reflect on His glory.

The next time you face a huge task, remember that God is your strength. And when you encounter a seemingly insignificant one, determine to do it with excellence to the glory of God. *DENNIS FISHER*

Lord, help me to do great things as though they were little, since I do them with your power; and little things as though they were great, since I do them in your name.

"Expect great things from God; attempt great things for God."

WILLIAM CAREY

Firm Foundation

Read: Matthew 7:21–27

Everyone who hears these words of mine and puts them into practice is like a wise man who built his house on the rock. —v. 24

Earthquakes are prevalent in the Pacific Rim region known as the "Ring of Fire." Ninety percent of the world's earthquakes and 81 percent of the world's largest earthquakes occur there. I learned that many buildings in the city of Hong Kong have been built on granite, which could help minimize damage in the event of an earthquake. The foundation of buildings is especially important in earthquake-prone regions of the world.

Jesus Christ told His followers that a stable foundation is critical in building lives. He said, "Therefore everyone who hears these words of mine and puts them into practice is like a wise man who built his house on the rock. The rain came down, the streams rose, and the winds blew and beat against that house; yet it did not fall, because it had its foundation on the rock" (MATT. 7:24–25). The foundation of Jesus Christ is what will give us the stability our hearts and lives need now and into the future.

By allowing the Lord's wisdom to guide us in our relationships, decisions, and priorities, we find that He provides the most trustworthy foundation any life could ever be built upon. *BILL CROWDER*

Gracious Father, you are the Lord God, the King of heaven, and I choose to place my hope in you because you alone are worthy of my trust.

Jesus is the best foundation upon which to build a solid life.

Fragrant Living

Read: Philippians 4:10–20

I am amply supplied, now that I have received . . . the gifts you sent. They are a fragrant offering . . . to God. —v. 18

I'm grateful that God has given us the sense of smell so we can enjoy the many fragrances of life. I think of how much I enjoy something as simple as the fresh and inviting aroma of after-shave lotion in the morning. Or the mellow smell of fresh-cut grass in the spring. I especially enjoy sitting in the backyard when the delicate scent of my favorite roses fills the air. And then there are the savory aromas of delicious food.

So it catches my attention when the apostle Paul says that our generous acts of love toward others are like a "fragrant offering, an acceptable sacrifice, pleasing to God" (PHIL. 4:18). When we think of helping those in need, we usually think of it as the right thing to do—or even the Christlike thing to do. But Paul says that our intentional act of reaching out to meet someone's need actually fills the throne room of God with a fragrance that brings pleasure to Him.

We can please God with the aromas that rise from being a blessing to others! What an added incentive this is for us to perform deeds of kindness in His name.

Who might need your act of kindness today? Ask the Lord to lead you to someone. Be a blessing. It's a fragrant thing to do! *JOE STOWELL*

What can you do for someone else today?

Blessing others is a blessing to God.

Who Are You?

Read: Matthew 21:1–11

When Jesus entered Jerusalem, the whole city was stirred and asked, "Who is this?" —v. 10

From time to time, we read of people who are offended at not being treated with what they consider due respect and deference. "Do you know who I am?" they shout indignantly. And we are reminded of the statement, "If you have to tell people who you are, you probably really aren't who you think you are." The polar opposite of this arrogance and self-importance is seen in Jesus, even as His life on earth was nearing its end.

Jesus entered Jerusalem to shouts of praise from the people (MATT. 21:7–9). When others throughout the city asked, "Who is this?" the crowds answered, "This is Jesus, the prophet from Nazareth in Galilee" (VV. 10–11). He didn't come claiming special privileges, but in humility He came to give His life in obedience to His Father's will.

The words Jesus said and the things He did commanded respect. Unlike insecure rulers, He never demanded that others respect Him. His greatest hours of suffering appeared to be His lowest point of weakness and failure. Yet, the strength of His identity and mission carried Jesus through the darkest hours as He died for our sins so that we might live in His love.

He is worthy of our lives and our devotion today. Do we recognize who He is?

DAVID MCCASLAND

Lord, I am in awe of your humility, strength, and love.
And I am embarrassed by my desires for self-importance.
May knowing you change every self-centered motive in my heart into a longing to live as you did in this world.

When once you have seen Jesus, you can never be the same.

OSWALD CHAMBERS

It's Beautiful!

Read: Mark 14:3–9

"Leave her alone," said Jesus. "Why are you bothering her? She has done a beautiful thing to me." —v. 6

After being away on business, Terry wanted to pick up some small gifts for his children. The clerk at the airport gift shop recommended a number of costly items. "I don't have that much money with me," he said. "I need something less expensive." The clerk tried to make him feel that he was being cheap. But Terry knew his children would be happy with whatever he gave them, because it came from a heart of love. And he was right—they loved the gifts he brought them.

During Jesus's last visit to the town of Bethany, Mary wanted to show her love for Him (MARK 14:3–9). So she brought "an alabaster jar of very expensive perfume" and poured it on his head (v. 3). The disciples asked angrily, "Why this waste?" (MATT. 26:8). Jesus told them to stop troubling her, for "she has done a beautiful thing to me" (MARK 14:6). Jesus delighted in her gift, for it came from a heart of love. Even anointing Him for burial was beautiful!

What would you like to give to Jesus to show your love? Your time, talent, treasure? It doesn't matter if it's costly or inexpensive, whether others understand or criticize. Whatever is given from a heart of love is beautiful to Him. *ANNE CETAS*

Nothing I could give you, Father, could repay you for your sacrifice.
But I want to give you what you would think is beautiful.
I give you my heart today in thankfulness for your love.

A healthy heart beats with love for Jesus.

Why Me?

Read: Mark 14:10–21

God demonstrates his own love for us in this: While we were still sinners, Christ died for us. —Romans 5:8

British pastor Joseph Parker was asked, "Why did Jesus choose Judas to be one of His disciples?" He thought deeply about the question for a while but could not come up with an answer. He said that he kept running into an even more baffling question: "Why did He choose me?"

That's a question that has been asked throughout the centuries. When people become painfully aware of their sin and are overcome with guilt, they cry out to Jesus for mercy. In joyous wonder they experience the truth that God loves them, that Jesus died for them, and that they are forgiven of all their sins. It's incomprehensible!

I too have asked, "Why me?" I know that the dark and sinful deeds of my life were motivated by a heart even darker, and yet God loved me! (ROM. 5:8). I was undeserving, wretched, and helpless, yet He opened His arms and His heart to me. I could almost hear Him whisper, "I love you even more than you loved your sin."

It's true! I cherished my sin. I protected it. I denied its wrongdoing. Yet God loved me enough to forgive me and set me free.

"Why me?" It's beyond my understanding. Yet I know He loves me—and He loves you too!

DAVE EGNER

How wonderful is your grace, Jesus! It's greater than all my sin.
You've taken away my burdens and set my spirit free.
Thank you.

God loves us not because of who we are, but because of who He is.

Pain with a Purpose

Read: John 16:17–24

[Jesus said,] "I will see you again and you will rejoice, and no one will take away your joy." –v. 22

I asked several friends what their most difficult, painful experience in life had been. Their answers included war, divorce, surgery, and the loss of a loved one. My wife's reply was, "The birth of our first child." It was a long and difficult labor in a lonely army hospital. But looking back, she said she considers it joyful "because the pain had a big purpose."

Just before Jesus went to the cross, He told His followers they were about to go through a time of great pain and sorrow. The Lord compared their coming experience to that of a woman during childbirth when her anguish turns to joy after her child is born (JOHN 16:20–21). "Now is your time of grief, but I will see you again and you will rejoice, and no one will take away your joy" (v. 22).

Sorrow comes to us all along the road of life. But Jesus, "for the joy set before him . . . endured the cross, scorning its shame" (HEB. 12:2), purchased forgiveness and freedom for all who open their hearts to Him. His painful sacrifice accomplished God's eternal purpose of opening the way to friendship and fellowship with Him.

The joy of our Savior outweighed His suffering, just as the joy He gives us overshadows all our pain. *DAVID MCCASLAND*

Dear Father, your precious Son Jesus chose suffering for me. Thank you for His sacrifice on my behalf. Thank you that even my pain can be a tool in your hands to make me more like your Son.

Suffering can be like a magnet that draws the Christian close to Christ.

Enjoying His Meal

Read: 1 Corinthians 11:23–34

Do this in remembrance of me. –v. 24

It's not about the table, whether it's square or round. It's not about the chairs—plastic or wooden. It's not about the food, although it helps if it has been cooked with love. A good meal is enjoyed when we turn off the TV and our cell phones and concentrate on those we're with.

I love gathering around the table, enjoying a good chat with friends and family and talking about a multitude of topics. However, instant technology has made it difficult. Sometimes we are more concerned about what others—sometimes miles away—have to say than what the person just across the table is saying.

We have been invited to another meal at the table when we come together in one place to celebrate the Lord's Supper. It's not about the church, if it's big or small. It's not about the type of bread. It's about turning off our thoughts from our worries and concerns and focusing on Jesus.

When was the last time we enjoyed being at the Lord's Table? Do we enjoy His presence, or are we more concerned with what's going on somewhere else? This is important, "for whenever you eat this bread and drink this cup, you proclaim the Lord's death until he comes" (1 COR. 11:26).

KEILA OCHOA

I want to learn, dear Lord, when I sit at your Table,
to concentrate only on your great love and sacrifice for us.
Help me to enjoy the fellowship of others as we remember together
what Jesus did for us at Calvary.

Remembering Christ's death gives us courage for today and hope for tomorrow.

And Then You Laugh

Read: 2 Corinthians 5:1–8

God made him who had no sin to be sin for us, so that in him we might become the righteousness of God. —v. 21

Noise. Vibration. Pressure. Fireball. Canadian astronaut Chris Hadfield used these words to describe being launched into space. As the rocket raced toward the International Space Station, the weight of gravity increased and breathing became difficult. Just when he thought he would pass out, the rocket made a fiery breakthrough into weightlessness. Instead of lapsing into unconsciousness, he broke into laughter.

His description made me think of the days leading to my mother's death. The heaviness of life kept increasing until she no longer had the strength to breathe. She was then released from her pain and broke free into the "weightlessness" of heaven. I like to think of her laughing when she took her first breath in Jesus's presence.

On the Friday we call "good," something similar happened to Jesus. God placed on Him the weight of the entire world's sin—past, present, and future—until He could no longer breathe. Then He said, "Father, into your hands I commit my spirit" (LUKE 23:46). After being suffocated by our sin, Jesus received back from God the life entrusted to Him and now lives where sin and death have no power. All who trust Christ will one day join Him, and I wonder if we'll look back at this life and laugh.

JULIE ACKERMAN LINK

Father in heaven, words cannot describe our gratitude for your Son Jesus, who bore the weight of our sins. Thank you that to be absent from this body with its heavy burdens is to be present with you forever.

The sacrifice of Jesus points us to the joy of heaven.

The Tree of Love

Read: Matthew 27:27–35

[Jesus] bore our sins in His own body on the tree. –1 Peter 2:24

The corkscrew willow tree stood vigil over our backyard for more than 20 years. It shaded all four of our children as they played in the yard, and it provided shelter for the neighborhood squirrels. But when springtime came and the tree didn't awaken from its winter slumber, it was time to bring it down.

Every day for a week I worked on that tree—first to fell it and then to chop two decades of growth into manageable pieces. It gave me a lot of time to think about trees.

I thought about the first tree—the one on which hung the forbidden fruit that Adam and Eve just couldn't resist (GEN. 3:6). God used that tree to test their loyalty and trust. Then there's the tree in Psalm 1 that reminds us of the fruitfulness of godly living. And in Proverbs 3:18, wisdom is personified as a tree of life.

But it is a transplanted tree that is most important—the crude cross of Calvary that was hewn from a sturdy tree. There our Savior hung between heaven and earth to bear every sin of every generation on His shoulders. It stands above all trees as a symbol of love, sacrifice, and salvation.

At Calvary, God's only Son suffered a horrible death on a cross. That's the tree of life for us. *DAVE BRANON*

Father, on this day between Good Friday and Easter Sunday,
we're grateful for the cross and for your Son who gave His life
so that we might have life. Thank you.

The cross of Christ reveals man's sin at its worst and God's love at its best.

Come to Me

Read: John 20:24–31

Blessed are those who have not seen and yet have believed. —v. 29

Charlotte Elliott wrote the hymn "Just As I Am" in 1834. She had been an invalid for many years, and though she wanted to help with a fundraiser for a girl's school, she was too ill. She felt useless, and this inner distress caused her to begin doubting her faith in Christ. She wrote "Just As I Am" as a response to her doubt. The crux of her distress is perhaps best expressed in these words:

Just as I am, though tossed about
With many a conflict, many a doubt,
Fightings and fears within, without,
O Lamb of God, I come!

Three days after His death and burial, Jesus rose from the grave and invited the disciple whom history has nicknamed "Doubting Thomas" to examine the marks of His crucifixion (JOHN 20:27). When Thomas touched Jesus's wounds, he finally believed in the resurrection. Christ responded, "Because you have seen me, you have believed; blessed are those who have not seen and yet have believed" (v. 29).

As Christians today, we are the ones who have not seen but still believe. Yet at times our earthly circumstances create serious questions in our souls. Even then, we cry out: "I do believe; help me overcome my unbelief!" (MARK 9:24). Jesus welcomes us to come to Him just as we are.

JENNIFER BENSON SCHULDT

Dear Jesus, help me to trust you when life doesn't make sense.
Please take my doubt and replace it with fresh faith in you.

The risen Christ opens the door for you to have fullness of life.

We're a Community

Read: 1 Corinthians 12:1–11

[The Lord] gave some . . . for the equipping of the saints for the work of ministry, for the edifying of the body of Christ. —Ephesians 4:11–12 NKJV

A pastor's wife was diagnosed with Parkinson's disease. That put the family in a difficult, stressful situation. The pastor wondered how he was going to be able to take good care of her while he still had responsibilities for his church family. But he needn't have worried because church members stepped up and volunteered to assist him with meals and some of her care.

The apostle Paul wrote to the Corinthian church about the purpose for which the Lord gave them their spiritual gifts. Before he listed the diversity of gifts in 1 Corinthians 12:8-10, he reminded them that "a spiritual gift is given to each of us so we can help each other" (v. 7 NLT). God does not give His spiritual gifts for our own selfish use but to serve others, and in so doing, we serve Him.

We are all given different gifts to be used at different times and in different ways. But they are all to be used in love "so that the body of Christ may be built up" (EPH. 4:12). Wherever God has placed us, we can use what He has gifted us to do as we see the need, remembering that we are all part of the church—the body of Christ (1 COR. 12:13–14). *C. P. HIA*

Thank you, Father, for the wonderful gifts you have given your church. Help me to understand how you have gifted me to encourage other believers, and to spread the message of your love to the world.

Use your gifts to exercise care for others.

Outrunning Cheetahs

Read: Isaiah 40:6–11, 28–31

The grass withers and the flowers fall . . . . But those who hope in the LORD will renew their strength. —vv. 7, 31

The majestic African cheetah is known for reaching speeds of 112 kph (70 mph) in short bursts, but it doesn't do so well over distances. A BBC news item reports that four members of a northeast Kenyan village actually outran two cheetahs in a 4-mile footrace.

It seems that two large cheetahs had been feeding on village goats. So the four men came up with a plan to stop them. They waited until the hottest part of the day and then gave chase to the cats, tracking them down when the animals couldn't run any farther. The exhausted cheetahs were safely captured and turned over to the Kenyan wildlife service for relocation.

Can we see ourselves in the cheetah? Our strengths might seem impressive, but they are short-lived. As the prophet Isaiah reminds us, we are like wildflowers that soon wither under the heat of the sun (40:6–8).

Yet it is at the end of ourselves that our God offers us comfort. A surprise rises up to meet those who wait on the Lord. In His time and ways, He can renew our strength. By His Spirit He can enable us to rise up on "wings like eagles" or to "run and not grow weary, [to] walk and not be faint" (v. 31).

MART DEHAAN

Lord, forgive us for the many times that we rely on our short-lived strength. Help us see that all good gifts come from you, and that you are the never-failing source of our strength, hope, and joy.

When we draw near to God, our minds are refreshed and our strength is renewed.

God's World

Read: Psalm 24

The earth is the LORD's, and everything in it. —v. 1

I knew my son would enjoy receiving a map of the world for his birthday. After some shopping, I found a colorful chart of the continents, which included illustrations in every region. A birdwing butterfly hovered over Papua, New Guinea. Mountains cascaded through Chile. A diamond adorned South Africa. I was delighted, but I wondered about the label at the bottom of the map: *Our World.*

In one sense, the earth is our world because we live in it. We're allowed to drink its water, mine its gold, and fish its seas—but only because God has given us the go-ahead (GEN. 1:28–30). Really, it's *God's World.* "The earth is the LORD's, and everything in it, the world, and all who live in it" (PS. 24:1). It amazes me that God has entrusted His incredible creation to mere humans. He knew that some of us would mistreat it, deny He made it, and claim it as ours. Still, He allows us to call it home and sustains it through His Son (COL. 1:16–17).

Today, take a moment to enjoy life in God's world. Savor the taste of some fruit. Eavesdrop on a bird and listen to its song. Revel in a sunset. Let the world you inhabit inspire you to worship the One who owns it.

JENNIFER BENSON SCHULDT

Help me, Lord, to stop occasionally. To look, to listen, to taste,
to think about the gifts you send for our enjoyment.
Thank you for expressing your creativity and love to me today.

The beauty of creation gives us reasons to sing God's praise.

A Father Who Runs

Read: Luke 15:11–24

The Son of Man came to seek and to save the lost. –Luke 19:10

Every day a father craned his neck to look toward the distant road, waiting for his son's return. And every night he went to bed disappointed. But one day, a speck appeared. A lonesome silhouette stood against the crimson sky. *Could that be my son?* the father wondered. Then he caught sight of the familiar saunter. *Yes, that has to be my son!*

And so while the son was "still a long way off, his father saw him and was filled with compassion for him; he ran to his son, threw his arms around him and kissed him" (LUKE 15:20). It is remarkable that the family patriarch did something that was considered undignified in Middle Eastern culture—he ran to meet his son. The father was full of unbridled joy at his son's return.

The son didn't deserve such a reception. When he had asked his father for his share of the inheritance and left home, it was as if he had wished his father dead. But despite all that the son had done to his father, he was still his son (v. 24).

This parable reminds me that I'm accepted by God because of His grace, not because of my merits. It assures me that I'll never sink so deep that God's grace can't reach me. Our heavenly Father is waiting to run to us with open arms. *POH FANG CHIA*

Father, I'm so grateful for all your Son did for me at the cross. I'm thankful for grace. I offer you a heart that desires to be like Jesus—merciful and gracious.

We deserve punishment and get forgiveness; we deserve God's wrath and get God's love. PHILIP YANCEY

Facing the Impossible

Read: Joshua 5:13–6:5

See, I have delivered Jericho into your hands. –6:2

In 2008, house values were tumbling in the United Kingdom. But 2 weeks after my husband and I put our home of 40 years on the market, a buyer offered us a good price and we agreed to a sale. Soon our builders started work on the house I had inherited, which would be our new home. But a few days before the sale of our old home was finalized, our buyer pulled out. We were devastated. Now we owned two properties—one whose value was tumbling rapidly, and the other a virtual ruin that we could neither sell nor move into. Until we found a new buyer, we had no money to pay the builder. It was an impossible situation.

When Joshua faced Jericho, a fortified city in lockdown, he may have felt as if he was facing an impossible situation (JOSH. 5:13–6:27). But then a Man with a drawn sword appeared to him. Some theologians think the Man was Jesus himself. Joshua anxiously asked if He would be backing the Israelites or their enemies in the forthcoming battle. "'Neither one,' he replied. 'I am the commander of the LORD's army'" (5:14 NLT). Joshua bowed in worship before he took another step. He still didn't know how Jericho would be delivered into his hand, but he listened to God and worshiped Him. Then he obeyed the Lord's instructions and the impossible happened. *MARION STROUD*

Dear Lord, often when I am faced with an impossible situation I choose worry rather than trust. Help me to trust you and to remember that nothing is too hard for you.

Nothing is impossible for the Lord.

A Happy Ending

Read: Ephesians 4:20–32

Be kind and compassionate to one another, forgiving each other, just as in Christ God forgave you. —v. 32

A friend told me about the time he was watching football on TV as his young daughter played nearby. Angered by his team's bad play, he grabbed the closest thing and threw it down. His little girl's favorite toy was shattered, along with her heart. My friend immediately embraced his daughter and apologized. He replaced the toy and thought all was well. But he didn't know how much his fury had frightened his 4-year-old, and she didn't know the depth of her pain. In time, however, forgiveness came.

Years later he sent an identical toy to his daughter when she was expecting a baby. She posted a photo of the toy on Facebook with the words, "This gift has a very long story going back to my childhood. It wasn't a happy story then, but it has a happy ending now! Redemption is a beautiful thing. Thanks, Grandpa!"

The Bible urges us to avoid angry outbursts by putting on the new self, "created to be like God in true righteousness and holiness" (EPH. 4:24). And if we are the victim of anger, God asks us to "be kind and compassionate to one another, forgiving each other, just as in Christ God forgave you" (v. 32).

Restored relationships are not easy, but they are possible by the grace of God. *DAVID MCCASLAND*

Lord, my temper can sometimes run hot. Grant me the grace to stop and think before I act or speak and the grace to apologize when I've hurt someone. Thank you for the gift of forgiveness.

Repentance and forgiveness are the glue that can repair a broken relationship.

Now Go!

Read: Exodus 4:10–17

Now go; I will help you speak and will teach you what to say. —v. 12

More than 10,000 evangelists and Christian leaders sat in a giant auditorium in Amsterdam in 1986 listening to world-renowned evangelist Billy Graham. I sat among them, listening as he narrated some of his experiences. Then, to my surprise, he said, "Let me tell you: every time I stand before the congregation of God's people to preach, I tremble and my knees wobble!"

What! I wondered. *How can such a great preacher who has enthralled millions with his powerful sermons exhibit trembling and wobbling knees?* Then he went on to describe not fear and stage fright, but intense humility and meekness as he felt inadequate for the daunting task to which God had called him. He relied on God for strength, not on his own eloquence.

Moses felt inadequate when God sent him to deliver the enslaved Israelites from their 400-year captivity in Egypt. Moses pleaded with the Lord to send someone else, with the excuse that he had never been a good speaker (SEE EX. 4:10, 13).

We may have similar fears when God calls us to do something for Him. But His encouragement to Moses can also spur us on: "Now go; I will help you speak and will teach you what to say" (v. 12).

As Billy Graham said that day, "When God calls you, do not be afraid of trembling and wobbling knees, for He will be with you!"

LAWRENCE DARMANI

What task does God have for you to do today?
Depend on Him by asking for His help.

Wherever God sends us, He comes alongside us.

APRIL 24

Hope Lives

Read: 1 Peter 1:3–9

Your faith—of greater worth than gold . . . may result in praise, glory and honor when Jesus Christ is revealed. —v. 7

When unspeakable tragedy shatters people's lives, they search for answers. Recently, a mother who had lost a teenager said to me, "I can't figure it out. I don't know if I can believe anymore. I try, but God doesn't make sense to me. What does it all mean?" There are no easy answers to such big concerns. But for those who have trusted Christ, there is hope—whether we are basking in blessings or grinding through grief.

Peter spells this out in his first letter. In glowing terms, he praises God for our "new birth into a living hope" (1 PETER 1:3) through our salvation. That hope can bring joy even in the middle of tragedy. He also assures us of the permanence of this hope (v. 4). He then tells us of the heart-breaking reality that we may "suffer grief in all kinds of trials" (v. 6). Those who have suffered loss turn hopeful hearts toward Peter's next words: These come so that your faith "may result in praise, glory and honor when Jesus Christ is revealed" (v. 7).

Trials—seemingly random and inexplicable—can be seen differently in the light of these words. In the midst of tragedy, the power and beauty of our salvation can shine through because of our great Savior. And that may be just enough light to get a troubled person through another day.

DAVE BRANON

Lord, you assure us that the grand salvation you provided is proved genuine in our pain and that it leads to glory for you. Help us to begin each new day with renewed hope in you.

The light of salvation shines clearly even in the darkest night.

Giving All

Read: Romans 12:1–8

Offer your bodies as a living sacrifice, holy and pleasing to God—this is your true and proper worship. —v. 1

During his only inaugural address as the US President, John F. Kennedy issued this challenge to Americans: "Ask not what your country can do for you; ask what you can do for your country." It was a renewed call for citizens to surrender their lives in sacrifice and service to others. His words especially inspired the sons and daughters of men and women who had served their country in war.

His meaning was clear: What their parents purchased, often with their very lives, must now be protected by peaceful means. An army of volunteers arose to answer that call, and through the decades they have accomplished an immeasurable amount of humanitarian work around the globe.

Centuries earlier, the apostle Paul issued a similar call to Christians in the opening verses of Romans 12. Here he urges us to give our bodies as living sacrifices in service to the One who paid with His life for our sins. This spiritual sacrifice must be more than mere words; it must be an investment of our lives in the physical, emotional, and spiritual well-being of others.

Best of all, our serving can be done right where we are.

Randy Kilgore

Father, show me this day the many ways my life can be surrendered to you, and then give me the strength to begin to act.

Don't always ask Jesus what He can do for you; ask Jesus what you can do for Him.

The Book Behind the Story

Read: Psalm 119:105–112

Your statutes are my heritage forever; they are the joy of my heart. —v. 111

Millions of people around the world have seen *Gone with the Wind*, which premiered in the United States on December 15, 1939. It won 10 Academy Awards and remains one of Hollywood's most commercially successful films. It was based on Margaret Mitchell's 1936 novel, which sold one million copies within 6 months, received a Pulitzer Prize, and has been translated into more than 40 languages. An epic movie often has its source in a powerful and timeless book.

The book that's the basis for the Christian faith is the Bible. From Genesis to Revelation, it is infused with God's plan for His creation, including us. Psalm 119 celebrates the power and necessity of God's Word in our lives. It lights our path (v. 105), revives our souls (v. 107), and guards our steps (v. 110). Through the Scriptures we find wisdom, guidance, life, and joy. "Your statues are my heritage forever; they are the joy of my heart" (v. 111).

Jesus our Lord calls us to base our lives on His Word and share the joy of knowing Him with people who are longing to find life. "My heart is set on keeping your decrees to the very end" (v. 112).

What a book! What a Savior! *DAVID MCCASLAND*

Dear Lord, your Word is a lamp to guide my feet and a light for my path.
your laws are my treasure; they are my heart's delight.
I am determined to keep your decrees to the very end.

The Bible, God's eternal truth, can be trusted today.

Love and Light

Read: Deuteronomy 11:8–15

The land you are crossing the Jordan to take possession of is a land . . . the LORD your God cares for. –vv. 11–12

Friends are starting to plan their summer vegetable gardens. Some get an early start by planting seeds indoors where they can control the conditions and provide the best environment for sprouting. After the danger of frost has passed, they will transplant the seedlings outdoors. Once the garden is planted, the work of weeding, feeding, watering, and guarding against rodents and insects begins. Producing food is a lot of work.

Moses reminded the Israelites of this before they entered the promised land. While living in Egypt, they had to do the hard work of irrigating crops by hand (DEUT. 11:10), but in the place where God was taking them He promised to ease their work by sending spring and autumn rains: "I will send rain on your land in its season, both autumn and spring rains" (v. 14). The only condition was that they "faithfully obey the commands" He gave them—"to love the LORD your God and to serve him with all your heart and with all your soul" (v. 13). The Lord was taking His people to a place where their obedience and His blessing would make them a light to those around them.

God wants the same for us and from us: He wants our love to be displayed in our obedience so that we might be His light to people around us. The love and obedience we have to offer, though, is far less than He deserves. But He is our provider, blessing us and enabling us to be a light that the world will notice. *JULIE ACKERMAN LINK*

Loving God doesn't make life effortless, but having His strength makes it easier.

In the Same Boat

Read: Matthew 8:23–27

He got into the boat and his disciples followed him. –v. 23

When the cruise ship pulled into port, the passengers got off as quickly as possible. They had spent the last few days enduring an outbreak of a virus, and hundreds of people had been sickened. One passenger, interviewed as he disembarked, said: "Well, I don't mean to complain so much. I mean I know everybody was in the same boat." His seemingly unintentional pun made the reporter smile.

In Matthew 8, we read about another trip on the water (vv. 23–27). Jesus got into the boat and the disciples followed Him (v. 23). Then a terrible storm arose, and Jesus's disciples feared for their lives. They awakened a sleeping Jesus, who they assumed was unaware of the crisis.

While Jesus was literally in the same boat as His followers, He was unconcerned about the weather. As the all-powerful Creator, He had no fear of a storm. "He got up and rebuked the winds and the waves, and it was completely calm" (v. 26).

But we are not all-powerful, and we are oh-so-prone to fear. So what are we to do when the storms of life rage around us? Whether they quickly blow over or last for a long time, we can be confident in this: We are in the same boat with the One whom even the winds and the sea obey.

CINDY HESS KASPER

Heavenly Father, this life is full of uncertainty.
But you have promised us your unfailing presence.
May we see you today—especially when we are tempted to panic
or to do things in our own strength.

No danger can come so near the Christian that God is not nearer.

Access to God

Read: 1 John 5:6–15

Let us then approach God's throne of grace with confidence, so that we may receive mercy and find grace to help us in our time of need. —Hebrews 4:16

Technology is a blessing in so many ways. Need a bit of information about a health problem? All you have to do is access the Internet where you instantaneously get a list of options to guide your search. Need to contact a friend? Just send a text, e-mail, or Facebook post. But technology can also be frustrating at times. The other day I needed to access some information in my bank account and was asked a list of security questions. Unable to recall the exact answers, I was blocked from my own account. Or think of the times when an important conversation is cut off because of a dead cellphone battery, with no way to reconnect until you find a plug to recharge it.

All of this makes me delighted with the reality that when I need to access God in prayer, there are no security questions and no batteries required. I love the assurance that John gives when he says, "This is the confidence we have in approaching God: that if we ask anything according to his will, he hears us" (1 JOHN 5:14).

God is always accessible, for He never slumbers nor sleeps! (PS. 121:4). And thanks to His love for us, He is waiting and ready to listen.

JOE STOWELL

Lord, thank you for desiring communication with me and for the reassurance that you are indeed listening and ready to help in time of need. Teach us to come to you with confidence in your attentive love for us.

God is always accessible in our time of need.

Image Consultants

Read: Colossians 3:1–11

[You] have put on the new self, which is being renewed in knowledge in the image of its Creator. —v. 10

In our media-saturated age, image consultants have become indispensable. Entertainers, athletes, politicians, and business leaders seem desperate to manage the way they are perceived in the eyes of the world. These high-priced consultants work to shape how their clients are viewed—even if sometimes there is a stark contrast between the public image and the real person inside.

In reality, what people need—what all of us need—is not an external makeover but an inner transformation. Our deepest flaws cannot be corrected cosmetically. They are directly related to who we are in heart and mind, and they reveal how far we have fallen from the image of God in which we were created. But such transformation is beyond any human ability to accomplish.

Only Christ offers us true transformation—not just a facelift or an outward adjustment. Paul said that those who have been raised to eternal life in Christ "have put on the new self, which is being renewed in knowledge in the image of its Creator" (COL. 3:10).

New! What a tremendous word full of hope! Christ transforms us into new people in Him—people with a new heart, not just fixed up to look good on the outside. *BILL CROWDER*

If anyone is in Christ, he is a new creation; old things have passed away; behold, all things have become new. 2 CORINTHIANS 5:17 NKJV

The Spirit develops in us the clear image of Christ.

Correct Gently

Read: Colossians 3:12–17

Clothe yourselves with compassion, kindness, humility, gentleness and patience. Bear with one another. –vv. 12–13

At the end of a conference in Nairobi, Kenya, our group traveled from the conference center to a guesthouse to prepare to fly back home the next morning. When we arrived, one person in our group reported that she had forgotten her luggage back at the conference center. After she left to retrieve it, our group leader (always meticulous on detail) criticized her sharply to us in her absence.

The next morning when we arrived at the airport, the leader discovered to his dismay that he too had left his luggage behind. It and his passport were back at the guesthouse. It was now going to cost us even more to go for his baggage. Later, he apologized and said to all of us, "I'll never criticize so harshly again!"

Because we all have faults and weaknesses, we should bear with one another and forgive each other when things go wrong (COL. 3:13). We need to be constructive in our criticism and "clothe [our]selves with compassion, kindness, humility, gentleness and patience" (v. 12).

When correction is necessary, it should be done with kindness and love. In that way we become imitators of our Lord Jesus Christ.

LAWRENCE DARMANI

Dear God, you know that there are times when I just don't feel patient and humble and gentle. Those days in my life, the fruit of your Spirit seems in short supply. Please enable me to love others today.

The keys to effective relationships are gentleness and humility.

In Every Generation

Read: Psalm 100

The LORD is good and his love endures forever; his faithfulness continues through all generations. —v. 5

It may seem surprising when children don't follow their parents' example of faith in God. Equally unexpected is a person with a deep commitment to Christ who emerges from a family where faith was not present. In every generation, each person has a choice.

Samuel was a great man of God who appointed his two sons, Joel and Abijah, as leaders over Israel (1 SAM. 8:1–2). Unlike their father, however, they were corrupt and "turned aside after dishonest gain and accepted bribes and perverted justice" (v. 3). Yet, years later, we find Heman, Joel's son, appointed as a musician in the house of the Lord (1 CHRON. 6:31–33). Heman, Samuel's grandson—along with Asaph, his right-hand man and the author of many of the psalms—served the Lord by singing joyful songs (15:16–17).

Even though a person seems indifferent toward the faith so precious to his or her parents, God is still at work. Things can change in later years, and seeds of faith may spring to life in generations to come.

No matter what the family situation may be, we know that "the LORD is good and his love endures forever; his faithfulness continues through all generations." *DAVID MCCASLAND*

Dear Lord, help me to remember that you are the one who causes the seed of faith to grow. We give our loved ones into your care, knowing that the end of the story has not yet been written.

God's faithfulness extends to all generations.

One Who Serves

Read: Luke 22:24–27

I am among you as one who serves. —v. 27

"I'm nobody's servant!" I cried out. That morning the demands of my family seemed too much as I frantically helped to find my husband's blue tie while feeding the crying baby and recovering the lost toy from under the bed for our 2-year-old.

Later on that day, as I was reading the Bible, I came across this verse: "For who is greater, the one who is at the table or the one who serves? Is it not the one who is at the table? But I am among you as one who serves" (LUKE 22:27).

Jesus didn't have to wash His disciples' feet, yet He did (JOHN 13:5). There were servants who did that job, but Jesus chose to serve them. Today's society insists that we should aim to "be somebody." We want the best-paying job, the highest position in the company, the top leadership in church. Yet whatever position we are in, we can learn from our Savior to serve.

We hold different roles as parents, children, friends, workers, leaders, or students. The question is this: Do we carry out those roles with an attitude of service? Even though my everyday routine is sometimes tiring, I'm thankful the Master will help me because I do want to follow His steps and willingly serve others.

May God help us to do this each day. *KEILA OCHOA*

Dear Lord, I know that you did not come to be served, but to serve.
Sometimes I fail to think of others, but I want to be like you.
Please give me a heart like yours.

We need a servant's attitude to be like Jesus.

The Best Wedding Ever

Read: Revelation 21:1–8

The wedding of the Lamb has come, and his bride has made herself ready. –19:7

Within the last 800 or so years, a new custom has been added to the Jewish wedding ceremony. At the very end, the groom crushes a wine glass under his foot. One explanation of this is that the shattering of the glass symbolizes the destruction of the temple in AD 70. Young couples are encouraged to remember, as they establish their own homes, that God's home had been destroyed.

God is not homeless, however. He has just chosen a new place to live—in us, His followers. In the metaphors of Scripture, believers are both the bride of Christ and the temple in which God lives. God is fitting His people together to build a new home that will be His permanent dwelling place. At the same time, He is preparing the bride and planning a wedding that will include all of God's family from the beginning of time.

Our part is easy though sometimes painful. We cooperate with God as He is at work in us to make us more like His Son Jesus. Then some day, at the best wedding ever, our Lord will present us to himself without spot or wrinkle. We will be holy and without blemish (EPH. 5:27). This wedding will bring an end to all sorrow and suffering. *JULIE ACKERMAN LINK*

Finish then Thy new creation; pure and spotless let us be;
let us see Thy great salvation perfectly restored in Thee.
WESLEY

The return of Jesus is sure.

Heart of Joy

Read: John 15:1–11

I have told you this so that my joy may be in you and that your joy may be complete. —v. 11

While waiting in the gate area of Singapore's Changi Airport to board my flight, I noticed a young family—mom, dad, and son. The area was crowded, and they were looking for a place to sit. Suddenly, the little boy began loudly singing "Joy to the World." He was about 6 years old, so I was pretty impressed that he knew all the words.

What captured my attention even more was the look on the boy's face—his beaming smile matched the words he was singing as he proclaimed to everyone at the gate the joy of the Christ who has come.

This joy is not limited to exuberant children nor should it be confined to the Christmas season. The overflowing joy of knowing Christ's presence in our lives was one of the themes of Jesus's final teaching with His disciples the night before He died on the cross. He told them of His extravagant love for them—that He loved them as the Father loved Him (JOHN 15:9). After sharing what this eternal relationship looks like, Jesus said, "I have told you this so that my joy may be in you and that your joy may be complete" (v. 11).

What a promise! Through Jesus Christ our hearts can be filled with joy—real joy!

BILL CROWDER

Lord, you have chosen me and redeemed me, crowned me with love and compassion. I can do nothing less than overflow with joy at your great love for me, for those I love, and for the world.

In every season of life we can know joy in Christ.

The School of Pain

Read: Psalm 119:65–80

I know, Lord, that your laws are righteous, and that in faithfulness you have afflicted me. —v. 75

In his book *The Problem of Pain*, C. S. Lewis observes that "God whispers to us in our pleasures, speaks in our conscience, but shouts in our pains: it is His megaphone to rouse a deaf world." Suffering often helps us to redirect our focus. It shifts our thinking from immediate circumstances so we can listen to God concerning His work in our lives. Life as usual is replaced by a spiritual schoolroom.

In the Old Testament, we read how the psalmist maintained a teachable heart even during painful circumstances. He accepted them as orchestrated by God, and in submission he prayed, "In faithfulness you have afflicted me" (PS. 119:75). Isaiah the prophet viewed suffering as a refining process: "See, I have refined you, though not as silver; I have tested you in the furnace of affliction" (ISA. 48:10). And Job, despite his laments, learned about the sovereignty and greatness of God through his troubles (JOB 40–42).

We are not alone in our experience of pain. God himself took on human form and suffered greatly: "To this you were called, because Christ suffered for you, leaving you an example, that you should follow in his steps" (1 PETER 2:21). The One with nail-scarred hands is near. He will comfort us and teach us in our suffering. *DENNIS FISHER*

Dear Lord, life is so hard sometimes. I confess that I don't always see your purpose in my trials. Help me to trust you, and teach me to become the person that you desire me to be.

We learn the lesson of trust in the school of trial.

The Squeaky Wheel

Read: Luke 18:1–8

The prayer of a righteous person is powerful and effective. –James 5:16

"The squeaky wheel gets the oil" is a popular proverb. As a child I rode my bicycle for long distances between home and school, and the squeaky sounds of the wheels drew my attention to the need to lubricate them.

In Luke 18, the widow's persistent request to the judge for justice against her adversary made her sound like a "squeaky wheel" until she got the result she needed. Luke explains that Jesus told this story to teach us the need to pray continually and not to give up, even if it appears that the answer to our prayer is delayed (vv. 1–5).

God is certainly not an unjust judge who must be harassed before He responds to us. He is our loving Father who cares about us and hears us when we cry to Him. Regular, persistent prayer draws us closer to Him. It may feel like we are a squeaky wheel, but the Lord welcomes our prayer and encourages us to approach Him with our cries. He hears us and will come to our aid in ways that we may not expect.

As Jesus teaches in Matthew 6:5-8, constant prayer does not require long periods of "an abundance of words." Rather, as we bring our needs before God "day and night" (LUKE 18:7) and walk with the One who already knows our needs, we learn to trust God and wait patiently for His response.

LAWRENCE DARMANI

Lord, we know that you are good and long for us to come to you in prayer. Thank you for caring about every aspect of our lives. Help us to wait patiently and accept whatever comes from your hand.

Don't give up—God hears you when you pray!

All Aboard

Read: 2 Peter 3:1–13

The Lord is . . . patient with you, not wanting anyone to perish. –v. 9

One day when I dropped my husband off at our local train station, I watched as the conductor scanned the area for stragglers. A woman with wet hair bounded from the parking lot and up into the train. Then, a man in a dark suit strode to the platform and climbed aboard. The conductor waited patiently while several more late-comers sprinted to the tracks and boarded at the last moment.

Just as the conductor was patient with people boarding the train, God patiently waits for people to come to know Him. However, someday Jesus will return and "the heavens will disappear with a roar; the elements will be destroyed by fire" (2 PETER 3:10). When this happens, or when our physical bodies die, it will be too late to establish a relationship with God.

The Lord is "patient with [us]," Peter says, "not wanting anyone to perish, but everyone to come to repentance" (v. 9). If you have delayed deciding to follow Christ, there is good news—you can still commit yourself to Him. "If you declare with your mouth 'Jesus is Lord,' and believe in your heart that God raised him from the dead, you will be saved" (ROM. 10:9). He is calling. Will you run in His direction? *JENNIFER BENSON SCHULDT*

Softly and tenderly Jesus is calling, calling for you and for me;
see, on the portals He's waiting and watching,
watching for you and for me.
THOMPSON

Now is the time to choose the Lord.

Remind the People

Read: Titus 3:1–8

Remind the believers to . . . show true humility to everyone. —vv. 1–2 NLT

In a typical week, many of us receive a number of e-mails reminding us of appointments or upcoming events or requests to pray for someone. All of them are needed reminders.

When Paul wrote his "papyrus mail" to Titus, he ended his note by saying, "Remind the believers . . ." (3:1 NLT). We can assume from Paul's word choice that he had already written about these things. But they were of such importance to the people in the church that he repeated them so they wouldn't forget.

Notice what Paul didn't want them to miss. He reminded the people—living under the oppressive Roman rule—"to be subject to rulers and authorities" (v. 1). It was important to be known for obedience; for doing what is good; for not slandering; for being peaceful and considerate; and for humility rather than for complaining. Their behavior was to showcase the change made in their lives by following Christ (vv. 3–5).

How could they—and we—do that? "The Holy Spirit, whom he poured out on us . . . through Jesus Christ" enables us to "devote [ourselves] to doing what is good" (vv. 5–6, 8). It is through Jesus's great gift of salvation that we are equipped to influence our world for good. That's a reminder we all need. *DAVE BRANON*

Lord, remind us how important it is that we obey you and treat others the way we want to be treated. Remind us that your salvation enables us to live as lights in a dark world.

A Christian's life is a window through which others can see Jesus.

No Need Is Too Trivial

Read: Isaiah 49:13–18

As a father has compassion on his children, so the Lord has compassion on those who fear him. —Psalm 103:13

Several mothers of small children were sharing encouraging answers to prayer. Yet one woman said she felt selfish about troubling God with her personal needs. "Compared with the huge global needs God faces," she explained, "my circumstances must seem trivial to Him."

Moments later, her little son pinched his fingers in a door and ran screaming to his mother. She didn't say, "How selfish of you to bother me with your throbbing fingers when I'm busy!" She showed him great compassion and tenderness.

As Psalm 103:13 reminds us, this is the response of love, both human and divine. In Isaiah 49, God said that even though a mother may forget to have compassion on her child, the Lord never forgets His children (v. 15). God assured His people, "I have engraved you on the palms of my hands" (v. 16).

Such intimacy with God belongs to those who fear Him and who rely on Him rather than on themselves. As that child with throbbing fingers ran freely to his mother, so may we run to God with our daily problems.

Our compassionate God doesn't neglect others to respond to our concerns. He has limitless time and love for each of His children. No need is too trivial for Him.

Joanie Yoder

You take great delight in me, Lord, and quiet me with your love.
You rejoice over me with singing, like a mother singing a lullaby
over her child. Thank you for your tender love for me.

God holds His children in the palm of His hand.

Tell Your Story

Read: 1 Timothy 1:12–20

Your awe-inspiring deeds will be on every tongue; I will proclaim your greatness.
—Psalm 145:6 NLT

Michael Dinsmore, a former prisoner and relatively new Christian, was asked to give his testimony in a prison. After he spoke, some inmates came to him and said, "This is the most exciting meeting we've ever been to!" Michael was amazed that God could use his simple story.

In 1 Timothy, after Paul had charged Timothy to stay the course preaching the gospel (1:1–11), he shared his personal testimony to encourage the young man (vv. 12–16). He told about God's mercy in his own life. Paul said that he had mocked the Lord, but He changed him. In His mercy, God not only counted him faithful and gave him a job to do, but He also enabled him to do His work (v. 12). Paul considered himself the worst of sinners, but God saved him (v. 15).

The Lord is able! That is what Paul wanted Timothy to see, and what we need to see too. Through Paul's testimony, we see God's mercy. If God could use someone like Paul, He can use us. If God could save the worst of sinners, then no one is beyond His reach.

Our story of God's work in our lives can encourage others. Let those around you know that the God of the Bible is still at work today!

POH FANG CHIA

Father, thank you for the salvation you offer and that no one, including me, is beyond the reach of your mercy, grace, and transforming power. Help me share my story with others so that people can see your love.

No one is beyond the reach of God's love.

Where Can We Lean?

Read: 2 Samuel 9

I will surely show you kindness for the sake of your father Jonathan. —v. 7

"What a wonderful funeral!" Cindy remarked as we walked out. Helen, our friend, had died. And friend after friend celebrated her by sharing stories of her all-around fun behavior. But Helen's life wasn't all jokes and laughter. Her nephew spoke of her faith in Jesus and her care for others. She had taken him into her home when he was young and struggling. Now in his twenties, he said of his Aunt Helen, "She was like a mom to me. She never gave up on me in my struggles. I am sure that if it wasn't for her, I would have lost my faith." Wow! What an influence! Helen leaned on Jesus and wanted her nephew to trust Him too.

In the Old Testament, we read that King David took a young man named Mephibosheth into his home with the purpose of showing him kindness for the sake of his father, Jonathan (David's friend who had died; SEE 2 SAM. 9:1). Years earlier, Mephibosheth had been injured when his nurse dropped him as they fled after the news that his father had been killed (4:4). He was surprised that the king would care for him; he even referred to himself as "a dead dog" (9:8). Yet the king treated him as his own son (9:11).

I'd like to be that kind of person, wouldn't you? Someone who cares for others and helps them hang on to faith in Jesus even when life looks hopeless.

ANNE CETAS

Lord, you showed the ultimate kindness by rescuing us when we were helpless in our sins. May our lives be marked by kindness so that others will see you in us.

God does most of His work for people through people.

The Riches of Obedience

Read: Psalm 119:14, 33–40

I have rejoiced in your laws as much as in riches. —v. 14 NLT

Publicly operated lotteries exist in more than 100 countries. In a recent year, lottery ticket sales totaled more than $85 billion in just the US and Canada, only part of the total sales worldwide. The lure of huge jackpots has created a mindset among many that all of life's problems would be solved "if I won the lottery."

There's nothing wrong with wealth itself, but it has the power to deceive us into thinking that money is the answer to all our needs. The psalmist, expressing a different point of view, wrote: "I have rejoiced in your laws as much as in riches. . . . I will delight in your decrees and not forget your word" (PS. 119:14, 16 NLT). This concept of spiritual treasure is focused on obedience to God and walking "in the path of [His] commands" (v. 35).

What if we were more excited about following the Lord's Word than about winning a jackpot worth millions? With the psalmist we might pray, "Turn my heart toward your statutes and not toward selfish gain. Turn my eyes away from worthless things; preserve my life according to your word" (vv. 36–37).

The riches of obedience—true riches—belong to all who walk with the Lord.

DAVID MCCASLAND

Dear Lord, may I commit each day to standing on the unchanging truth of your Word and to growing in my relationship with you, the only measure of success in this life and in eternity.

Success is knowing and loving God.

Listening with Love

Read: Luke 18:9–14

All those who exalt themselves will be humbled, and those who humble themselves will be exalted. —v. 14

One August evening in Vermont, a young missionary spoke at our small church. The country where he and his wife served was in religious turmoil, and it was considered too dangerous for children. In one of his stories, he told us about a heart-wrenching episode when his daughter pleaded with him not to leave her behind at a boarding school.

I was a new dad at that time, having recently been blessed with a daughter, and the story upset me. *How could loving parents leave their daughter alone like that?* I muttered to myself. By the time the talk was finished, I was so worked up that I ignored the offer to visit with the missionary. I charged out of the church, saying out loud as I left: "I'm sure glad I'm not like . . ."

In that instant, the Holy Spirit stopped me cold. I couldn't even finish the sentence. Here I was, saying almost word for word what the Pharisee said to God: "I thank you that I am not like other people" (LUKE 18:11). How disappointed I was in myself! How disappointed God must have been! Since that evening, I've asked God to help me listen to others with humility and restraint as they pour their hearts out in confession, profession, or pain.

RANDY KILGORE

Lord, may we be quick to listen and slow to speak and to judge.
A proud attitude so easily infects our lives.
Give us instead a humility that reflects your heart and love.

We don't get closer to God by passing judgment on others.

A Survivor's Thoughts

Read: Romans 9:1–5

I could wish that I myself were cursed and cut off from Christ for the sake of my people. —v. 3

After a 71-year-old South Korean woman was rescued during the tragic sinking of a ferry boat, she struggled with survivor's guilt. From her hospital bed she said she couldn't understand how it could be right for her to have lived through an accident that had taken the lives of many who were so much younger. She also regretted not knowing the name of the young man who had pulled her out of the water after she had given up hope. Then she added, "I want to buy him a meal at least, or hold his hand, or give him a hug."

This woman's heart for others reminds me of the apostle Paul. He was so concerned about his neighbors and countrymen that he said he wished he could trade his own relationship with Christ for their rescue: "I have great sorrow and unceasing anguish in my heart. For I could wish that I myself were cursed and cut off from Christ for the sake of my people" (ROM. 9:2–3).

Paul also expressed a deep sense of personal gratitude. He knew he didn't understand the ways and judgments of God (VV. 14–24). So while doing everything he could to proclaim the gospel to all, he found peace and joy in trusting the heart of a God who loves the whole world so much more than we ever could.

MART DEHAAN

Lord God, your ways are so far beyond our comprehension,
yet we know without doubt that you love us.
Help us trust your loving heart with the things we don't understand.

Gratitude to God leads to growth in godliness.

Motivated by Love

Read: 2 Corinthians 5:11–17

Christ's love compels us. —v. 14

In the 1920s, Bobby Jones dominated the golfing world, despite being an amateur. In one film about his life, *Bobby Jones: Stroke of Genius*, there is a scene where a professional golfer asks Bobby when he is going to quit being an amateur and grab for the money like everyone else does. Jones answers by explaining that the word *amateur* comes from the Latin *amo*—to love. His answer was clear: He played golf because he loved the game.

Our motives, why we do what we do, make all the difference. This certainly applies to those who are followers of Jesus Christ. In his letter to the Corinthian church, Paul gives us an example of this. Throughout the epistle he defended his conduct, character, and calling as an apostle of Christ. In response to those who questioned his motives for ministry, Paul said, "Christ's love compels us, because we are convinced that one died for all, and therefore all died. And he died for all, that those who live should no longer live for themselves but for him who died for them and was raised again" (2 COR. 5:14–15).

Christ's love is the greatest of all motivators. It causes those who follow Him to live for Him, not for themselves. *BILL CROWDER*

What are some of the ways your understanding of Christ and His love has shaped your motives and your actions? In what ways would you like to see God work in you now?

We are shaped and fashioned by what we love most.

Power in Praise

Read: 2 Chronicles 20:15–22

Praise the Lord, for His mercy endures forever. —v. 21 NKJV

Willie Myrick was kidnapped from his driveway when he was 9 years old. For hours, he traveled in a car with his kidnapper, not knowing what would happen to him. During that time, Willie decided to sing a song called "Every Praise." As he repeatedly sang the words, his abductor spewed profanity and told him to shut up. Finally, the man stopped the car and let Willie out—unharmed.

As Willie demonstrated, truly praising the Lord requires us to concentrate on God's character while forsaking what we fear, what is wrong in our lives, and the self-sufficiency in our hearts.

The Israelites reached this place of surrender when they faced attackers. As they prepared for battle, King Jehoshaphat organized a choir to march out in advance of their enemy's army. The choir sang, "Praise the Lord, for His mercy endures forever" (2 CHRON. 20:21 NKJV). When the music started, Israel's enemies became confused and destroyed each other. As the prophet Jahaziel had predicted, Israel didn't need to fight at all (v. 17).

Whether we're facing a battle or feeling trapped, we can glorify God in our hearts. Truly, "Great is the Lord and most worthy of praise" (PS. 96:4).

JENNIFER BENSON SCHULDT

Dear God, you are holy and good. I worship you today despite the problems that cloud my vision of you. Let my soul tell of your glory forever.

Worship is a heart overflowing with praise to God.

One Step Closer

Read: Romans 13:10–14

Now our salvation is nearer now than when we first believed. —v. 11

Some years ago a friend and I set out to climb Mount Whitney. At 14,505 feet, it is the tallest mountain in the contiguous United States. We arrived at Whitney Portal late one evening, rolled out our sleeping bags at base camp, and tried to get some sleep before we began our ascent at first light. Whitney is not a technical climb but rather a long, exhausting walk—11 miles of relentless ascent.

The climb, though hard-going, was exhilarating, with stunning vistas, beautiful blue lakes, and lush meadows along the way. But the trail grew long and exhausting, a test for legs and lungs. I thought of turning back as the day wore on and the trail seemed to stretch endlessly before us.

Occasionally, however, I caught a glimpse of the summit and realized that each step was bringing me one step closer. If I just kept walking, I would get there. That was the thought that kept me going.

Paul assures us, "Our salvation is nearer now than when we first believed" (ROM. 13:11). Every day brings us one day closer to that great day when we shall "summit" and see our Savior's face. That's the thought that can keep us going.

DAVID ROPER

Dear Lord, may I, for the joy set before me, endure with patience the hardship of the trail. When my journey is over, I will see you face to face and live with you forever.

Now we see Jesus in the Bible, but someday we'll see Him face to face.

The Great Healer

Read: Genesis 2:7–15

I am the LORD, who heals you. —Exodus 15:26

The doctors I know are smart, hard-working, and compassionate. They have relieved my suffering on many occasions, and I am grateful for their expertise in diagnosing illnesses, prescribing medication, setting broken bones, and stitching up wounds. But this does not mean that I place my faith in physicians rather than in God.

For reasons known only to God, He appointed humans to be His partners in the work of caring for creation (GEN. 2:15), and doctors are among them. Doctors study medical science and learn how God designed the body. They use this knowledge to help restore us to a healthy condition. But the only reason doctors can do anything to make us better is that God created us with the ability to heal. Surgeons would be useless if incisions didn't heal.

Scientists can learn how God created our bodies to function, and they devise therapies to help restore or cure us, but they are not healers; God is (EX. 15:26). Doctors simply cooperate with God's original intent and design.

So I am grateful for science and doctors, but my praise and thanksgiving go to God, who designed an orderly universe and who created us with minds that can discover how it works. I believe, therefore, that all healing is divine because no healing takes place apart from God.

JULIE ACKERMAN LINK

Father God, you are the Great Physician, and I ask for healing, whether mind, body, spirit, or in all of these. I believe you will give what is best. Thank you for your goodness, kindness, and love in all things.

When you think of all that's good, give thanks to God.

Guard Your Focus

Read: 1 Corinthians 3:1–9

Fixing our eyes on Jesus, the pioneer and perfecter of faith. —Hebrews 12:2

"That's my disciple," I once heard a woman say about someone she was helping. As followers of Christ we are all tasked with making disciples—sharing the good news of Christ with people and helping them grow spiritually. But it can be easy to focus on ourselves instead of Jesus.

The apostle Paul was concerned that the Corinthian church was losing its focus on Christ. The two best-known preachers in those days were Paul and Apollos. The church was divided: "I follow Paul." "Well, I follow Apollos!" They had begun focusing on the wrong person, following the teachers rather than the Savior. But Paul corrected them. We are God's co-workers. It doesn't matter who plants and who waters, for only God can give the growth. Christians are "God's field, God's building" (1 COR. 3:6–9). The Corinthian believers didn't belong to Paul nor to Apollos.

Jesus tells us to go and make disciples and to teach them about Him (MATT. 28:20). And the author of the book of Hebrews reminds us to focus on the Author and Finisher of our faith (12:2 NKJV). Christ will be honored when we focus on Him; He is superior to any human being and He will meet our needs.

C. P. HIA

Father, I confess that it is easy to shift my focus from you to less important things. Thank you for putting people in my life that help point me to you. Help me point others to you in a way that makes you more and me less.

Put Jesus first.

New Start for a Broken Heart

Read: Isaiah 61:1–3

He has sent me to bind up the brokenhearted. —v. 1

The Museum of Broken Relationships in Zagreb, Croatia, is filled with anonymously donated remnants of love gone wrong. There is an axe that a jilted lover used to destroy the furniture of an offending partner. Stuffed animals, love letters framed in broken glass, and wedding dresses all speak volumes of heartache. While some visitors to the museum leave in tears over their own loss, some couples depart with hugs and a promise not to fail each other.

The Old Testament prophet Isaiah wrote, "The Spirit of the Sovereign LORD is upon me, because the LORD has anointed me to proclaim good news to the poor. He has sent me to bind up the brokenhearted" (ISA. 61:1). When Jesus read from Isaiah 61 at the synagogue in Nazareth, He said, "Today this scripture is fulfilled in your hearing" (LUKE 4:21). Extending far beyond help for an emotional wound, Isaiah's words speak of a changed heart and a renewed spirit that come by receiving God's gift of "beauty instead of ashes, the oil of joy instead of mourning, a garment of praise instead of a spirit of despair" (ISA. 61:3).

All of us have experienced regret and broken promises in our lives. Whatever has happened, the Lord invites us to find healing, hope, and new life in Him.

DAVID MCCASLAND

Lord, you are the promise-keeping God who has said He will make all things new.
Today we give you our ashes in exchange for your beauty,
our mourning for the joy of finding comfort in you. Thank you!

God can transform tragedies into triumphs.

Wisdom Seekers

Read: Proverbs 3:1–18

Blessed are those who find wisdom. —v. 13

Every spring colleges and universities hold commencement ceremonies to celebrate the success of students who have completed their studies and earned their degrees. After the students cross the stage, these graduates will enter a world that will challenge them. Just having academic knowledge won't be good enough. The key to success in life will be in wisely applying everything they have learned.

Throughout Scripture, wisdom is celebrated as a treasure that is worth seeking. It is better than riches (PROV. 3:13–18). Its source is God, who alone is perfectly wise (ROM. 16:27). And it is found in the actions and attitude of Jesus, in whom "all the treasures of wisdom" are found (COL. 2:3). Wisdom comes from reading and applying the Scripture. We have an example of this in the way Jesus applied His knowledge when He was tempted (LUKE 4:1–13). In other words, the truly wise person tries to see life from God's point of view and chooses to live according to His wisdom.

What's the payoff for this kind of life? Proverbs tells us that wisdom is like sweetness of honey on the tongue (PROV. 24:13–14). "Blessed are those who find wisdom" (3:13). So seek wisdom, for it is more profitable than silver or gold! *JOE STOWELL*

Lord, strengthen my resolve to live by the wisdom that comes only from you. Give me the discernment to live all of life from your point of view that I might know the blessings of a life lived wisely.

Blessing comes from seeking wisdom and living by it.

Stuck in the Mud

Read: Psalm 40:1–5

He lifted me . . . out of the mud and mire; he set my feet on a rock. —v. 2

We were absolutely stuck! While I was laying the wreath in place on my parents' grave, my husband eased the car off the road to allow another car to pass. It had rained for weeks and the parking area was sodden. When we were ready to leave, we discovered that the car was stuck. The wheels spun, sinking further and further into the mud.

We weren't going anywhere without a push, but my husband had a damaged shoulder, and I had just come out of the hospital. We needed help! At a distance I saw two young men, and they responded cheerfully to my frantic waves and shouts. Thankfully, their combined strength pushed the car back onto the roadway.

Psalm 40 recounts God's faithfulness when David cried for help. "I waited patiently for the Lord to help me, and he . . . heard my cry. He lifted me out of the pit of despair, out of the mud and the mire" (vv. 1–2 NLT). Whether this psalm refers to an actual pit or to challenging circumstances, David knew that he could always call on God for deliverance.

God will help us too when we call on Him. Sometimes He intervenes directly, but more often He works through other people. When we admit our need to Him—and perhaps to others—we can count on His faithfulness.

MARION STROUD

I praise you, heavenly Father, that you can rescue me from any pit, no matter how deep. Help me to accept the help of others and to be ready to offer it to those in need.

Hope comes with help from God and others.

Chipmunk Chatter

Read: Isaiah 41:10–13

Do not fear; I will help you. —v. 13

I had laid out some landscape netting in my yard, upon which I was going to spread decorative stones. As I was preparing to finish the job, I noticed a chipmunk tangled up in the netting.

I put on my gloves and gingerly began clipping away at the netting. The little guy was not happy with me. He kicked his hind feet and tried to bite me. I calmly told him, "I'm not going to hurt you, buddy. Just relax." But he didn't understand, so in fear he resisted. I finally snipped the last restricting loop and sent him scampering home.

Sometimes humans feel entangled and react in fear to the Lord. Through the centuries, He has offered rescue and hope to people—yet we resist Him, not understanding the help He provides. In Isaiah 41, the prophet quotes the Lord as saying, "For I am the LORD your God who takes hold of your right hand and says to you, Do not fear; I will help you" (v. 13).

As you think about your situation, how do you see God's role? Are you afraid to turn things over to Him—for fear that He might harm you? He is good and He is near, wanting to free you from life's entanglements. You can trust Him with your life. *DAVE BRANON*

In what area of your life do you need freedom?
Ask the Lord to show you and to give you the faith to trust Him
for His deliverance.

Faith is the best antidote for fear.

Our Strength and Song

Read: Exodus 15:1–2, 13–18

The Lord shall reign forever and ever. –15:18

Often called "The March King," composer and band director John Philip Sousa created music that has been played by bands around the world for more than a hundred years. As Loras John Schissel, music historian and conductor of the Virginia Grand Military Band, said, "Sousa is to marches what Beethoven is to symphonies." Sousa understood the power of music to motivate, encourage, and inspire people.

In Old Testament times, the people of Israel were often inspired to compose and sing songs to celebrate God's help during times of need. When the Lord saved His people from certain destruction by Pharaoh's army, "Then Moses and the Israelites sang this song to the Lord: 'I will sing to the Lord, for he is highly exalted. Both horse and driver he has hurled into the sea. The Lord is my strength and my defense; he has become my salvation'" (Ex. 15:1–2).

Music has the power to lift our spirits by reminding us of God's faithfulness in the past. When we're discouraged, we can sing songs and hymns that raise our eyes from the challenging circumstances we face to see the power and presence of the Lord. We are reminded that He is our strength, our song, and our salvation. *David McCasland*

Trust in Him, ye saints, forever—He is faithful, changing never;
neither force nor guile can sever those He loves from Him.
Kelly

Songs of praise raise our eyes to see God's faithfulness.

Calming the Storm

Read: Mark 4:35–41

He got up, rebuked the wind and said to the waves, "Quiet! Be still!" Then the wind died down and it was completely calm. —v. 39

While Hurricane Katrina headed toward the coast of Mississippi, a retired pastor and his wife left their home and went to a shelter. Their daughter pleaded with them to go to Atlanta where she could take care of them, but the couple couldn't get any money to make the trip because the banks were closed. After the storm had passed, they returned to their home to get a few belongings, and were able to salvage only a few family photos floating in the water. Then, when the man was taking his father's photo out of its frame so it could dry, $366 fell out—precisely the amount needed for two plane tickets to Atlanta. They learned they could trust Jesus for what they needed.

For the disciples, trusting Jesus in a storm was the curriculum for the day in the dramatic narrative of Mark 4:35-41. Jesus had instructed His disciples to cross to the other side of the Sea of Galilee and then He went to sleep in the boat. When a quick and violent storm blew in, the disciples dripped as much with fear and anxiety as water from the waves. They woke Jesus, saying, "Teacher, don't you care if we drown?" (v. 38). Jesus stood up and with three words, "Peace, be still!" He muzzled the storm.

We all experience storms—persecutions, financial troubles, illnesses, disappointments, loneliness—and Jesus does not always prevent them. But He has promised never to leave us nor forsake us (HEB. 13:5). He will keep us calm in the storm. *MARVIN WILLIAMS*

Are you in a storm? What do you know about God's character that could help bring calm to your heart?

In the storms of life, we can see the character of our God.

Marked by His Name

Read: Acts 11:19–26

The disciples were called Christians first at Antioch. –v. 26

In July 1860, the world's first nursing school opened at St. Thomas Hospital in London. Today that school is part of the King's College, where nursing students are called Nightingales. The school—like modern nursing itself—was established by Florence Nightingale, who revolutionized nursing during the Crimean War. When prospective nurses complete their training, they take the "Nightingale Pledge," a reflection of her ongoing impact on nursing.

Many people, like Florence Nightingale, have had a significant impact on our world. But no one has had a greater effect than Jesus, whose birth, death, and resurrection have been transforming lives for 2,000 years.

Around the world, Christ's name marks those who are His followers, going back to the earliest days of the church. "When [Barnabas] found [Saul], he brought him to Antioch. So for a whole year Barnabas and Saul met with the church and taught great numbers of people. The disciples were called Christians first at Antioch" (ACTS 11:26).

Those who bear Christ's name identify with Him because we have been changed by His love and grace. We declare to the world that He has made an eternal difference in our lives and we long for that in the hearts of others too.

BILL CROWDER

Father, give me the grace and wisdom to honor you.
May my life be so marked by the person of Christ that His great name—and salvation—will be embraced by others as well.

Followers of Christ—Christians—are marked by His name.

I'm Stumped

Read: Proverbs 30:1–4

I am afraid that . . . your minds may somehow be led astray from your sincere and pure devotion to Christ. —2 Corinthians 11:3

The riddle stumped me: What is greater than God—and more evil than the devil? The poor have it. The rich need it. And if you eat it you will die.

I missed the solution by allowing my mind to be distracted from the obvious answer: "Nothing."

That riddle reminds me of another test of wits that would have been far more difficult to solve when it was originally posed. An ancient wise man named Agur asked: "Who has gone up to heaven and come down? Whose hands have gathered up the wind? Who has wrapped up the waters in a cloak? Who has established all the ends of the earth? What is his name, and what is the name of his son? Surely you know!" (PROV. 30:4).

Today, we know the answer to those questions. But sometimes when we're in the middle of the questions, worries, and needs of our lives we may lose sight of the obvious. The details of life can so easily distract us from the One who answers the most important riddle: Who is One with God; more powerful than the devil; the poor can have Him; the rich need Him; and if you eat and drink from His table, you'll never die? Jesus Christ, the Lord.

MART DEHAAN

Father, in the details and distractions of our spiritual journey,
it is so easy to look right past you and your Son.
May we see you today in a new and fresh way.

Focusing on God helps us to take our eyes off our circumstances.

Mysterious Ways

Read: Job 40:1–14

As the heavens are higher than the earth, so are my ways higher than your ways. —Isaiah 55:9

When my son began attending Chinese language classes, I marveled at the papers he brought home after his first session. As a native English speaker, it was difficult for me to understand how the written characters related to the spoken words. The language seemed incredibly complex to me—almost incomprehensible.

Sometimes I feel the same sense of bewilderment when I consider the way God operates. I know He has said, "My thoughts are not your thoughts, neither are your ways my ways" (ISA. 55:8). Still, there's a part of me that feels like I should be able to understand why God allows certain things to happen. After all, I read His Word regularly and His Holy Spirit lives inside of me.

When I feel entitled to understand God's ways, I try to recommit myself to humility. I remember that Job did not get an explanation for all his heartache (JOB 1:5, 8). He struggled to understand, but God asked him: "Will the one who contends with the Almighty correct him?" (40:2). Job contritely responded, "How can I reply to you? I put my hand over my mouth" (v. 4). Job was speechless before God's greatness.

Although God's ways may seem to be mysterious and unfathomable at times, we can rest confidently that they are higher than our ways.

JENNIFER BENSON SCHULDT

Father, please help me to trust you even when I don't understand why things happen as they do. Comfort my heart and remind me of your goodness and love.

Since God's hand is in everything, you can leave everything in God's hand.

The Gift of Tears

Read: John 11:32–44

Jesus wept. –v. 35

I called a longtime friend when his mother died. She had been a close friend of my mother, and now both had passed on. As we spoke, our conversation slipped easily into a cycle of emotion—tears of sorrow now that Beth was gone and tears of laughter as we recalled the caring and fun person she had been.

Many of us have experienced that strange crossover from crying one moment and laughing the next. It's an amazing gift that emotions of both sorrow and joy can provide a physical release in this way.

Since we are made in God's image (GEN. 1:26), and humor is such an integral part of almost every culture, I imagine that Jesus must have had a wonderful sense of humor. But we know that He also knew the pain of grief. When his friend Lazarus died, Jesus saw Mary weeping, and "he was deeply moved in spirit and troubled." A short time later, He too began to weep (JOHN 11:33–35).

Our ability to express our emotions with tears is a gift, and God keeps track of each tear we cry. Psalm 56:8 says, "You keep track of all my sorrows. You have collected all my tears in your bottle. You have recorded each one in your book" (NLT). But one day—we are promised (REV. 7:17)—God "will wipe away every tear." *CINDY HESS KASPER*

Lord, you have made us to laugh, to cry, to yearn, to love—
and to miss those who have gone before us. Help us to love even more deeply,
confident in your goodness and in the resurrection you promise.

Our loving heavenly Father, who washed away our sins,
will also wipe away our tears.

The Blame Game

Read: Leviticus 16:5–22

The next day John saw Jesus coming toward him and said, "Look, the Lamb of God, who takes away the sin of the world!" —John 1:29

I've been blamed for a lot of things, and rightly so. My sin, failure, and incompetence have caused grief, anxiety, and inconvenience for friends and family (and probably even for strangers). I've also been blamed for things that were not my fault, things I was powerless to change.

But I have stood on the other side of the fence hurling accusations at others. If they had just done something different, I tell myself, I would not be in the mess I'm in. Blame hurts. So whether guilty or not, we waste lots of time and mental energy trying to find someone else to carry it for us.

Jesus offers us a better way to deal with blame. Even though He was blameless, He took upon himself the sin of the world and carried it away (JOHN 1:29). We often refer to Jesus as the sacrificial lamb, but He was also the final scapegoat for everything that is wrong with the world (LEV. 16:10).

Once we acknowledge our sin and accept Christ's offer to take it away, we no longer have to carry the weight of our guilt. We can stop looking for someone to blame for what's wrong with us, and we can stop accepting blame from others trying to do the same.

Thanks to Jesus, we can stop playing the blame game.

JULIE ACKERMAN LINK

Help me, Lord, to be honest when I am at fault and to confess that to you—instead of looking for someone else to blame. Thank you for taking my blame on yourself.

Honesty about our sin brings forgiveness.

Light in the Darkness

Read: John 12:42–50

I have come into the world as a light so that no one who believes in me should stay in darkness. —v. 46

During a trip to Peru, I visited one of the many caves found throughout that mountainous country. Our guide told us that this particular cave had already been explored to a depth of 9 miles—and it went even deeper. We saw fascinating bats, nocturnal birds, and interesting rock formations. Before long, however, the darkness of the cave became unnerving—almost suffocating. I was greatly relieved when we returned to the surface and the light of day.

That experience was a stark reminder of how oppressive darkness can be and how much we need light. We live in a world made dark by sin—a world that has turned against its Creator. And we need the Light.

Jesus, who came to restore all of creation—including humanity—to its intended place referred to himself as that "light" (JOHN 8:12). "I have come into the world as a light," He said, "so that no one who believes in me should stay in darkness" (12:46).

In Him, we not only have the light of salvation but the only light by which we can find our way—His way—through our world's spiritual darkness.

BILL CROWDER

How have you seen God's light displayed in our broken world?
In what ways have you shared His light?

When we walk in the Light, we won't stumble in the darkness.

Feeling Insignificant?

Read: Psalm 139:7–16

I will praise you because I am fearfully and wonderfully made. —v. 14

We are among seven billion people who coexist on a tiny planet that resides in a small section of a rather insignificant solar system. Our earth, in reality, is just one miniscule blue dot among millions of celestial bodies that God created. On the gigantic canvas that is our universe, our beautiful, majestic Earth appears as a tiny speck of dust.

That could make us feel extremely unimportant and inconsequential. However, God's Word suggests that just the opposite is true. Our great God, who "measured the waters in the hollow of his hand" (ISA. 40:12), has singled out each person on this planet as supremely important, for we are made in His image.

For instance, He has created everything for us to enjoy (1 TIM. 6:17). Also, for all who have trusted Jesus as Savior, God has given purpose (EPH. 2:10). And then there's this: Despite the vastness of this world, God cares specifically about each of us. Psalm 139 says He knows what we are going to say and what we are thinking. We can't escape His presence, and He planned our earthly existence before we were born.

We don't need to feel unimportant when the God of the universe is that interested in us! *DAVE BRANON*

Lord, I look out into the vastness of the heavens and I see
the grandeur of your infinite power, yet you look at me from heaven
and see someone you know, love, and care about.
Thank you that you find value in me.

The God who created the universe is the God who loves you.

Something New

Read: Ephesians 2:10–22

We are God's handiwork, created in Christ Jesus to do good works, which God prepared in advance for us to do. —v. 10

It was only scrap wood, but Charles Hooper saw much more than that. Salvaging old timbers from a long-abandoned corncrib, he sketched some simple plans. Then he felled a few oak and poplar trees from his wooded property and painstakingly squared them with his grandfather's broadax. Piece by piece, he began to fit together the old lumber with the new.

Today you can see Charles and Shirley Hooper's postcard-perfect log cabin, tucked away in the trees on Tennessee Ridge. Part guesthouse, part museum for family heirlooms, the structure stands as an enduring tribute to Charles's vision, skill, and patience.

Writing to a Gentile audience, Paul told the church at Ephesus how Jesus was creating something new by bringing together Jewish and non-Jewish believers as a single entity. "You who once were far away have been brought near by the blood of Christ," Paul wrote (EPH. 2:13). This new structure was "built on the foundation of the apostles and prophets, with Christ Jesus himself as the chief cornerstone. In him the whole building is joined together and rises to become a holy temple in the Lord" (vv. 20–21).

The work continues today. God takes the brokenness of our lives, artfully fits us together with other broken and rescued people, and patiently chips away our rough edges. He loves His work, you know. *TIM GUSTAFSON*

Lord, we can't thank you enough for your passionate love for us.
Help us to see that you bring us together in this beautiful
body of believers known as your church.

Our rough edges must be chipped away to bring out the image of Christ.

My Father Is with Me

Read: Mark 14:32–50

You will be scattered, each to your own home. You will leave me all alone. Yet I am not alone, for my Father is with me. —John 16:32

A friend struggling with loneliness posted these words on her Facebook page: "It's not that I feel alone because I have no friends. I have lots of friends. I know that I have people who can hold me and reassure me and talk to me and care for me and think of me. But they can't be with me all the time for all time."

Jesus understands that kind of loneliness. I imagine that during His earthly ministry He saw loneliness in the eyes of lepers and heard it in the voices of the blind. But above all, He must have experienced it when His close friends deserted Him (MARK 14:50).

However, as He foretold the disciples' desertion, He also confessed His unshaken confidence in His Father's presence. He said to His disciples: "You will leave me all alone. Yet I am not alone, for my Father is with me" (JOHN 16:32). Shortly after Jesus said these words, He took up the cross for us. He made it possible for you and me to have a restored relationship with God and to be a member of His family.

Being humans, we will all experience times of loneliness. But Jesus helps us understand that we always have the presence of the Father with us. God is omnipresent and eternal. Only He can be with us all the time, for all time.

POH FANG CHIA

Heavenly Father, thank you for your promise that you will never leave me or forsake me. When I feel lonely, help me to remember you are always with me.

If you know Jesus, you'll never walk alone.

What We Do

Read: Philippians 3:7–17

One thing I do . . . I press on toward the goal to win the prize for which God has called me heavenward in Christ Jesus. —vv. 13–14

When Pulitzer Prize-winning film critic Roger Ebert died, a fellow journalist wrote of him: "With all his notoriety, honors, and celebrity, all his exclusive interviews and star-dusted encounters with movie greats, Ebert never forgot the essence of what we do—review movies. And he reviewed them with an infectious zeal and probing intellect" (Dennis King, *The Oklahoman*).

The apostle Paul never forgot the essence of what God wanted him to be and do. Focus and enthusiasm were at the heart of his relationship with Christ. Whether he was reasoning with philosophers in Athens, experiencing shipwreck in the Mediterranean, or being chained to a Roman soldier in prison, he focused on his calling to know Christ and "the power of his resurrection and participation in his sufferings" and to teach about Him (PHIL. 3:10).

While he was in prison, Paul wrote: "I do not consider myself yet to have taken hold of it. But one thing I do: Forgetting what is behind and straining toward what is ahead, I press on toward the goal to win the prize for which God has called me heavenward in Christ Jesus" (3:13–14). Whatever his circumstances, Paul continually pressed forward in his calling as a disciple of Christ.

May we always remember the essence, the heart, of who we are called to be and what we are called to do as followers of Jesus. *DAVID MCCASLAND*

Father, may I be willing to do what I can with all that I have, wherever I am.

Paul was in earnest over one thing only, and that was his relationship to Jesus Christ. OSWALD CHAMBERS

Start from Here!

Read: Acts 9:1–9

Lord, what do You want me to do? —v. 6 NKJV

On June 6, 1944, three American officers huddled in a bombshell crater on Utah Beach in Normandy, France. Realizing the tide had carried them to the wrong place on the beach, the trio made an impromptu decision: "We'll start the battle from right here." They needed to move forward from a difficult starting point.

Saul found himself in a difficult place, needing to make a decision after meeting Jesus on the road to Damascus (ACTS 9:1–20). Suddenly, the location and direction of his life was revealed to him as a mistake, his prior life perhaps even feeling like a waste. Moving forward would be difficult and would require hard and uncomfortable work, perhaps even facing the Christian families whose lives he had torn apart. But he responded, "Lord, what do You want me to do?" (v. 6 NKJV).

We often find ourselves in unexpected places, places we never planned nor wanted to be. We may be drowning in debt, inhibited by physical barriers, or suffering under the weight of sin's consequences. Whether Christ finds us this day in a prison cell or a palace, whether He finds us broken and broke or absorbed by our own selfish desires, Scripture tells us to heed Paul's advice to forget what lies behind and to press forward toward Christ (PHIL. 3:13–14). The past is no barrier to moving forward with Him.

RANDY KILGORE

Are you paralyzed by your past? Have you drifted away from Christ? Or perhaps never even met Him? Today is the day to begin anew with Christ, even if you've tried and failed before.

It's not too late for a fresh start.

The Greatest Thing

Read: Luke 10:38–42

Mary . . . sat at the Lord's feet listening to what he said. —v. 39

During a church service I spotted an infant several rows ahead. As the baby peeked over his father's shoulder, his eyes were wide with wonder as he looked at the members of the congregation. He grinned at some people, drooled, and chewed his chunky fingers, but never quite found his thumb. The pastor's words grew distant as my eyes kept sliding back to that sweet baby.

Distractions come in all shapes and sizes. For Martha, distraction took the form of cooking and cleaning—trying to serve Christ instead of listening to Him and talking with Him. Mary refused to be sidetracked. "Mary . . . sat at the Lord's feet listening to what he said" (LUKE 10:39). When Martha grumbled because Mary wasn't helping her, Jesus said, "Mary has chosen what is better, and it will not be taken away from her" (v. 42).

Jesus's words remind us that our relationship with Him is more important than any of the good things that might temporarily capture our attention. It has been said that good things are the enemies of great things. For followers of Jesus, the greatest thing in this life is to know Him and to walk with Him. *JENNIFER BENSON SCHULDT*

What do you think Martha's distractions were? Was she wanting to be seen as a good host? Or was she jealous of her sister? What attitudes cause you not to make Jesus your top priority?

Teach me, Lord, to get to know you, for that's when I'll learn to love you more than anything.

On a Hill Far Away

Read: Genesis 22:1–12

Take your son, your only son, whom you love—Isaac. —v. 2

I often find myself thinking back to the years when my children were young. One particular fond memory is our morning wake-up routine. Every morning I'd go into their bedrooms, tenderly call them by name, and tell them that it was time to get up and get ready for the day.

When I read that Abraham got up early in the morning to obey God's command, I think of those times when I woke up my children and wonder if part of Abraham's daily routine was going to Isaac's bed to waken him—and how different it would have been on that particular morning. How heart-rending for Abraham to waken his son that morning!

Abraham bound his son and laid him on an altar, but then God provided an alternate sacrifice. Hundreds of years later, God would supply another sacrifice—the final sacrifice—His own Son. Think of how agonizing it must have been for God to sacrifice His Son, His only Son whom He loved! And He went through all of that because He loves you.

If you wonder whether you are loved by God, wonder no more.

JOE STOWELL

Lord, I am amazed that you would love me so much
that you would sacrifice your Son for me.
Teach me to live gratefully in the embrace of your unfailing love.

God has already proven His love for you.

Deceptive Currents

Read: Deuteronomy 8:11–20

When they were satisfied, they became proud; then they forgot me. —Hosea 13:6

In his book *The Hidden Brain*, science writer Shankar Vedantam describes the day he went for a leisurely swim. The water was calm and clear, and he felt strong and proud for covering a long distance so easily. He decided to swim out of the bay and into open water. But when he tried to return he couldn't make any progress. He had been deceived by the current. The ease of swimming had not been due to his strength but to the movement of the water.

In our relationship with God something similar can happen. "Going with the flow" can lead us to believe we're stronger than we are. When life is easy, our minds tell us that it's due to our own strength. We become proud and self-confident. But when trouble hits, we realize how little strength we have and how helpless we are.

This happened with the Israelites. God would bless them with military success, peace, and prosperity. But thinking they had achieved it on their own, they would then become proud and self-sufficient (DEUT. 8:11–12). Assuming that they no longer needed God, they would go their own way until an enemy attacked and they would realize how powerless they were without God's help.

When life is going well we too need to beware of self-deception. Pride will take us where we do not want to go. Only humility will keep us where we ought to be—grateful to God and dependent on His strength.

JULIE ACKERMAN LINK

Lord, we don't dare trust in our own strength to do our tasks today.
you are the Giver of our talents and opportunities. Help us use them not for our own advancement, but to help others.

True humility credits God for every success.

The Unlikely

Read: 1 Corinthians 1:25–31

God chose the foolish things of the world to shame the wise. —v. 27

Fanny Kemble was a British actress who moved to America in the early 1800s and married a southern plantation owner named Pierce Butler. Fanny enjoyed the life afforded by the wealth of the plantation, until she saw the cost of that luxury—a cost paid by the slaves who worked her husband's plantations.

Having written a memoir of the cruel treatment slaves often suffered, Kemble was eventually divorced from her husband. Her writings were widely circulated among abolitionists and published in 1863 as *Journal of a Residence on a Georgian Plantation in 1838–1839*. Because of her opposition to slavery, the former wife of a slave owner became known as "The Unlikely Abolitionist."

In the body of Christ, God often wonderfully surprises us. He regularly uses the unlikely—people and circumstances—to accomplish His purposes. Paul wrote, "But God chose the foolish things of the world to shame the wise; God chose the weak things of the world to shame the strong. God chose the lowly things of this world and the despised things" (1 COR. 1:27–28).

This reminds us that God, in His grace, can use anyone. If we will allow His work to be done in us, we might be surprised at what He can do through us!

BILL CROWDER

How will you let God use you today?

God desires willing hearts ready to be used.

Strength in Stillness

Read: Exodus 14:10–14

In quietness and trust is your strength. —Isaiah 30:15

Early in my Christian life the demands of commitment made me wonder if I could make it past a year without returning to my old sinful ways. But this Scripture verse helped me: "The Lord will fight for you; you need only to be still" (EX. 14:14). These are the words Moses spoke to the Israelites when they had just escaped from slavery in Egypt and were being pursued by Pharaoh. They were discouraged and afraid.

As a young believer, with temptations engulfing my world, this call "to be still" encouraged me. Now, some 37 years later, remaining still and calm while trusting Him in the midst of stress-laden situations has been a constant desire for my Christian living.

"Be still, and know that I am God," the psalmist says (PS. 46:10). When we remain still, we get to know God, "our refuge and strength, an ever-present help in trouble" (v. 1). We see our weakness apart from God and recognize our need to surrender to Him. "When I am weak, then I am strong," says the apostle Paul (2 COR. 12:10).

Daily we grind through stress and other frustrating situations. But we can trust that He will be faithful to His promise to care for us. May we learn to be still.

LAWRENCE DARMANI

Dear Father, you are Lord of heaven, and you have promised to be with me. I don't have to fear, for you are my God. Please quiet me with your love.

The Lord may calm your storm, but more often He'll calm you.

Don't Lose Heart

Read: Galatians 6:1–10

At the proper time we will reap a harvest if we do not give up. —v. 9

Cooking can become tedious work when I do it three times a day, week after week. I get tired of peeling, cutting, slicing, mixing, and then waiting for food to bake, grill, or boil. But eating is never tedious! It's actually something we truly enjoy even though we do it day after day.

Paul used the illustration of sowing and reaping because he knew that doing good can be tiring (GAL. 6:7–10). He wrote, "Let us not become weary in doing good, for at the proper time we will reap a harvest if we do not give up" (v. 9). It's difficult to love our enemies, discipline our children, or pray without ceasing. However, reaping the good we have sown isn't tedious! What a joy when we do get to see love conquering strife, or children following God's ways, or answers to prayer.

While the cooking process can take hours, my family usually finishes a meal in 20 minutes or less. But the reaping that Paul talks about will be eternal. As we have the opportunity, let's do what is good and wait for the blessings in God's timing. Don't lose heart today as you go about following God's ways. Remember that joy is guaranteed for more than a lifetime.

KEILA OCHOA

Dear Lord, help me not to become weary of doing good today. I'm thankful that some day I will be with you for a joy-filled eternity!

Keep running the race with eternity in view.

What Is That to You?

Read: John 21:15–22

Jesus answered, ". . . You must follow me." –v. 22

Social media is useful for many things, but contentment is not one of them. At least not for me. Even when my goals are good, I can become discouraged by continual reminders that others are accomplishing them first or with greater results. I am prone to this kind of discouragement, so I frequently remind myself that God has given me everything I need to accomplish the work He wants me to do.

This means I don't need a bigger budget or the assurance of success. I don't need a better work environment or a different job. I don't need the approval or permission of others. I don't need good health or more time. God may give me some of those things, but everything I need I already have, for when He assigns work He provides the resources. My only assignment is to use whatever time and talents He has given in a way that blesses others and gives God the glory.

Jesus and Peter had a conversation that got around to this subject. After making breakfast on the shore of Galilee, Jesus told Peter what would happen at the end of his life. Pointing at another disciple, Peter asked, "What about him?" Jesus responded, "What is that to you?"

That is the question I need to ask myself when I compare myself to others. The answer is, "None of my business." My business is to follow Jesus and to be faithful. *JULIE ACKERMAN LINK*

In what **ways** *do I need to learn not to compare myself with others?*
How has God blessed me to fulfill His purposes?

Resentment comes from looking at others; contentment comes from looking at God.

Never Stop Learning

Read: 2 Timothy 3:10–17

Continue in what you have learned . . . from infancy you have known the Holy Scriptures. —vv. 14–15

Sheryl is a voracious reader. While others are watching television or playing video games, she is deeply engrossed in the pages of a book.

Much of this zeal can be traced back to her early childhood. Her family often visited a great aunt and uncle who owned a bookstore. There, Sheryl would sit on Uncle Ed's lap as he read to her and introduced her to the wonders and delights of books.

Centuries ago a young man named Timothy had his steps guided on the road to learning. In Paul's last recorded letter, he acknowledged that Timothy was first introduced to the Bible by his grandmother and mother (2 TIM. 1:5). Then Paul exhorted Timothy to continue in the Christian way because "from infancy you have known the Holy Scriptures" (2 TIM. 3:14–15).

For the believer, learning about the spiritual life should never cease to delight us and help us grow. Reading and study can be a big part of that, but we also need others to encourage and teach us.

Who has helped you grow in your faith? And who in turn can you help? That's a great way to enhance our appreciation of God and strengthen our relationship with Him. *DENNIS FISHER*

Lord, give us the desire to learn throughout life, so that we may grow increasingly closer to you each day. Thank you for those who have inspired us to learn about you.

Reading the Bible is meant not to inform but to transform.

Look Up!

Read: Psalm 121

My help comes from the LORD, the Maker of heaven and earth. —v. 2

In a park near our home there's a trail I enjoy walking on. Along one section there's a panoramic view of red sandstone rocks in the Garden of the Gods with the majestic 14,115-foot Pikes Peak behind them. From time to time, though, I find myself walking that section occupied with some problem and looking down at the wide, smooth trail. If no one is around, I may stop and say aloud, "David, look up!"

The psalms known as "Songs of Ascents" (PS. 120–134) were sung by the people of Israel as they walked the road up to Jerusalem to attend the three annual pilgrim festivals. Psalm 121 begins, "I lift up my eyes to the mountains—where does my help come from?" (v. 1). The answer follows, "My help comes from the LORD, the Maker of heaven and earth" (v. 2). The Creator is not an aloof being, but a companion who is always with us, always awake to our circumstances (vv. 3–7), guiding and guarding our journey through life "both now and forevermore" (v. 8).

Along life's path, how we need to keep our eyes fixed on God, our source of help. When we're feeling overwhelmed and discouraged, it's all right to say aloud, "Look up!"

DAVID MCCASLAND

I look up to you, Father, for you are the One who can help me.
Thank you for the joys and trials in my life right now.
I'm grateful that I never walk alone.

Keep your eyes on God—your source of help.

Our Anchor

Read: Hebrews 6:13–20

We have this hope as an anchor for the soul, firm and secure. —v. 19

After Estella Pyfrom retired from teaching, she bought a bus, decked it out with computers and desks, and now drives the "Brilliant Bus" through Palm Beach County, Florida, providing a place for at-risk children to do their homework and learn technology. Estella is providing stability and hope to children who might be tempted to throw away their dream for a better tomorrow.

In the first century, an avalanche of suffering and discouragement threatened the Christian community. The author of Hebrews wrote to convince these followers of Christ not to throw away their confidence in their future hope (2:1). Their hope—a faith in God for salvation and entrance into heaven—was found in the person and sacrifice of Christ. When Jesus entered heaven after His resurrection, He secured their hope for the future (6:19–20). Like an anchor dropped at sea, preventing a ship from drifting away, Jesus's death, resurrection, and return to heaven brought assurance and stability to the believers' lives. This hope for the future cannot and will not be shaken loose.

Jesus anchors our souls, so that we will not drift away from our hope in God.

MARVIN WILLIAMS

Jesus, in the face of all kinds of trouble and uncertainty,
help me to have a confident expectation that is grounded
in your unfailing love for me.

Our hope is anchored in Jesus.

Wise Words

Read: Prov. 10:18–21; 12:17–19

The tongue of the wise brings healing. –12:18

What is the strongest muscle in the human body? Some say it's the tongue, but it's hard to determine which muscle is the most powerful because muscles don't work alone.

But we do know that the tongue is strong. For a small muscle, it can do a lot of damage. This active little muscular organ that helps us eat, swallow, taste, and begin digestion has a tendency to also assist us in saying things we shouldn't. The tongue is guilty of flattery, cursing, lying, boasting, and harming others. And that's just the short list.

It sounds like a pretty dangerous muscle, doesn't it? But here's the good thing: It doesn't have to be that way. When we are controlled by the Holy Spirit, our tongues can be turned to great good. We can speak of God's righteousness (PS. 35:28) and justice (37:30). We can speak truth (15:2), show love (1 JOHN 3:18), and confess sin (1 JOHN 1:9).

The writer of Proverbs 12:18 spells out one of the best uses of the tongue: "The tongue of the wise brings healing." Imagine how we could glorify the One who made our tongues when He helps us use it to bring healing—not harm—to everyone we talk to. *DAVE BRANON*

Please guard each word we say so we reflect you and your love.
Help our tongues speak words of healing and not harm.

Encourage one another and build each other up. 1 THESSALONIANS 5:11

Failure Is Not Fatal

Read: John 18:15–27

You are the Christ, the Son of the living God. —6:69 NKJV

Prime Minister Winston Churchill knew how to bolster the spirits of the British people during World War II. On June 18, 1940, he told a frightened populace, "Hitler knows that he will have to break us . . . or lose the war. . . . Let us therefore brace . . . and so bear ourselves that, if the British Empire [lasts] for a thousand years, men will still say, 'This was their finest hour!' "

We would all like to be remembered for our "finest hour." Perhaps the apostle Peter's finest hour was when he proclaimed, "You are the Christ, the Son of the living God" (JOHN 6:69 NKJV). Sometimes, however, we let our failures define us. After Peter repeatedly denied that he knew Jesus, he went out and wept bitterly (MATT. 26:75; JOHN 18).

Like Peter, we all fall short—in our relationships, in our struggle with sin, in our faithfulness to God. But "failure is not fatal," as Churchill also said. Thankfully, this is true in our spiritual life. Jesus forgave the repentant Peter for his failure (JOHN 21) and used him to preach and lead many to the Savior.

Failure is not fatal. God lovingly restores those who turn back to Him.

CINDY HESS KASPER

Dear Father, thank you for your forgiveness.
Thank you that your mercy and grace are given freely
through the shed blood of your Son, Jesus.

When God forgives, He removes the sin and restores the soul.

Look at the Tassels

Read: Numbers 15:37–41

So you will remember all the commandments of the LORD, that you may obey them. —v. 39

Best-selling author Chaim Potok began his novel *The Chosen* by describing a baseball game between two Jewish teams in New York City. Reuven Malter, the book's main character, notices that the opposing players' uniforms have a unique accessory—four long ropelike tassels that extend below each teammate's shirt. Reuven recognizes the tassels as a sign of strict obedience to God's Old Testament laws.

The history of these fringes—known as *tzitzit*—began with a message from God. Through Moses, God told His people to create tassels containing some strands of blue thread and attach them to the four corners of their top garments (NUM. 15:38). God said, "You will have these tassels to look at and so you will remember all the commandments of the LORD, that you may obey them" (v. 39).

God's memory device for the ancient Israelites has a parallel for us today. We can look at Christ who consistently kept the whole law in our place and obeyed His heavenly Father (JOHN 8:29). Having received His work on our behalf, "clothe yourself with the Lord Jesus Christ, and do not think about how to gratify the desires of the flesh" (ROM. 13:14). Keeping our eyes on God's Son helps us to honor our heavenly Father.

JENNIFER BENSON SCHULDT

Dear Jesus, thank you for being my spiritual role model. Help me to walk in your steps so that I can honor and obey God with the Holy Spirit's help.

If Christ is the center of your life, you'll always be focused on Him.

A Missing Sheep

Read: Luke 15:1–10

We are his people, and the sheep of his pasture. —Psalm 100:3

Laura loaded a borrowed goat and sheep into a trailer to transport them to church for a rehearsal of a live nativity. The animals head-butted and chased each other for a bit and then settled down. Laura started for the church but first had to stop for gas.

While pumping the gas, she noticed the goat standing in the parking lot! And the sheep was gone! In the commotion of getting them settled she had forgotten to lock one of the latches. Laura called the sheriff and some friends who searched frantically along a stretch of businesses, cornfields, and woods during the last daylight hours. Many were praying that she would find the borrowed animal.

The next morning Laura and a friend went out to post "Lost Sheep" flyers at local businesses. Their first stop was the gas station. A customer overheard them asking the cashier about posting a flyer and said, "I think I know where your sheep is!" The sheep had wandered to his neighbor's farm, where he had put it in the barn for the night.

The Lord cares about lost sheep—including you and me. Jesus came from heaven to earth to show us His love and provide salvation (JOHN 3:16). He goes to great lengths to seek and find us (LUKE 19:10).

When the sheep was found, Laura nicknamed her Miracle. And God's salvation of us is a miracle of His grace. *ANNE CETAS*

Heavenly Father, as we care for the things dear to us,
how much more do you care for us, your children!
Thank you for answered prayer and for the miracle of your grace.

The Good Shepherd gives His life for His sheep. JOHN 10:11

A Loving Father

Read: Psalm 103:7–13

As a father has compassion on his children, so the LORD has compassion on those who fear him. —v. 13

The parents were obviously weary from dragging their two energetic preschoolers through airports and airplanes, and now their final flight was delayed. As I watched the two boys running around the crowded gate area, I wondered how Mom and Dad were going to keep the little guys settled down for our half-hour flight into Grand Rapids. When we finally boarded, I noticed that the father and one of the sons were in the seats behind me. Then I heard the weary father say to his son, "Why don't you let me read one of your storybooks to you." And during the entire flight, this loving father softly and patiently read to his son, keeping him calm and focused.

In one of his psalms David declares, "As a father has compassion on his children, so the LORD has compassion on those who fear him" (PS. 103:13). The word *pities* refers to showing love and compassion. This tender word gives us a picture of how deeply our heavenly Father loves His children, and it reminds us what a great gift it is to be able to look to God and cry, "Abba, Father" (ROM. 8:15).

God longs for you to listen again to the story of His love for you when you are restless on your own journey through life. Your heavenly Father is always near, ready to encourage you with His Word. *BILL CROWDER*

I rejoice in your presence and your love for me, Lord.
Today I choose joy in knowing your love is constant and unchanging, forever fixed.

God's great love for His child is one of His greatest gifts.

The Challenge of Transition

Read: Joshua 1:6–11

Be strong and very courageous. —v. 7

After former professional athlete Chris Sanders suffered a career-ending injury, he told a group of military veterans that although he had never experienced combat, "I understand the pressures of transitions."

Whether it's the loss of a job, the loss of a marriage, a serious illness, or a financial setback, every major change brings challenges. The former athlete told the soldiers that the key to success when you are transitioning into a new way of living is to reach out and get help.

The book of Joshua is recommended reading whenever we find ourselves in transition. After 40 years of wandering and setbacks, God's people were poised to enter the Promised Land. Moses, their great leader, had died, and Joshua, his assistant, was in charge.

God told Joshua to "be strong and very courageous. Be careful to obey all the law my servant Moses gave you; do not turn from it to the right or to the left, that you may be successful wherever you go" (JOSH. 1:7). God's words of direction were to be the bedrock of Joshua's leadership in every situation.

The Lord's charge and promise to Joshua apply to us as well: "Be strong and courageous. Do not be afraid; do not be discouraged, for the LORD your God will be with you wherever you go" (v. 9).

He is with us in every transition. *DAVID MCCASLAND*

Father, I'm bringing you my trials and frustrations. you know each and every detail.
Please comfort me as only you can, and provide exactly what I need for today.
Help me give my unfulfilled expectations to you,
trusting you're working out a plan for me.

God remains faithful in every change.

Shopping with Liam

Read: Genesis 3:14–19

He will crush your head, and you will strike his heel. —v. 15

My son Liam loves to pick dandelions for his mother. To date, she hasn't wearied of receiving them. One man's weed is a little boy's flower.

One day I took Liam shopping with me. As we hurried past the floral section, he pointed excitedly to an arrangement of yellow tulips. "Daddy," he exclaimed, "you should get those dandelions for Mommy!" His advice made me laugh. It made a pretty good Facebook post on his mother's page too. (By the way, I bought the tulips.)

Some see in weeds a reminder of Adam's sin. By eating the forbidden fruit, Adam and Eve brought on themselves the curse of a fallen world—relentless work, agonizing birth, and eventual death (GEN. 3:16–19).

But Liam's youthful eyes remind me of something else. There is beauty even in weeds. The anguish of childbirth holds hope for us all. Death is ultimately defeated. The "offspring" God spoke of in Genesis 3:15 would wage war with the serpent's offspring. That offspring is Jesus himself, who rescued us from the curse of death (GAL. 3:16).

The world may be broken, but wonder awaits us at every turn. Even weeds remind us of the promise of redemption and a Creator who loves us.

TIM GUSTAFSON

Help us, Father, to find you even in the midst of all life's pain and aggravations. Forgive us for so often overlooking the beauty you have planted everywhere.

Creation reminds us of the promise of redemption.

Walking on Water

Read: Matthew 14:22–33

Take courage! It is I. Don't be afraid. —v. 27

When I learned to sail, I had to walk along a very unsteady floating platform to reach the little boats in which we had our lessons. I hated it. I don't have a good sense of balance and was terrified of falling between the platform and the boat as I attempted to get in. I nearly gave up. "Fix your eyes on me," said the instructor. "I'm here, and I'll catch you if you slip." I did what he said, and I am now the proud possessor of a basic sailing proficiency certificate!

Do you avoid taking risks at all costs? Many of us are reluctant to step out of our comfort zones in case we fail, get hurt, or look stupid. But if we allow that fear to bind us, we'll end up afraid to do anything.

The story of Peter's water-walking adventure and why it supposedly failed is a popular choice for preachers (MATT. 14:22–33). But I don't think I've ever heard any of them discuss the behavior of the rest of the disciples. In my opinion, Peter was a success. He felt the fear but responded to the call of Jesus anyway. Maybe it was those who never tried at all who failed.

Jesus risked everything for us. What are we prepared to risk for Him?

MARION STROUD

Father, thank you for stretching out your hand and saying, "Come."
Help me to get out of the boat, knowing that it is totally safe
to walk on water with you.

"Life is either a daring adventure, or nothing." HELEN KELLER

Worth It All

Read: 1 Corinthians 15:30–38

What you sow does not come to life unless it dies. —v. 36

By the end of the 4th century, followers of Christ were no longer being fed to the lions for the entertainment of Roman citizens. But the games of death continued until the day one man jumped out of the crowd in a bold attempt to keep two gladiators from killing each other.

His name was Telemachus. As a desert monk, he had come to Rome for the holidays only to find himself unable to tolerate the bloodlust of this popular pastime. According to the 5th-century bishop and church historian Theodoret, Telemachus cried out for the violence to stop but was stoned to death by the crowd. The Emperor Honorius heard about his courageous act and ordered an end to the games.

Some may question Telemachus. Was his action the only way to protest a tragic blood sport? The apostle Paul asked a similar question of himself: "Why do we endanger ourselves every hour?" (1 COR. 15:30). In 2 Corinthians 11:22-33, he chronicled some of his travails for the love of Christ, many of which could have killed him. Had it all been worth it?

In Paul's mind the matter was settled. Trading things that will soon come to an end for honor that will last forever is a good investment. In the resurrection, a life that has been lived in behalf of Christ and others is seed for an eternity we will never regret. *MART DEHAAN*

Give us courage, Father, to make and live by choices that
show the difference the love of Jesus makes in our lives.
Help us not to trade away eternal values for convenience and comfort.

Now is the time to invest in eternity.

Hidden Mysteries

Read: 2 Kings 6:15–23

Don't be afraid. . . . Those who are with us are more than those who are with them. –v. 16

Most of what goes on in the universe we never see. Many things are too small or move too fast or even too slow for us to see. Using modern technology, however, filmmaker Louis Schwartzberg is able to show stunning video images of some of those things—a caterpillar's mouth, the eye of a fruit fly, the growth of a mushroom.

Our limited ability to see the awesome and intricate detail of things in the physical world reminds us that our ability to see and understand what's happening in the spiritual realm is equally limited. God is at work all around us doing things more wonderful than we can imagine. But our spiritual vision is limited and we cannot see them. The prophet Elisha, however, actually got to see the supernatural work that God was doing. God also opened the eyes of his fearful colleague so he too could see the heavenly army sent to fight on their behalf (2 KINGS 6:17).

Fear makes us feel weak and helpless and causes us to think we are alone in the world. But God has assured us that His Spirit in us is greater than any worldly power (1 JOHN 4:4).

Whenever we become discouraged by the evil we can see, we need to think instead about the good work God is doing that we cannot see.

JULIE ACKERMAN LINK

Lord, I'm tempted to fear what I cannot understand or control. But my security rests in you and not in what happens to me or around me. Help me to rest in your unfailing love.

Eyes of faith see God at work in everything.

The Whole Story

Read: Acts 8:26–37

Philip began with that very passage of Scripture and told him the good news about Jesus. —v. 35

Recently my 5-year-old grandson, Dallas, asked, "Why did Jesus die on the cross?" So we had a little talk. I explained to him about sin and Jesus's willingness to be our sacrifice. Then he ran off to play.

A few minutes later, I overheard him talking to his 5-year-old cousin, Katie, explaining to her why Jesus died. Katie said to him, "But Jesus isn't dead." Dallas replied, "Yes. He's dead. Grampy told me. He died on the cross."

I realized I hadn't completed the story. So we had another talk as I explained to Dallas that Jesus rose from the dead. We went over the story again until he understood that Jesus is alive today, even though He did die for us.

What a reminder that people need to hear the whole gospel. When a man from Ethiopia asked Philip about a portion of Scripture he did not understand, Philip "began with that very passage of Scripture and told him the good news about Jesus" (ACTS 8:35).

Tell others the good news about Jesus: that we are all sinners needing salvation; that the perfect Son of God died to save us; and that He rose from the grave, showing His power over death. Jesus, our Savior, is alive and is offering now to live His life through us.

When someone wants to know about Jesus, let's make sure to tell the whole story! *DAVE BRANON*

Lord, your story is amazing. Help us to tell all of it so others can put their faith in you and enjoy the salvation you offer to all who trust and believe.

Jesus said . . . , "I am the resurrection and the life. The one who believes in me will live, even though they die." JOHN 11:25

A Voice in the Night

Read: Psalm 134

Lift up your hands in the sanctuary and praise the LORD. —v. 2

Psalm 134 has only three verses, but it is proof that little things can mean a lot. The first two verses are an admonition to the priests who serve in God's house night after night. The building was dark and empty; nothing of consequence was occurring—or so it seemed. Yet these ministers were encouraged to "lift up [their] hands to the holy place and bless the LORD!" (v. 2 ESV). The third verse is a voice from the congregation calling into the darkness and loneliness of the night: "May the LORD bless you . . . , he who made heaven and earth" (ESV).

I think of other servants of the Lord today—pastors and their families who serve in small churches in small places. They're often discouraged, tempted to lose heart, doing their best, serving unnoticed and unrewarded. They wonder if anyone cares what they're doing; if anyone ever thinks of them, prays for them, or considers them a part of their lives.

I would say to them—and to anyone who is feeling lonely or insignificant: Though your place is small, it is a holy place. The one who made and moves heaven and earth is at work in and through you. "Lift up your hands" and praise Him. *DAVID ROPER*

Lord, show me how I can be an encourager of others who might feel they are in a "small" place. Let them know that their lives leave an eternal impact on those they serve.

Anyone doing God's work in God's way is important in His sight.

Rescuing the Reluctant

Read: Genesis 19:12–25

The men led them safely out of the city, for the LORD was merciful to them. —v. 16

Many years ago during a water safety class, we were taught how to save a drowning person who is resisting rescue. "Approach the person from behind," the instructor told us. "Place one arm across the person's chest and flailing arms, and swim toward safety. If you approach from the front, the person may grab you and pull both of you down." Panic and fear can paralyze the ability to think and act wisely.

When two angels sent by God came to rescue Lot and his family from the impending destruction of the cities of Sodom and Gomorrah (GEN. 19:12–13), they encountered resistance. Lot's sons-in-law thought the warning was a joke (V. 14). When the angels told Lot to hurry and leave, he hesitated (V. 15). At that point, the two angels "grasped his hand and the hands of his wife and of his two daughters," and "led them safely out of the city, for the LORD was merciful to them" (V. 16).

When we reflect on our journey of faith in Christ, we can see God's faithfulness in overcoming our reluctance and resistance. When we encounter people lashing out in spiritual desperation and fear, may we have God's wisdom to show His love to them—and to every person who is reluctant to be rescued by Him. *DAVID MCCASLAND*

Father, as I look at my own heart, I know I have resisted you and have been reluctant at times to come to you. Thank you for your mercy. Help me to share with others who you are.

God's mercy can overcome our resistance.

Christ the Redeemer

Read: Job 19:23–29

I know that my redeemer lives. —v. 25

The famous statue *Christ the Redeemer* overlooks the city of Rio de Janeiro. The statue is a model of Christ with His arms extended so that His body forms the shape of a cross. Brazilian architect Heitor da Silva Costa designed the figure. He imagined that the city's residents would see it as the first image to emerge from the darkness at dawn. At dusk, he hoped the city dwellers would view the setting sun as a halo behind the statue's head.

There is value in keeping our eyes on our Redeemer each day, during the good times and the difficult times. As he suffered, Job said, "I know that my redeemer lives, and that in the end he will stand on the earth" (JOB 19:25).

The cry of Job's heart points us to Jesus—our living Savior who will visit the earth again one day (1 THESS. 4:16–18). Keeping our eyes on Jesus means remembering that we have been rescued from our sin. Jesus "gave himself for us to redeem us from all wickedness and to purify for himself a people that are his very own" (TITUS 2:14).

Anyone who has accepted Jesus as Savior has a reason to be glad today. No matter what we endure on earth, we can have hope today and look forward to enjoying eternity with Him. *JENNIFER BENSON SCHULDT*

Dear Jesus, you are my rescuer. Because you died and rose again,
I am free from the consequences of my sin forever.
Thank you for redeeming my life.

Through His cross and resurrection, Jesus rescues and redeems.

Raise Your Hand

Read: John 4:7–15, 28–30

God did not send his Son into the world to condemn the world, but to save the world through him. –3:17

The St. Olaf Choir from Northfield, Minnesota, is renowned for making beautiful music. One reason for its excellence is the selection process. Applicants are chosen based not only on how well they sing but also on how they sound as part of the whole. Another reason is that all members agree to make the choir their first priority and commit to a rigorous rehearsal and performance schedule.

One of the things that intrigues me the most about this choir is what happens during rehearsals. Whenever members make a mistake, they raise their hand. Instead of trying to hide the blunder, they call attention to it! This allows the conductor to help each singer learn the difficult part, and it increases the likelihood of a flawless performance.

I think this is the kind of community Jesus was establishing when He told Nicodemus that God sent His Son into the world to save it, not condemn it (JOHN 3:17). Shortly after this conversation, Jesus encountered a Samaritan woman at the public well. He made it easy for her to admit failure by promising her a better way of life where she could enjoy His forgiveness (JOHN 4).

As members of Christ's body on Earth, we should not fear admitting our wrongs but welcome it as an opportunity to together experience and rejoice in the forgiveness of God. *JULIE ACKERMAN LINK*

Lord, it's our tendency to hide our sins and flaws.
May we come to you in full honesty, understanding that we are
loved and forgiven by you.

We can't put our sins behind us until we are ready to face them.

Fiery Conversation

Read: James 3:2–10

Let your conversation be always full of grace, seasoned with salt. —Colossians 4:6

Where I come from in northern Ghana, bush fires are regular occurrences in the dry season between December and March. I've witnessed many acres of farmland set ablaze when the winds carried tiny embers from fireplaces or from cigarette butts carelessly thrown by the roadside. With the dry grassland vegetation, all that is needed to start a devastating fire is a little spark.

That is how James describes the tongue, calling it "a world of evil among the parts of the body. It corrupts the whole body, sets the whole course of one's life on fire, and is itself set on fire by hell" (JAMES 3:6). A false statement made here or backbiting there, a vicious remark somewhere else, and relationships are destroyed. "The words of the reckless pierce like swords," says Proverbs 12:18, "but the tongue of the wise brings healing." Just as fire has both destructive and useful elements, so "the tongue has the power of life and death" (18:21).

For conversation that reflects God's presence in us and pleases Him, let it always be "full of grace" (COL. 4:6). When expressing our opinions during disagreements, let's ask God to help us choose wholesome language that brings honor to Him. *LAWRENCE DARMANI*

Guide my conversation today, Lord. May the words I choose bless and encourage others and build them up rather than tear them down. May you be pleased with what you hear.

Anger can make us speak our mind when we should be minding our speech.

A Letter from the Battlefield

Read: 2 Timothy 4:1–8

I have fought the good fight, I have finished the race, I have kept the faith. —v. 7

For more than two decades, Andrew Carroll has been urging people not to throw away the letters written by family members or friends during a time of war. Carroll, director of the Center for American War Letters at Chapman University in California, considers them an irreplaceable link to tie families together and open a door of understanding. "Younger generations are reading these letters," Carroll says, "and asking questions and saying, 'Now I understand what you endured, what you sacrificed.'"

When the apostle Paul was imprisoned in Rome and knew his life would soon end, he wrote a letter to a young man whom he considered a "son in the faith," Timothy. Like a soldier on the battlefield, Paul opened his heart to him: "The time for my departure is near. I have fought the good fight, I have finished the race, I have kept the faith. Now, there is in store for me the crown of righteousness, which the Lord, the righteous Judge, will award to me on that day—and not only to me, but also to all who have longed for his appearing" (2 TIM. 4:6–8).

When we read the letters in the Bible that the heroes of the Christian faith have left for us and grasp what they endured because of their love for Christ, we gain courage to follow their example and to stand strong for those who come after us. *DAVID MCCASLAND*

Lord, give us strength for the spiritual battles we face today, knowing that you have won the ultimate victory and that we will one day live eternally with you.

Run the race with eternity in view.

The Cyrus Cylinder

Read: Ezra 1:1–4

The LORD moved the heart of Cyrus king of Persia. –v. 1

In 1879, archaeologists discovered a remarkable little item in an area now known as Iraq (biblical Babylon). Just 9 inches long, the Cyrus Cylinder records something that King Cyrus of Persia did 2,500 years ago. It says that Cyrus allowed a group of people to return to their homeland and rebuild their "holy cities."

It's the same story told in Ezra 1. There we read that "the LORD moved the heart of Cyrus king of Persia" to make a proclamation (v. 1). Cyrus said he was releasing the captives in Babylon to go home to Jerusalem, reestablish their homes, and rebuild their temple (vv. 2–5). But there's more to the story. Daniel confessed his sins and his people's sins and pleaded with God to end the Babylonian captivity (DAN. 9). In response, God sent an angel to speak to Daniel (v. 21). Later He moved Cyrus to release the Hebrews. (SEE ALSO JER. 25:11–12; 39:10.)

Together, the Cyrus Cylinder and God's Word combine to show us that the king's heart was changed and he allowed the exiled Hebrews to go home and worship.

This story has great implications for us today. In a world that seems out of control, we can rest assured that God can move the hearts of leaders. We read in Proverbs 21:1 that "the king's heart is in the hand of the Lord" (NKJV). And Romans 13:1 says that "there is no authority except that which God has established."

The Lord, who is able to change our own hearts as well as our leaders', can be trusted for He is in control. Let's ask Him to work. *DAVE BRANON*

Father, the world seems out of control. We know you are sovereign over everything. We pray that your will be done in the hearts of our leaders.

Rather than complain, pray.

Come to Me

Read: John 6:30–40

I am the bread of life. Whoever comes to me will never go hungry. —v. 35

When Jesus lived on this earth, He invited people to come to Him, and He still does today (JOHN 6:35). But what do He and His Father in heaven have that we need?

Salvation. Jesus is the only way to have forgiveness of sin and the promise of heaven. "Whoever believes in Him should not perish but have eternal life" (JOHN 3:15 NKJV).

Purpose. We are to give all of our heart, soul, mind, and strength to following Jesus. "Whoever wants to be my disciple must deny themselves and take up their cross and follow me" (MARK 8:34).

Comfort. In trial or sorrow, the "God of all comfort . . . comforts us in all our troubles" (2 COR. 1:3–4).

Wisdom. We need wisdom beyond our own for making decisions. "If any of you lacks wisdom, you should ask God, . . . and it will be given to you" (JAMES 1:5).

Strength. When we're weary, "the LORD gives strength to his people" (PS. 29:11).

Abundant life. The fullest life is found in a relationship with Jesus. "I have come that they may have life, and have it to the full" (JOHN 10:10).

Jesus said, "Whoever comes to me I will never drive away" (JOHN 6:37). Come!

ANNE CETAS

How can I grow closer to God today?

Jesus invites us to come to Him for life.

July 6

Darkness and Light

Read: Psalm 91:1–8

You will not fear the terror of night, . . . nor the pestilence that stalks in the darkness. —vv. 5–6

When I was a boy, I delivered newspapers to about 140 homes on two streets that were connected by a cemetery. Since I delivered a morning newspaper, I had to be out at 3:00 a.m. walking through that cemetery in the darkness. Sometimes I would be so frightened that I would actually run! I was afraid until I was standing safely under a streetlight on the other side. The scary darkness was dispelled by the light.

The psalmist understood the connection between fear and darkness, but he also knew that God is greater than those fears. He wrote, "You will not fear the terror of night, nor the arrow that flies by day, nor the pestilence that stalks in the darkness" (PS. 91:5–6). Neither terrors of night nor evil in the darkness need to drive us to fear. We have a God who sent His Son, the Light of the World (JOHN 8:12).

In the light of God's love and grace and truth, we can find courage, help, and strength to live for Him. *BILL CROWDER*

Lord, I come to you, the Light of the World.
I want you to bring your light into
the darkness of my fears.

You need not fear the darkness if you are walking with the Light of the World.

The Slow Walk

Read: Job 16:1–5

I will pray the Father, and He will give you another Helper, that He may abide with you forever. –John 14:16

Caleb was sick. Really sick! Diagnosed with a nervous system disease, the 5-year-old suffered from temporary paralysis. His anxious parents prayed. And waited. Slowly, Caleb began to recover. Months later, when doctors cleared him to attend school, all Caleb could manage was a slow, unsteady walk.

One day his dad visited him at school. He watched his son haltingly descend the steps to the playground. And then he saw Caleb's young friend Tyler come alongside him. For the entire recess, as the other kids raced and romped and played, Tyler slowly walked the playground with his frail friend.

Job must have ached for a friend like Tyler. Instead, he had three friends who were certain he was guilty. "Who, being innocent, has ever perished?" asked Eliphaz (JOB 4:7). Such accusations prompted Job to bitterly declare, "You are miserable comforters, all of you!" (16:2).

How unlike Jesus. On the eve of His crucifixion He took time to comfort His disciples. He promised them the Holy Spirit, who would be with them forever (JOHN 14:16), and assured them, "I will not leave you as orphans; I will come to you" (v. 18). Then, just before He returned to His Father, He said, "I am with you always, to the very end of the age" (MATT. 28:20).

The One who died for us also walks with us, step by painstaking step.

TIM GUSTAFSON

Father, we tend to say too much to our hurting friends.
Help us choose our words wisely. Teach us to walk slowly with
those in pain, as you walk patiently with us.

Sometimes the best way to be like Jesus is to sit quietly with a hurting friend.

Ordinary People

Read: Judges 6:11–16

We have this treasure in jars of clay to show that this all-surpassing power is from God and not from us. –2 Corinthians 4:7

Gideon was an ordinary person. His story, recorded in Judges 6, inspires me. He was a farmer, and a timid one at that. When God called him to deliver Israel from the Midianites, Gideon's initial response was "How can I save Israel? My clan is the weakest in Manasseh, and I am the least in my family" (JUDG. 6:15). God promised that He would be with Gideon and that he would be able to accomplish what he had been asked to do (V. 16). Gideon's obedience brought victory to Israel, and he is listed as one of the great heroes of faith (HEB. 11:32).

Many other individuals played a significant part in this plan to save the Israelites from a strong enemy force. God provided Gideon with 300 men, valiant heroes all, to win the battle. We are not told their names, but their bravery and obedience are recorded in the Scriptures (JUDG. 7:5–23).

Today, God is still calling ordinary people to do His work and assuring us that He will be with us as we do. Because we are ordinary people being used by God, it's obvious that the power comes from God and not from us.

POH FANG CHIA

Lord, I **am** *just an ordinary person, but you are an all-powerful God.*
I want to serve you. Please show me how
and give me the strength.

God uses ordinary people to carry out His extraordinary plan.

Grace in Our Hearts

Read: Ephesians 2:4–10

Let your conversation be always full of grace. —Colossians 4:6

A few years ago, four-star General Peter Chiarelli (the No. 2 general in the US Army at that time) was mistaken for a waiter by a senior presidential advisor at a formal Washington dinner. As the general stood behind her in his dress uniform, the senior advisor asked him to get her a beverage. She then realized her mistake, and the general graciously eased her embarrassment by cheerfully refilling her glass and even inviting her to join his family sometime for dinner.

The word *gracious* comes from the word *grace,* and it can mean an act of kindness or courtesy, like the general's. But it has an even deeper meaning to followers of Christ. We are recipients of the incredible free and unmerited favor—grace—that God has provided through His Son, Jesus (EPH. 2:8).

Because we have received grace, we are to show it in the way we treat others—for example, in the way we speak to them: "Words from the mouth of the wise are gracious" (ECCL. 10:12). Grace in our hearts pours out in our words and deeds (COL. 3:16–17).

Learning to extend the grace in our hearts toward others is a by-product of the life of a Spirit-filled follower of Christ Jesus—the greatest of grace-givers.

CINDY HESS KASPER

Dear heavenly Father, help me today to season my words with grace.
May all that I say and do be gracious to others and pleasing to you,
O Lord, my strength and my redeemer.

God's grace in the heart brings out good deeds in the life.

Help for a Heavy Load

Read: Numbers 11:4–17

[The men] will share the burden of the people with you so that you will not have to carry it alone. —v. 17

It's amazing what you can haul with a bicycle. An average adult with a specialized trailer (and a bit of determination) can use a bicycle to tow up to 300 pounds at 10 mph. There's just one problem: Hauling a heavier load means moving more slowly. A person hauling 600 pounds of work equipment or personal possessions would only be able to move at a pace of 8 miles in one hour.

Moses carried another kind of weight in the wilderness—an emotional weight that kept him at a standstill. The Israelites' intense craving for meat instead of manna had reduced them to tears. Hearing their ongoing lament, an exasperated Moses said to God, "I cannot carry all these people by myself; the burden is too heavy for me" (NUM. 11:14).

On his own, Moses lacked the resources necessary to fix the problem. God responded by telling him to select 70 men to stand with him and share his load. God told Moses, "[The men] will share the burden of the people with you so that you will not have to carry it alone" (v. 17).

As followers of Jesus, we don't have to handle our burdens alone either. We have Jesus himself, who is always willing and able to help us. And He has given us brothers and sisters in Christ to share the load. When we give Him the things that weigh us down, He gives us wisdom and support in return.

JENNIFER BENSON SCHULDT

Who has come alongside you? Have you thanked them?

God's help is only a prayer away.

Desert Places

Read: Isaiah 48:16–22

They did not thirst when he led them through the deserts. –v. 21

Dry. Dusty. Dangerous. A desert. A place where there is little water, a place hostile to life. It's not surprising, then, that the word *deserted* describes a place that is uninhabited. Life there is hard. Few people choose it. But sometimes we can't avoid it.

In Scripture, God's people were familiar with desert life. Much of the Middle East, including Israel, is desert. But there are lush exceptions, like the Jordan Valley and areas surrounding the Sea of Galilee. God chose to "raise His family" in a place surrounded by wilderness, a place where He could make His goodness known to His children as they trusted Him for protection and daily provision (ISA. 48:17–19).

Today, most of us don't live in literal deserts, but we often go through desert-like places. Sometimes we go as an act of obedience. Other times we find ourselves there through no conscious choice or action. When someone abandons us, or disease invades our bodies, we end up in desert-like circumstances where resources are scarce and life is hard to sustain.

But the point of going through a desert, whether literally or figuratively, is to remind us that we are dependent on God to sustain us—a lesson we need to remember even when we're living in a place of plenty.

JULIE ACKERMAN LINK

Are you living in a place of plenty or of need?
In what ways is God sustaining you?

In every desert, God has an oasis of grace.

Seeing Beyond Loss

Read: Psalm 77:1–15

I will remember the deeds of the Lord; yes, I will remember your miracles of long ago. —v. 11

Author William Zinsser described his last visit to see the house where he grew up, a place he greatly loved as a boy. When he and his wife arrived at the hill overlooking Manhasset Bay and Long Island Sound, they found that the house had been demolished. All that remained was a huge hole. Disheartened, they walked to the nearby seawall. Zinsser looked across the bay, absorbing the sights and sounds. Later, he wrote of this experience, "I was at ease and only slightly sad. The view was intact: the unique configuration of land and sea I remember so well that I still dream about it."

The psalmist wrote of a difficult time when his soul refused to be comforted and his spirit was overwhelmed (Ps. 77:2–3). But in the midst of his trouble, he shifted his focus from his sadness to his Savior, saying, "I will remember the deeds of the Lord; yes, I will remember your miracles of long ago" (v. 11).

In dealing with disappointment, we can either focus on our loss or on God himself. The Lord invites us to look to Him and see the scope of His goodness, His presence with us, and His eternal love. *David McCasland*

Heavenly Father, this life can be both wonderful and disappointing.
We know that things are not the way they ought to be.
Our disappointments cause us to turn to you,
the only true hope for the world.

Faith in God's goodness keeps hope alive.

Not Saying Goodbye

Read: Philippians 4:1–9

Whatever you have learned or received or heard from me, or seen in me—put it into practice. And the God of peace will be with you. —v. 9

Francis Allen led me to Jesus, and now it was nearly time for Francis to meet Jesus face to face. I was at his home as it grew time for him to say goodbye. I wanted to say something memorable and meaningful.

For nearly an hour I stood by his bed. He laughed hard at the stories I told on myself. Then he got tired, we got serious, and he spent his energy rounding off some rough edges he still saw in my life. I listened, even as I tried to sort out how to say goodbye.

He stopped me before I got the chance. "You remember, Randy, what I've always told you. We have nothing to fear from the story of life because we know how it ends. I'm not afraid. You go do what I've taught you." Those challenging words reminded me of what the apostle Paul said to the believers in Philippi: "Whatever you have learned or received or heard from me, or seen in me—put it into practice." (PHIL. 4:9).

Francis had the same twinkle in his eye this last day I saw him as he had the first day I met him. He had no fear in his heart.

So many of the words I write, stories I tell, and people I serve are touched by Francis. As we journey through life, may we remember those who have encouraged us spiritually. *RANDY KILGORE*

Who has been your mentor? Are you mentoring others?

Live so that when people get to know you, they will want to know Christ.

Prayerful Thinking

Read: Psalm 8

What is mankind that you are mindful of them, human beings that you care for them? —v. 4

Augustine was one of the most brilliant Christian thinkers of all time. Interestingly, he did some of his most effective and intimate praying while engaged in deep thought. He was what might be called a "prayerful thinker." Often Augustine began a line of reasoning and then concluded it with a prayer. Here is a sample from *Confessions*, one of his works on theology:

"Too late came I to love You, O Beauty both ancient and ever new; too late came I to love You. . . . You called to me; yes, You even broke open my deafness. Your beams shined unto me and cast away my blindness."

These are not the dry musings of some pseudo-theologian or armchair philosopher. They are the thoughts of someone with a passionate prayer life.

Prayerful thinking is not unique to Augustine. David pondered the beauty of creation and felt compelled to worship his Creator: "When I consider your heavens, the work of your fingers, the moon and the stars, which you have set in place, what is mankind that you are mindful of them?" (PS. 8:3–4).

As we walk life's journey, our deep thoughts and feelings and our praying can be interwoven. Seeing the beauty of nature or even solving a problem can be opportunities for prayerful thinking. *DENNIS FISHER*

What does it mean that God has "crowned man with glory and honor"? (PSALM 8:5). *What does that mean for me today at work and at home?*

Prayerful thinking leads to purposeful thanking.

Transformed Hearts

Read: Ezekiel 36:22–31

Above all else, guard your heart, for everything you do flows from it. —Proverbs 4:23

During the early 1970s in Ghana, a poster titled "The Heart of Man" appeared on walls and public notice boards. In one picture, all kinds of reptiles—symbols of the vile and despicable—filled the heart-shaped painting with the head of a very unhappy man on top of it. In another image, the heart-shape was clean and serene with the head of a contented man. The caption beneath the images read: "What is the condition of your heart?"

In Matthew 15:18-19, Jesus explained what pollutes a person. "The things that come out of a person's mouth come from the heart, and these defile them. For out of the heart come evil thoughts—murder, adultery, sexual immorality, theft, false testimony, slander." That is the condition of a heart separated from God—the situation ancient Israelites found themselves in when their sins forced them into exile (EZEK. 36:23).

God's promise in Ezekiel 36:26 is beautiful: "I will give you a new heart, and I will put a new spirit in you. I will take out your stony, stubborn heart and give you a tender, responsive heart" (NLT; SEE ALSO 11:19). God will take away our stubborn hearts that have been corrupted by all kinds of evil and give to us a clean heart that is responsive to Him. Praise God for such a wonderful gift. *LAWRENCE DARMANI*

Father in heaven, thank you that when we confess our sin to you, you give us a new heart and a new life. I pray that the life I live reflects the goodness of your gift and that others may see the difference a new heart has made in me.

For a new start, ask God for a new heart.

A Given Name

Read: Matthew 1:18–25

She will give birth to a son, and you are to give him the name Jesus, because he will save his people from their sins. —v. 21

Most families have their own family stories. One in our family has to do with how I got my name. Apparently, when my parents were in the early days of their marriage, they disagreed about what to name their first son. Mom wanted a son named after Dad, but Dad wasn't interested in naming a son "Junior." After much discussion, they reached a compromise, agreeing that only if a son was born on Dad's birthday would he be given Dad's name. Amazingly, I was born on my dad's birthday. So I was given his name with a "Junior" attached to it.

The naming of children is as old as time. As Joseph wrestled with the news that his fiancée, Mary, was pregnant, the angel brought him insight from the Father about naming the Baby: "She will give birth to a son, and you are to give him the name Jesus, because he will save his people from their sins" (MATT. 1:21). Not only would Jesus be His name, but it would also explain the reason for His coming into the world: To take on himself the punishment we deserve for our sin. His redemptive purpose behind the manger is wrapped up in the perfectly given Name above all names.

May our heart's desire be to live in a way that honors His wonderful name!

BILL CROWDER JR.

Thank you, Father, for sending your Son to rescue us from sin and bring us into relationship with you.

Jesus: His name and His mission are one and the same.

Tears of a Teen

Read: Romans 9:1–5

I have great sorrow and unceasing anguish in my heart. —v. 2

As I sat with four teenagers and a 20-something homeless man at a soup kitchen in Alaska, I was touched by the teens' compassion for him. They listened as he talked about what he believed and then they gently presented the gospel to him—lovingly offering him hope in Jesus. Sadly, the man refused to seriously consider the gospel.

As we were leaving, one of the girls, Grace, expressed through her tears how much she didn't want the man to die without knowing Jesus. From the heart, she grieved for this young man who, at least at this point, was rejecting the love of the Savior.

The tears of this teen remind me of the apostle Paul who served the Lord humbly and had great sorrow in his heart for his countrymen, desiring that they trust in Christ (ROM. 9:1–5). Paul's compassion and concern must have brought him to tears on many occasions.

If we care enough for others who have not yet accepted God's gift of forgiveness through Christ, we will find ways to share with them. With the confidence of our own faith and with tears of compassion, let's take the good news to those who need to know the Savior. *DAVE BRANON*

Is there someone you need to talk to about Jesus today?

Sharing the gospel is one person telling another good news.

My Way

Read: 2 Kings 5:1–15

Now I know that there is no God in all the world, except in Israel. —v. 15

Two small boys were playing a complicated game with sticks and string. After a few minutes the older boy turned to his friend and said crossly, "You're not doing it properly. This is my game, and we play it my way. You can't play anymore!" The desire to have things our own way starts young!

Naaman was a person who was accustomed to having things his way. He was commander of the army of the king of Syria. But Naaman also had an incurable disease. One day his wife's servant girl, who had been captured from the land of Israel, suggested that he seek healing from Elisha, the prophet of God. Naaman was desperate enough to do this, but he wanted the prophet to come to him. He expected to be treated with great ceremony and respect. So when Elisha simply sent a message that he should bathe seven times in the Jordan River, Naaman was furious! He refused (2 KINGS 5:10–12). Only when he finally humbled himself and did it God's way was he cured (vv. 13–14).

We've probably all had times when we've said "I'll do it my way" to God. But His way is always the best way. So let's ask God to give us humble hearts that willingly choose His way, not our own. *MARION STROUD*

Father, forgive me for my pride and for so often thinking I know best. Give me a humble heart that is willing to follow your way in everything.

Humility is to make a right estimate of one's self. CHARLES SPURGEON

Eulogize the Living God

Read: Ephesians 1:3–14

Praise be to the God and Father of our Lord Jesus Christ, who has blessed us in the heavenly realms with every spiritual blessing in Christ. —v. 3

In 2005, when American civil rights hero Rosa Parks died, Oprah Winfrey counted it a privilege to eulogize her. Oprah said of the woman who refused to give up her bus seat to a white man in 1955, "I often thought about what that took—knowing the climate of the times and what could have happened to you—what it took to stay seated. You acted without concern for yourself and made life better for us all."

We often use the word *eulogy* to refer to the words spoken at a funeral. But it can also refer to other situations where we give high praise to someone. In the opening lines of Ephesians, the apostle Paul eulogized the living God. When he said, "Praise be to the God and Father," he used a word for "praise" that means "eulogy." Paul invited the Ephesians to join him in praising God for all kinds of spiritual blessings: God had chosen and adopted them; Jesus had redeemed, forgiven, and made known to them the mystery of the gospel; and the Spirit had guaranteed and sealed them. This great salvation was purely an act of God and His grace.

Let us continue to center our thoughts on God's blessings in Christ. When we do, like Paul, we will find our hearts overflowing with a eulogy that declares: "To the praise of his glory" (1:14). MARVIN WILLIAMS

Blessed Father, I am overwhelmed by your grace.
My only adequate response is ceaseless praise.
Thank you for choosing me, adopting me, redeeming me, forgiving me,
and making known to me the mystery of the gospel.

Praise is the song of a soul set free.

Faithful Service

Read: 2 Timothy 2:1–10

Join with me in suffering, like a good soldier of Jesus Christ. —v. 3

Having served in World War I, C. S. Lewis was no stranger to the stresses of military service. In a public address during the Second World War, he eloquently described the hardships a soldier has to face: "All that we fear from all the kinds of adversity . . . is collected together in the life of the soldier on active service. Like sickness, it threatens pain and death. Like poverty, it threatens ill lodging, cold, heat, thirst, and hunger. Like slavery, it threatens toil, humiliation, injustice, and arbitrary rule. Like exile, it separates you from all you love."

The apostle Paul used the analogy of a soldier suffering hardship to describe the trials a believer may experience in service to Christ. Paul—now at the end of his life—had faithfully endured suffering for the sake of the gospel. He encourages Timothy to do the same: "Join with me in suffering, like a good soldier of Christ Jesus" (2 TIM. 2:3).

Serving Christ requires perseverance. We may encounter obstacles of poor health, troubled relationships, or difficult circumstances. But as a good soldier we press on—with God's strength—because we serve the King of Kings and Lord of Lords who sacrificed himself for us! *DENNIS FISHER*

Dear Father, help me to be faithful in my service to you.
Thank you for the strength you provide to help me
persevere through suffering.

God's love does not keep us from trials, but sees us through them.

Be Near

Read: Psalm 34:4–18

The LORD is close to the brokenhearted. —v. 18

My friend was going through some difficult challenges in her life and family. I didn't know what to say or do, and I told her so. She looked at me and said, "Just be near." That's what I did, and later on we started talking about God's love.

Many times we don't know how to respond when others are grieving, and words may do more harm than good. Serving others requires that we understand them and find out what they need. Often we can help by meeting practical needs. But one of the best ways to encourage those who are suffering is to be near—to sit beside them and listen.

God is near to us when we call out to Him. "The righteous cry out, and the LORD hears them; he delivers them from all their troubles," the psalmist says. "The LORD is close to the brokenhearted and saves those who are crushed in spirit" (PS. 34:17–18).

By putting ourselves in the shoes of others and allowing our hearts to feel compassion, we can help those who are hurting. We can be near them as God is with us and sit close to them. At the right time, the Holy Spirit will give us the words to say, if they are needed. *KEILA OCHOA*

Who needs my help or for me to sit alongside them this week?

The best way to encourage others may be to just be near.

An Exchange

Read: Psalm 32:1–11

I said, "I will confess my transgressions to the Lord," and you forgave the guilt of my sin. —v. 5

Jen sat on her patio pondering a scary question: Should she write a book? She had enjoyed writing a blog and speaking in public but felt God might want her to do more. "I asked God if He wanted me to do this," she said. She talked with Him and asked for His leading.

She began to wonder if God wanted her to write about her husband's pornography addiction and how God was working in his life and their marriage. But then she thought that it might publicly disrespect him. So she prayed, "What if we wrote it together?" and she asked her husband Craig. He agreed.

While he didn't say what sin he committed, King David engaged in a public conversation about his struggles. He even put them into song. "When I kept silent, my bones wasted away," he wrote (Ps. 32:3). So he said, "I will confess my transgressions to the Lord" (v. 5). Not everyone should go public with their private battles. But when David confessed his sin, he found peace and healing that inspired him to worship God.

Craig and Jen say that the process of writing their deeply personal story has brought them closer than ever. How like God, who loves to exchange our guilt, shame, and isolation for His forgiveness, courage, and community!

Tim Gustafson

Do you need to make an exchange with God of guilt for forgiveness? He is listening.

God forgives those who confess their guilt.

Miracle Material

Read: Isaiah 46:1–10

To whom will you compare me? Or who is my equal? —40:25

CNN calls a derivative of graphite a "miracle material" that could revolutionize our future. Only one atom thick, graphene is being hailed as a truly two-dimensional material in a 3-D world. One hundred times stronger than steel, it is harder than diamond, conducts electricity 1,000 times better than copper, and is more flexible than rubber.

In and of themselves, such technological advances are neither moral nor evil. But we are wise to remember the limitations of anything we make for ourselves.

Isaiah spoke to a generation who found themselves carrying into captivity gods they had made with their own hands. The prophet wanted the Israelites to see the irony of needing to care for the silver and gold idols they had crafted to inspire, help, comfort, and protect them.

What was true of Israel holds true for us as well. Nothing we have made or bought for ourselves can meet the needs of our heart. Only God, who has been carrying us "since [we] were born" (ISA. 46:3–4), can carry us into the future.

MART DEHAAN

Father, thank you for the miracle of relationship with you.
Help us not to rely on our own efforts, strength, or possessions
but instead sense your loving care for us.

An idol is anything that takes God's rightful place.

Speak Up

Read: Luke 22:54–65

Then seizing [Jesus], they led him away and took him into the house of the high priest. Peter followed at a distance. —v. 54

When I hear stories about young people who have been bullied, I notice there are always at least two levels of hurt. The first and most obvious comes from the mean-spirited nature of those actually doing the bullying. That's terrible on its own. But there's another, deeper hurt that may end up being even more damaging than the first: The silence of everyone else.

It hurts the one being bullied because they're stunned that no one will help. That often makes bullies more brazen, leading them to intensify their meanness. Worse, it heightens the embarrassment, false shame, and loneliness of the victim. So it is imperative to speak up for others and speak out against the behavior (SEE PROV. 31:8).

Jesus knows precisely what it feels like to be bullied and to be left to suffer completely alone. Without cause, He was arrested, beaten, and mocked (LUKE 22:63–65). Matthew 26:56 says that "all the disciples deserted him and fled." Peter, one of His closest friends, even denied three times that he knew Him (LUKE 22:61). While others may not understand fully, Jesus does.

When we see others being hurt, we can ask Him for the courage to speak up.

RANDY KILGORE

Make us brave, Lord, for those who need our courage.
Help us to speak for others and show them that you know their
hurt and loneliness.

The voice of a courageous Christian is an echo of the voice of God.

Walking with the Lord

Read: Psalm 37:23–31

The LORD makes firm the steps of the one who delights in him. —v. 23

A small pamphlet I received from a friend was titled "An Attempt to Share the Story of 86 Years of Relationship with the Lord." In it, Al Ackenheil noted key people and events in his journey of faith over nearly nine decades. What seemed to be ordinary choices at the time—memorizing Bible verses, meeting for prayer with others, telling his neighbors about Jesus—became turning points that changed the direction of his life. It was fascinating to read how God's hand guided and encouraged Al.

The psalmist wrote, "The LORD makes firm the steps of the one who delights in him" (PS. 37:23). The passage continues with a beautiful description of God's faithful care for everyone who wants to walk with Him. "The law of their God is in their hearts; their feet do not slip" (v. 31).

Each of us could create a record of God's leading and faithfulness, reflecting on God's guidance—the people, places, and experiences that are landmarks on our pathway of faith. Every remembrance of the Lord's goodness encourages us to keep walking with Him and to thank someone who influenced us for good.

The Lord guides and guards all who walk with Him. *DAVID MCCASLAND*

Heavenly Father, your faithfulness to us is unfailing. Thank you for leading, guiding, and providing so many spiritual encouragers and mentors. Bless those today who have helped us so much.

You are headed in the right direction when you walk with God.

A Devoted Heart

Read: 2 Chronicles 17:1–11

He did what was right in the eyes of the Lord. –20:32

A successful Christian businessman shared his story with us at church. He was candid about his struggles with faith and abundant wealth. He declared, "Wealth scares me!"

He quoted Jesus's statement, "It is easier for a camel to go through the eye of a needle than for someone who is rich to enter the kingdom of God" (LUKE 18:25). He cited Luke 16:19-31 about the rich man and Lazarus and how in this story it was the rich man who went to hell. The parable of the "rich fool" (LUKE 12:16–21) disturbed him.

"But," the businessman stated, "I've learned a lesson from Solomon's verdict on the abundance of wealth. It's all 'meaningless' " (ECCL. 2:11). He determined not to let wealth get in the way of his devotion to God. Rather, he wanted to serve God with his assets and help the needy.

Throughout the centuries, God has blessed some people materially. We read of Jehoshaphat in 2 Chronicles 17:5, "The Lord established the kingdom . . . so that he had great wealth and honor." He did not become proud or bully others with his wealth. Instead, "his heart was devoted to the ways of the Lord" (v. 6). Also, "he followed the ways of his father Asa and did not stray from them; he did what was right in the eyes of the Lord" (20:32).

The Lord is not against wealth for He has blessed some with it—but He's definitely against the unethical acquisition and wrong use of it. He is worthy of devotion from all His followers. *LAWRENCE DARMANI*

Giving thanks to God often helps us learn contentment with what we do have. What are you thankful for?

Wealth or no wealth, devoted hearts please the Lord.

The Checkup

Read: Psalm 139:17–24

Search me, God. . . . See if there is any offensive way in me. –vv. 23–24

It's that time of year when I go to the doctor for my annual physical. Even though I feel well and I'm not experiencing any health problems, I know that routine checkups are important because they can uncover hidden problems that if left undiscovered can grow to be serious health issues. I know that giving permission to my doctor to find and remedy the hidden problems can lead to long-term health.

Clearly the psalmist felt that way spiritually. Pleading for God to search for hidden sin, he prayed, "Search me, God. . . . See if there is any offensive way in me, and lead me in the way everlasting" (PS. 139:23–24). Pausing to give God the opportunity for a full and unconditional inspection, he then surrendered to the righteous ways of God that would keep him spiritually healthy.

So, even if you are feeling good about yourself, it is time for a checkup! Only God knows the true condition of our heart, and only He can forgive, heal, and lead us to a cleansed life and productive future. *JOE STOWELL*

Lord, you know me better than I know myself.
Search the deepest parts of my heart for anything that is
displeasing to you. Cleanse me of my wandering ways and
lead me in your good and righteous way.

God's work in us isn't over when we receive salvation—it has just begun.

Pencil Battle

Read: Judges 2:11–22

They refused to give up their evil practices and stubborn ways. —v. 19

As I learned to write my letters, my first-grade teacher insisted that I hold my pencil in a specific way. As she watched me, I held it the way she wanted me to. But when she turned away, I obstinately reverted the pencil to the way I found more comfortable.

I thought I was the secret winner in that battle of the wills, and I still hold my pencil in my own peculiar way. Decades later, however, I realize that my wise teacher knew that my stubborn habit would grow into a bad writing practice that would result in my hand tiring more quickly.

Children rarely understand what is good for them. They operate almost entirely on what they want at the moment. Perhaps the "children of Israel" were aptly named as generation after generation stubbornly insisted on worshiping the gods of the nations around them rather than the one true God. Their actions greatly angered the Lord because He knew what was best, and He removed His blessing from them (JUDG. 2:20–22).

Pastor Rick Warren says, "Obedience and stubbornness are two sides of the same coin. Obedience brings joy, but our stubbornness makes us miserable."

If a rebellious spirit is keeping us from obeying God, it's time for a change of heart. Return to the Lord; He is gracious and merciful.

CINDY HESS KASPER

Heavenly Father, you are loving and gracious, and eager to forgive when we return to you. May we pursue you with our whole heart and not cling to our stubborn tendency to want things our way.

First we make our habits; then our habits make us.

Whose Mess?

Read: Matthew 15:7–21

Out of the heart come evil thoughts. . . . These are what defile a person. —vv. 19–20

"Could they not carry their own garbage this far?" I grumbled to Jay as I picked up empty bottles from the beach and tossed them into the trash bin less than 20 feet away. "Did leaving the beach a mess for others make them feel better about themselves? I sure hope these people are tourists. I don't want to think that any locals would treat our beach with such disrespect."

The very next day I came across a prayer I had written years earlier about judging others. My own words reminded me of how wrong I was to take pride in cleaning up other people's messes. The truth is, I have plenty of my own that I simply ignore—especially in the spiritual sense.

I am quick to claim that the reason I can't get my life in order is because others keep messing it up. And I am quick to conclude that the "garbage" stinking up my surroundings belongs to someone other than me. But neither is true. Nothing outside of me can condemn or contaminate me—only what's inside (MATT. 15:19–20). The real garbage is the attitude that causes me to turn up my nose at a tiny whiff of someone else's sin while ignoring the stench of my own. *JULIE ACKERMAN LINK*

Forgive me, Lord, for refusing to throw away my own "trash."
Open my eyes to the damage that pride does to your natural and spiritual creation.
May I have no part of it.

Most of us are farsighted about sin—we see the sins of others but not our own.

Grey Power

Read: Joshua 14:6–12

I'm just as vigorous to go out to battle now as I was then. –v. 11

Dutch artist Yoni Lefevre created a project called "Grey Power" to show the vitality of the aging generation in the Netherlands. She asked local schoolchildren to sketch their grandparents. Lefevre wanted to show an "honest and pure view" of older people, and she believed children could help supply this. The youngsters' drawings reflected a fresh and lively perspective of their elders—grandmas and grandpas were shown playing tennis, gardening, painting, and more!

Caleb, of ancient Israel, was vital into his senior years. As a young man, he infiltrated the Promised Land before the Israelites conquered it. Caleb believed God would help his nation defeat the Canaanites, but the other spies disagreed (JOSH. 14:8). Because of Caleb's faith, God miraculously sustained his life for 45 years so he might survive the wilderness wanderings and enter the Promised Land. When it was finally time to enter Canaan, 85-year-old Caleb said, "I'm just as vigorous to go out to battle now as I was then" (v. 11). With God's help, Caleb successfully claimed his share of the land (NUM. 14:24).

God does not forget about us as we grow older. Although our bodies age and our health may fail, God's Holy Spirit renews us inwardly each day (2 COR. 4:16). He makes it possible for our lives to have significance at every stage and every age. *JENNIFER BENSON SCHULDT*

Heavenly Father, I know that my physical strength and health can fail. But I pray that you will continually renew me spiritually so I can serve you faithfully as long as I live.

With God's strength behind you and His arms beneath you, you can face whatever lies ahead of you.

He Found Me

Read: Luke 19:1–10

The Son of Man came to seek and to save the lost. –v. 10

The film *Amazing Grace* was set in the late 1700s. It tells the story of William Wilberforce, a politician who was driven by his faith in Christ to commit his money and energy to abolishing the slave trade in England. In one scene, Wilberforce's butler finds him praying. The butler asks, "You found God, Sir?" Wilberforce responds, "I think He found me."

The Bible pictures humanity as wayward and wandering sheep. It says, "We all, like sheep, have gone astray, each of us has turned to our own way; and the LORD has laid on him the iniquity of us all" (ISA. 53:6). In fact, this wayward condition is so deeply rooted in us that the apostle Paul said: "There is no one righteous, not even one; there is no one who understands; there is no one who seeks God. All have turned away" (ROM. 3:10–12). That is why Jesus came. We would never seek Him, so He came seeking us. Jesus declared His mission with the words, "For the Son of Man came to seek and to save the lost" (LUKE 19:10).

Wilberforce was exactly right. Jesus came to find us, for we could never have found Him if left to ourselves. It is a clear expression of the Creator's love for His lost creation that He pursues us and desires to make us His own.

BILL CROWDER

Amazing grace—how sweet the sound—that saved a wretch like me!
I once was lost but now am found, was blind, but now I see.
JOHN NEWTON

Once lost, now found. Eternally thankful!

How to Have Peace

Read: Colossians 1:15–23

We have peace with God through our Lord Jesus Christ. —Romans 5:1

The Kamppi Chapel of Silence in Helsinki, Finland, stands out in its urban setting. The curved structure, covered with wood, buffers the noise from the busy city outside. Designers created the chapel as a quiet space and a "calm environment for visitors to compose themselves." It's a welcome escape from the hustle and bustle of the city.

Many people long for peace, and a few minutes of silence may soothe our minds. But the Bible teaches that real peace—peace with God—comes from His Son. The apostle Paul said, "Therefore, since we have been justified through faith, we have peace with God through our Lord Jesus Christ" (ROM. 5:1). Without Christ, we are enemies of God because of our sin. Thankfully, accepting Jesus's sacrifice reconciles us to God and ends the hostility that existed between us (COL. 1:19–21). He now sees us as Christ presents us—"holy in his sight, without blemish and free from accusation" (v. 22).

Having peace with God does not ensure problem-free living. However, it does steady us during difficult times. Jesus told His followers, "In this world you will have trouble," but He also said, "In me you may have peace" (JOHN 16:33). Because of Christ, the true peace of God can fill our hearts (COL. 3:15).

JENNIFER BENSON SCHULDT

Father, we long for your peace in the midst of our turmoil.
Please help us to rest in you.

Peace floods the soul when Christ rules the heart.

God's Good Heart

Read: Romans 5:1–11

Consider it pure joy . . . whenever you face trials of many kinds. –James 1:2

Roger had been through a lot. He had open-heart surgery to repair a leaky valve. Then, within just a couple of weeks, doctors had to perform the surgery again because of complications. He had just begun to heal with physical therapy when he had a biking accident and broke his collarbone. Added to this, Roger also experienced the heartbreak of losing his mother during this time. He became very discouraged. When a friend asked him if he had seen God at work in any small ways, he confessed that he really didn't feel he had.

I appreciate Roger's honesty. Feelings of discouragement or doubt are part of my life too. In Romans, the apostle Paul says, "We can rejoice . . . when we run into problems and trials, for we know that they help us develop endurance. And endurance develops strength of character, and character strengthens our confident hope of salvation" (5:3–4 NLT). But that doesn't mean we always feel the joy. We may just need someone to sit down and listen to us pour out our hearts to them, and to talk with God. Sometimes it takes looking back on the situation before we see how our faith has grown during trials and doubts.

Knowing that God wants to use our difficulties to strengthen our faith can help us to trust His good heart for us. *ANNE CETAS*

In what ways has God used trials in your life?
Are you learning to trust Him more?

God may lead us into troubled waters to deepen our trust in Him.

On the Edge

Read: Romans 6:16–23

Everyone who sins is a slave to sin. –John 8:34

There's an underground lava tube south of Kuna, Idaho, that has gained a certain amount of local notoriety. The only entrance, as far as I know, is a yawning shaft that plunges straight down into darkness.

Some years ago I stood at the edge of that shaft and looked down. I was drawn to venture closer and almost lost my balance. I felt a moment of heart-pounding terror and stepped away from the opening.

Sin is like that: Curiosity can draw us toward the darkness. How often have men and women gotten too close to the edge, lost their balance, and fallen into the darkness? They've destroyed their families, reputations, and careers through adulterous affairs that began with a "mere" flirtation but then progressed to thoughts and actions. Looking back they almost always say, "I never thought it would come to this."

We think we can flirt with temptation, get very close to the edge, and walk away, but that's a fool's dream. We know an action is wrong and yet we toy with it. Then, inescapably, we are drawn into deeper and darker perversions. Jesus put it simply: "Everyone who sins is a slave to sin" (JOHN 8:34).

And so, seeing our own need for God's help, we pray as David did in Psalm 19:13, "Keep your servant also from willful sins; may they not rule over me."

DAVID ROPER

Heavenly Father, whether we are being tempted now, or have fallen,
we thank you that you are always there, and you love us with relentless love.
We have nowhere to turn but to you.

A big fall begins with a little stumble.

Web Wisdom

Read: Proverbs 26:1–12

A quarrelsome person starts fights as easily as hot embers light charcoal or fire lights wood. —v. 21 NLT

Scroll to the bottom of many online news sites and you'll find the "Comments" section where readers can leave their observations. Even the most reputable sites have no shortage of rude rants, uninformed insults, and name-calling.

The book of Proverbs was collected about 3,000 years ago, but its timeless wisdom is as up-to-date as today's breaking news. Two proverbs in chapter 26 seem at first glance to contradict each other, yet they apply perfectly to social media. "Do not answer a fool according to his folly, or you yourself will be just like him" (v. 4). And then, "Answer a fool according to his folly, or he will be wise in his own eyes" (v. 5).

The balance in those statements is in the "according to": Don't answer in the way a fool would answer. But respond so that foolishness is not considered wisdom.

My problem is that the foolishness I encounter is often my own. I have at times posted a sarcastic comment or turned someone else's statement back on them. God hates it when I treat my fellow human beings with such disrespect, even when they're also being foolish.

God gives us an amazing range of freedoms. We are free to choose what we will say, and when and how we say it. And we are always free to ask Him for wisdom.

TIM GUSTAFSON

Things to keep in mind: Is what I am saying true, and is it loving?
What is my motive? Will it help anyone?
Will this reflect the character of Jesus?

Let love be your highest goal.

More Than Wishing

Read: Matthew 6:5–15

Do not be like them, for your Father knows what you need before you ask him. —v. 8

As a child, C. S. Lewis enjoyed reading the books of E. Nesbit, especially *Five Children and It*. In this book, brothers and sisters on a summer holiday discover an ancient sand fairy who grants them one wish each day. But every wish brings the children more trouble than happiness because they can't foresee the results of getting everything they ask for.

The Bible tells us to make our requests known to God (PHIL. 4:6). But prayer is much more than telling God what we want Him to do for us. When Jesus taught His disciples how to pray, He began by reminding them, "Your Father knows what you need before you ask him" (MATT. 6:8).

What we call the "Lord's Prayer" is more about living in a growing, trusting relationship with our heavenly Father than about getting what we want from Him. As we grow in faith, our prayers will become less of a wish list and more of an intimate conversation with the Lord.

Toward the end of his life, C. S. Lewis wrote, "If God had granted all the silly prayers I've made in my life, where should I be now?"

Prayer is placing ourselves in the presence of God to receive from Him what we really need. *DAVID MCCASLAND*

Our Father in heaven, hallowed be your name, your kingdom come, your will be done, on earth as it is in heaven. Give us today our daily bread. And forgive us our debts, as we also have forgiven our debtors. And lead us not into temptation, but deliver us from the evil one. —Matthew 6:9–13

Our highest privilege is to talk to God; our highest duty is to listen to Him.

Family Privilege

Read: John 1:6–14

To all who did receive him . . . he gave the right to become children of God. —v. 12

When I was in primary school in Ghana, I had to live with a loving and caring family away from my parents. One day, all the children assembled for a special family meeting. The first part involved all of us sharing individual experiences. But next, when only "blood children" were required to be present, I was politely excluded. Then the stark reality hit me: I was not a "child of the house." Despite their love for me, the family required that I should be excused because I was only living with them; I was not a legal part of their family.

This incident reminds me of John 1:11–12. The Son of God came to His own people and they rejected Him. Those who received Him then, and receive Him now, are given the right to become God's children. When we are adopted into His family, "the Spirit himself testifies with our spirit that we are God's children" (ROM. 8:16).

Jesus doesn't exclude anybody who is adopted by the Father. Rather, He welcomes us as a permanent part of His family. "To all who did receive him, to those who believed in his name, he gave the right to become children of God" (JOHN 1:12).

LAWRENCE DARMANI

Thank you, Father, for making it possible for me to be your child.
I'm grateful to be yours and not to have to worry about
whether you will remove me from your family.
I am yours and you are mine.

Assurance of salvation is not in what you know but who you know.

Faultfinders Anonymous

Read: Philippians 1:1–11

And this is my prayer: that your love may abound more and more. —v. 9

Like many people, when I read a newspaper or magazine I notice the misteaks in grammar and spelling. (You saw that, didn't you!) I'm not trying to find errors; they leap off the page at me! My usual reaction is to criticize the publication and the people who produce it. "Why don't they use 'spell check' or hire a proofreader?"

You may have a similar experience in your area of expertise. It seems that often, the more we know about something, the more judgmental we become over mistakes. It can infect our relationships with people as well.

Yet Philippians 1:9 expresses a different approach. Paul wrote, "And this is my prayer: that your love may abound more and more in knowledge and depth of insight." God's plan is that the more we know and understand, the more we love. Rather than cultivating a critical spirit and pretending we don't notice or don't care, our understanding should nourish empathy. Criticism is replaced by compassion.

Instead of our being faultfinders, the Lord calls us to be "filled with the fruit of righteousness that comes through Jesus Christ—to the glory and praise of God" (v. 11).

When the Lord fills our hearts, we can overlook mistakes, hold our criticism, and love others, no matter how much we know about them!

DAVID MCCASLAND

Lord, by your grace, please replace my critical spirit with your love and compassion for others.

To err is human; to forgive, divine. ALEXANDER POPE

Unpredictable

Read: Psalm 46

Be still, and know that I am God; I will be exalted among the nations, I will be exalted in the earth. –v. 10

In the 2003 US Women's Open, the relatively unknown Hilary Lunke secured the greatest prize in women's golf—and a place in history. Not only did she win the US Open in an 18-hole playoff, but it was also her only professional victory. Her surprising and inspiring win underscores the fact that one of the most exciting things about sports is its unpredictability.

The unpredictability of life is not always so thrilling, however. We devise and strategize. We make plans, projections, and proposals about what we would like to see happen in life, but often they are little more than our best guess. We have no idea what a year, a month, a week, or even a day might bring. So we pray and plan, and then we trust the God who knows fully and completely what we can never predict. That is why I love the promise of Psalm 46:10: "Be still, and know that I am God; I will be exalted among the nations, I will be exalted in the earth."

Life is unpredictable. There are countless things I can never know with certainty. What I can know, however, is that there is a God who knows all and loves me deeply. And by knowing Him, I can "be still"—I can be at peace.

BILL CROWDER

What plans do I need to surrender to God today?

God's care is the certainty we take into life's uncertainties.

Batter in the Bowl

Read: Ruth 2:1–12

Please let me glean . . . among the sheaves behind the harvesters. —v. 7

My daughter and I consider brownies to be one of the seven wonders of the culinary world. One day, as we were mixing the ingredients of our favorite chocolate treat, my daughter asked if I would leave some batter in the bowl after pouring most of it into the baking pan. She wanted to enjoy what was left over. I smiled and agreed. Then, I told her, "That's called gleaning, you know, and it didn't start with brownies."

As we enjoyed the remnants of our baking project, I explained that Ruth had gathered leftover grain in order to feed herself and her mother-in-law Naomi (RUTH 2:2–3). Because both of their husbands had died, the women had returned to Naomi's homeland. There Ruth met a wealthy landowner named Boaz. She asked him, "Please let me glean . . . among the sheaves behind the harvesters" (v. 7). He willingly consented and instructed his workers to purposely let grain fall for her (v. 16).

Like Boaz, who provided for Ruth from the bounty of his fields, God provides for us out of His abundance. His resources are infinite, and He lets blessings fall for our benefit. He willingly provides us with physical and spiritual nourishment. Every good gift we receive comes from Him.

JENNIFER BENSON SCHULDT

Dear God, thank you for the blessings I enjoy!
You minister to your children out of your limitless abundance.
I worship you as my provider.

Our greatest needs cannot exceed God's great resources.

I've Come to Help

Read: James 1:19–27

Do not merely listen to the word, and so deceive yourselves. Do what it says. —v. 22

Reporter Jacob Riis's vivid descriptions of poverty in 19th-century New York City horrified a generally complacent public. His book *How the Other Half Lives* combined his writing with his own photographs to paint a picture so vivid that the public could not escape the certainty of poverty's desperate existence. The third of fifteen children himself, Riis wrote so effectively because he had lived in that world of terrible despair.

Shortly after the release of his book, he received a card from a young man just beginning his political career. The note read simply, "I have read your book, and I have come to help. Theodore Roosevelt." (This politician later became a US President.)

True faith responds to the needs of others, according to James (1:19–27). May our hearts be moved from inaction to action, from words alone to deeds that back them up. Compassionate action not only aids those mired in life's difficulties, but it may also make them open to the greater message from our Savior who sees their need and can do so much more for them.

RANDY KILGORE

O Lord, it is so easy to be overwhelmed, or to judge and therefore to refrain from helping others. Lift our eyes above our own thoughts and circumstances, and let us care as you care.

Others will know what the words "God is love" mean when they see it in our lives.

Debits and Credits

Read: John 16:1–11

In this world you will have trouble. But take heart! I have overcome the world. —v. 33

When my husband was teaching an accounting class at a local college, I took one of the tests just for fun to see how well I could do. The results were not good. I answered every question wrong. The reason for my failure was that I started with a faulty understanding of a basic banking concept. I reversed debits and credits.

We sometimes get our debits and credits confused in the spiritual realm as well. When we blame Satan for everything that goes wrong—whether it's bad weather, a jammed printer, or financial trouble—we're actually giving him credit that he doesn't deserve. We are ascribing to him the power to determine the quality of our lives, which he does not have. Satan is limited in time and space. He has to ask God's permission before he can touch us (JOB 1:12; LUKE 22:31).

However, as the father of lies and prince of this world (JOHN 8:44; 16:11), Satan can cause confusion. Jesus warned of a time when people would be so confused that they wouldn't know right from wrong (16:2). But He added this assurance: "The prince of this world now stands condemned" (v. 11).

Problems will disrupt our lives, but they cannot defeat us. Jesus has already overcome the world. To Him goes all the credit.

JULIE ACKERMAN LINK

Thank you, Father, for being Lord over everything in our lives. We praise you for overcoming the world through your Son.

While Satan accuses and confuses, God controls.

A Portrait of Jesus

Read: Isaiah 53:4–12

Each of us has turned to our own way; and the LORD has laid on him the iniquity of us all. –v. 6

In *Portraits of Famous American Women*, Robert Henkes writes, "A portrait is not a photograph, nor is it a mirror image." A portrait goes beyond the outer appearance to probe the emotional depth of the human soul. In a portrait, a true artist tries "to capture what the person is really about."

Over the centuries, many portraits have been painted of Jesus. Perhaps you've seen them in a church or museum of art or even have one in your home. Not one of these is a true portrait, of course, because we have no photograph or mirror image of our Lord's physical appearance. We do, however, have a magnificent word portrait of Him in Isaiah 53. This God-inspired description captures in vivid detail what He is all about: "Surely he took up our pain and bore our suffering . . . . But he was pierced for our transgressions, he was crushed for our iniquities; . . . and by his wounds we are healed" (vv. 4–5).

This passage enables us to see love and sorrow, anguish and pain on Jesus's face. But His lips do not accuse or condemn. He has no sins of His own to grieve; only ours to bear. And deep inside, He knows that "he will see the light of life and be satisfied" (v. 11).

What a portrait of our Savior!

DAVID MCCASLAND

What amazing love you have for us, Jesus! As I think of how awesome you are, I bow in silence before you.

Love was when God became a man.

Not Again!

Read: 2 Thess. 2:13–17

God from the beginning chose you for salvation through sanctification by the Spirit and belief in the truth. –v. 13 NKJV

As I was reading the text message on my mobile phone, my temperature started to rise and my blood began to boil. I was on the verge of shooting back a nasty message when an inner voice told me to cool down and reply tomorrow. The next morning after a good night's sleep, the issue that had upset me so greatly seemed so trivial. I had blown it out of proportion because I didn't want to put another person's interest before my own. I was unwilling to inconvenience myself so I could help someone.

Regretfully, I am tempted to respond in anger more often than I would like to admit. I constantly find myself having to put into practice familiar Bible truths, such as "In your anger do not sin" (EPH. 4:26) and "Let each of you look out not only for his own interests, but also for the interests of others" (PHIL. 2:4 NKJV).

Thankfully, God has given us His Spirit who will assist us in our battle with our sin. The apostles Paul and Peter called it the "sanctifying work of the Spirit" (2 THESS. 2:13; 1 PETER 1:2). Without His power, we are helpless and defeated; but with His power, we can have victory. *POH FANG CHIA*

I'm grateful, Lord, that you are at work in me.
I want you to change my heart; please help me to listen
and to cooperate with you.

The growth of a saint is the work of a lifetime.

Einstein and Jesus

Read: John 9:1–7

[Jesus] said, "I am the light of the world." –John 8:12

We remember Albert Einstein for more than his disheveled hair, big eyes, and witty charm. We know him as the genius and physicist who changed the way we see the world. His famous formula of $E=mc^2$ revolutionized scientific thought and brought us into the nuclear age. Through his "Special Theory of Relativity" he reasoned that since everything in the universe is in motion, all knowledge is a matter of perspective. He believed that the speed of light is the only constant by which we can measure space, time, or physical mass.

Long before Einstein, Jesus talked about the role of light in understanding our world, but from a different perspective. To support His claim to be the Light of the World (JOHN 8:12), Jesus healed a man who had been blind from birth (9:6). When the Pharisees accused Christ of being a sinner, this grateful man said, "Whether he is a sinner or not, I don't know. One thing I do know: I was blind but now I see" (v. 25).

While Einstein's ideas would later be proven difficult to test, Jesus's claims can be tested. We can spend time with Jesus in the Gospels. We can invite Him into our daily routine. We can see for ourselves that He can change our perspective on everything. *MART DEHAAN*

Lord Jesus, you are the one constant in this chaotic world. Thank you for being the one true Light that the darkness can never extinguish.

Only as we walk in Christ's light can we live in His love.

The Waving Girl

Read: Romans 15:1–7

Accept one another, then, just as Christ accepted you, in order to bring praise to God. —v. 7

In the late 1800s and early 1900s, a familiar sight greeted ships as they pulled into the port of Savannah, Georgia. That sight was Florence Martus, "The Waving Girl." For 44 years, Florence greeted the great ships from around the world, waving a handkerchief by day or a lantern by night. Today, a statue of Florence and her faithful dog stands in Savannah's Morrell Park, permanently welcoming incoming vessels.

There is something in a warm welcome that speaks of acceptance. In Romans 15:7, Paul urged his readers: "Accept one another, then, just as Christ accepted you." Paul had in view our treatment of each other as followers of Christ, for in verses 5-6 he challenged us to live in harmony with one another. The key is to have "the same attitude of mind toward each other that Christ Jesus had, so that with one mind and one voice you may glorify the God and Father of our Lord Jesus Christ."

Our acceptance of our fellow believers in Christ demonstrates more than just our love for each other—it reflects the great love of the One who has permanently welcomed us into His family. *BILL CROWDER*

Father, give me a heart for my brothers and sisters in Christ. Please give us, together, a heart for one another, so that we will love and honor you in all we do.

The closer Christians get to Christ, the closer they get to one another.

Silent Helper

Read: Isaiah 25:1–9

I will exalt you and praise your name, for . . . you have done wonderful things. –v. 1

The discovery of penicillin revolutionized health care. Prior to the 1940s, bacterial infections were often fatal. Since then, penicillin has saved countless lives by killing harmful bacteria. The men who recognized its potential and developed it for widespread use won a Nobel Prize in 1945.

Long before the discovery of penicillin, other silent killers were at work saving lives by destroying bacteria. These silent killers are white blood cells. These hard workers are God's way of protecting us from disease. No one knows how many invasions they have stopped or how many lives they have saved. They receive little recognition for all the good they do.

The Lord gets similar treatment. He often gets blamed when something goes wrong, but He seldom gets credit for all the things that go right. Every day people get up, get dressed, drive to work or school or the grocery store, and return safely to their families. No one knows how many times God has protected us from harm. But when there is a tragedy, we ask, "Where was God?"

When I consider all the wonderful things that God does silently on my behalf each day (ISA. 25:1), I see that my list of praises is much longer than my list of petitions. *JULIE ACKERMAN LINK*

In what ways does God's goodness undergird your life?
What are you thanking Him for today?

God keeps giving us reasons to praise Him.

Baking with Jess

Read: John 6:22–34

Do not work for food that spoils, but for food that endures to eternal life. —v. 27

One morning as Lilia prepared for work, her 4-year-old daughter Jess set to work too. The family had purchased a conveyor toaster, and the concept of cycling bread through the small countertop oven fascinated Jess. Minutes later, Lilia discovered a loaf and a half of toast piled on the counter. "I'm a very good baker!" Jess declared.

It's no miracle that an inquisitive girl could turn bread into toast. But when Jesus transformed a boy's five loaves and two fish into a meal for thousands, the crowd on the hillside recognized the miraculous nature of the event and wanted to make Him king (SEE JOHN 6:1–15).

Jesus's kingdom, of course, is "not of this world" (JOHN 18:36), and so He slipped away. When the crowd found Him the next day, Christ identified a flaw in their motives: "You are looking for me, not because you saw the signs I performed but because you ate the loaves and had your fill" (6:26). They mistakenly thought "King" Jesus would give them full stomachs and national freedom. But Jesus counseled them, "Do not work for food that spoils, but for food that endures to eternal life" (v. 27).

An earthbound view will cause us to treat Jesus as a means to an end. He is, in fact, our Bread of Life. *TIM GUSTAFSON*

Lord, our cares and worries can keep us from a genuine relationship with you. May we see you as our very food and not only as our divine problem-solver.

Seek first the kingdom of God, and all these things will be added to you. JESUS

Under Siege

Read: Philippians 2:1–11

Value others above yourselves, not looking to your own interests but . . . to the interests of the others. —vv. 3–4

During the Bosnian War (1992–1996), more than 10,000 people—civilians and soldiers—were killed in the city of Sarajevo as gunfire and mortar rounds rained down from the surrounding hills. Steven Galloway's gripping novel *The Cellist of Sarajevo* unfolds there, during the longest siege of a capital city in modern warfare. The book follows three fictional characters who must decide if they will become completely self-absorbed in their struggle to survive, or will somehow rise above their numbing circumstances to consider others during a time of great adversity.

From a prison in Rome, Paul wrote to the Christians in Philippi, saying: "Value others above yourselves, not looking to your own interests but each of you to the interests of the others" (PHIL. 2:3–4). Paul cited Jesus as the great example of a selfless focus on others: "Christ Jesus: Who, being in very nature God, . . . made himself nothing . . . humbled himself by becoming obedient to death—even death on a cross!" (vv. 5–8). Rather than seeking sympathy from others, Jesus gave all He had to rescue us from the tyranny of sin.

Our continuing challenge as followers of Jesus is to see through His eyes and respond to the needs of others in His strength, even in our own difficult times. *DAVID MCCASLAND*

Are you going through something hard right now?
What can you still do for another?

Embracing God's love for us is the key to loving others.

Reflecting God's Glory

Read: Exodus 31:1–11

The heavens declare the glory of God; the skies proclaim the work of his hands. —Psalm 19:1

The 12th-century Chinese artist Li Tang painted landscapes animated with people, birds, and water buffalo. Because of his genius with fine line sketches on silk, Li Tang is considered a master of Chinese landscape art. For centuries, artists from around the world have depicted what they see in God's art gallery of creation: "The heavens declare the glory of God; the skies proclaim the work of his hands" (PS. 19:1). The Bible tells us that our creativity as human beings comes from being made in the image of the Master Creator (GEN. 1:27).

God chose artists who worked with wood, gold, silver, bronze, and gems to create the furnishings, utensils, altars, and garments that were to be used when the ancient Israelites worshiped Him in the tabernacle (EX. 31:1–11). These artistic renderings of spiritual realities prompted and guided the priests and the people in their worship of the Lord who had called them to be His people.

Through many types of artistic expression, we reflect the beauty of creation and honor the Creator and Redeemer of this marvelous world.

DENNIS FISHER

Lord of the universe, you are the Creator and have given us creative abilities. May we honor you through them.

We were created to bring God the glory.

Who Is My Neighbor?

Read: Luke 10:30–37

Go and do likewise. –v. 37

Mary enjoyed her midweek church group meeting when she and several friends gathered to pray, worship, and discuss questions from the previous week's sermon. This week they were going to talk about the difference between "going" to church and "being" the church in a hurting world. She was looking forward to seeing her friends and having a lively discussion.

As she picked up her car keys, the doorbell rang. "I'm so sorry to bother you," said her neighbor Sue, "but are you free this morning?" Mary was about to say that she was going out when Sue continued, "I have to take my car to the repair shop. Normally I would walk or cycle home, but I've hurt my back and can't do either at the moment." Mary hesitated for a heartbeat and then smiled. "Of course," she said.

Mary knew her neighbor only by sight. But as she drove her home, she learned about Sue's husband's battle with dementia and the utter exhaustion that being a caregiver can bring with it. She listened, sympathized, and promised to pray. She offered to help in any way she could.

Mary didn't get to church that morning to talk about sharing her faith. Instead she took a little bit of Jesus's love to her neighbor who was in a difficult situation.

MARION STROUD

Lord, help me to be ready at any time to be your hands and feet to those in need.

Faith is seen in our actions.

Continuing with Christ

Read: 1 Kings 19:19–21

Whoever loses their life for me will find it. —Matthew 16:25

As a child, my favorite week of the summer was the one I spent at a Christian youth camp. At the end of the week, I'd sit elbow-to-elbow with friends in front of an enormous bonfire. There, we would share what we had learned about God and the Bible and sing. One song I still remember focused on deciding to follow Jesus. The chorus contained an important phrase: "no turning back."

When Elisha decided to follow the prophet Elijah, Elisha did something incredible that made it difficult, impossible really, for him to return to his prior occupation of farming. After going home and having a farewell banquet, Elisha "took his yoke of oxen and slaughtered them" (1 KINGS 19:21). Leaving his way of life, he burned up his plowing equipment. He roasted the freshly butchered meat over the blaze and fed everyone present. Then "[Elisha] set out to follow Elijah and became his servant" (v. 21).

Giving ourselves to God, who deserves our devotion, often comes with a price. At times, it means making difficult decisions about relationships, finances, and living arrangements. However, nothing compares with what we gain when we continue on with Christ. Jesus said, "Whoever wants to save their life will lose it, but whoever loses their life for me will find it" (MATT. 16:25).

JENNIFER BENSON SCHULDT

Father, help me to see if there's something you want me to leave behind to follow you completely.

Jesus is looking for fulltime followers.

It's What We Do

Read: Psalm 112

Whoever fears the LORD has a secure fortress, and for their children it will be a refuge. —Proverbs 14:26

My father was critically injured when he took a bullet in the leg as a second lieutenant leading his men on Hill 609 in North Africa during World War II. Dad was never again 100 percent physically. I was born several years after this, and when I was young I didn't even know he had been wounded. I found out later when someone told me. Although he felt constant pain in his leg, my dad never complained about it, and he never used it as an excuse for not providing for our family.

My parents loved the Savior and raised us to love, trust, and serve Him. Through good times and bad, they simply trusted God, worked hard, and loved us unconditionally. Proverbs 14:26 says that "Whoever fears the LORD has a secure fortress, and for their children it will be a refuge." My dad did that for our family. No matter what difficulties he faced, he provided a safe place for us spiritually, emotionally, and physically.

We parents can provide a safe haven for our families with the help of our perfect heavenly Father, whose love for His children is deep and eternal.

DAVE BRANON

How has God been a Father to you?
In what ways do you honor Him in your family life?

The Father's love knows no limit.

Turn It Off

Read: Mark 6:30–32, 45–47

Come with me by yourselves to a quiet place and get some rest. —v. 31

When our kids were young, we took a trip to northern Wisconsin to visit my grandparents. They didn't get very good reception on their television, but TV wasn't much of a priority with them. After I had seen our son Scott fiddling with the TV set for a while, he asked with frustration, "What do you do if you can get only one channel and you don't like what's on that one?"

"Try turning it off," I said with a smile. Not exactly the advice he was hoping for. It's even more difficult to do now, especially when there are so many devices that entertain, inform, and distract us.

Sometimes we do need to just turn it all off and rest our minds for a little while; we simply need to "unplug." Jesus often drew aside for a time—especially when He wanted to take time to pray (MATT. 14:13). He encouraged the disciples to step away as well—even for a brief time (MARK 6:31). That kind of solitude and time for reflection is beneficial for each of us. In those moments we are able to draw near to God.

Follow the example and wisdom of Christ. Get away by yourself and "get some rest." It will be good for your body, mind, and spirit.

CINDY HESS KASPER

Lord, help me to seek those things which are from above.
I want to turn off all that distracts me and draw near to you.

Turning down the volume of life allows you to listen carefully to God.

Coming Alongside

Read: 2 Corinthians 1:3–11

Praise be to the God and Father of our Lord Jesus Christ, . . . who comforts us in all our troubles, so that we can comfort those in any trouble. –vv. 3–4

When my sister Carole was diagnosed with breast cancer, our family worried. That diagnosis, with its surgeries and treatments, caused us to fear for her well-being, which drove our family to prayer on her behalf. Over the ensuing months, Carole's updates were honest about the challenges. But we all celebrated when the report came back that the surgery and treatments had been successful. Carole was on the road to recovery!

Then, less than a year later, my sister Linda faced the same battle. Immediately, Carole came alongside Linda, helping her understand what to expect and how to prepare for what she would face. Carole's experience had equipped her to walk with Linda through her own trial.

This is what Paul calls for in 2 Corinthians 1:3–4, where we read, "Praise be to the God and Father of our Lord Jesus Christ, the Father of compassion and the God of all comfort, who comforts us in all our troubles, so that we can comfort those in any trouble with the comfort we ourselves receive from God."

Thankfully, the Lord doesn't waste anything. Our struggles not only give us an opportunity to experience His comfort, but they also open the door for us to share that comfort with others in their struggles.

BILL CROWDER

Today, how can I be an encouragement to others whose hearts are weighed down by the cares of life?

God's presence brings us comfort; our presence brings others comfort.

When Things Don't Go Well

Read: Romans 8:28–30

We know that in all things God works for the good of those who love him. —v. 28

The first words that many people like to quote when misfortune hits are: "We know that in all things God works for the good of those who love him, who have been called according to his purpose" (ROM. 8:28). But that's hard to believe in hard times. I once sat with a man who had lost his third son in a row, and I listened as he lamented, "How can this tragedy work for my good?" I had no answer but to sit silently and mourn with him. Several months later, he was thankful as he said, "My sorrow is drawing me closer to God."

Tough as Romans 8:28 may be to understand, countless testimonies give credence to the truth of it. The story of hymn writer Fanny Crosby is a classic example. The world is the beneficiary of her memorable hymns, yet what worked together for good was born out of her personal tragedy, for she became blind at the age of 5. At only age 8, she began to write poetry and hymns. Writing over 8,000 sacred songs and hymns, she blessed the world with such popular songs as "Blessed Assurance," "Safe in the Arms of Jesus," and "Pass Me Not, O Gentle Savior." God used her difficulty to bring good for her and us and glory for Him.

When tragedy befalls us, it's hard to understand how anything good can come from it, and we won't always see it in this life. But God has good purposes and always remains with us. *LAWRENCE DARMANI*

What trial in your life have you found to be for your good? What good things have come from it? What are you now suffering that you pray will bring something good?

God always has good purposes for our trials.

The Power of Words

Read: Proverbs 18:1–8, 20–21

The tongue has the power of life and death, and those who love it will eat its fruit. —v. 21

Nelson Mandela, who opposed the South African apartheid regime and was imprisoned for almost 3 decades, knew the power of words. He is often quoted today, but while in prison his words could not be quoted for fear of repercussion. A decade after his release he said: "It is never my custom to use words lightly. If 27 years in prison have done anything to us, it was to use the silence of solitude to make us understand how precious words are, and how real speech is in its impact on the way people live and die."

King Solomon, author of most of the Old Testament book of Proverbs, wrote often about the power of words. He said, "The tongue has the power of life and death" (PROV. 18:21). Words have the potential to produce positive or negative consequences (V. 20). They have the power to give life through encouragement and honesty or to crush and kill through lies and gossip. How can we be assured of producing good words that have a positive outcome? The only way is by diligently guarding our hearts: "Above all else, guard your heart, for everything you do flows from it" (4:23).

Jesus can transform our hearts so that our words can truly be their best—honest, calm, appropriate, and suitable for the situation.

MARVIN WILLIAMS

May these words of my mouth and this meditation of my heart be pleasing in your sight, LORD, my Rock and my Redeemer.

PSALM 19:14

Our words have the power to build up or tear down.

Purpose in Routine

Read: 1 Corinthians 9:19–27

I run with purpose in every step. –v. 26 NLT

A rolling-ball clock in the British Museum struck me as a vivid illustration of the deadening effects of routine. A small steel ball traveled in grooves across a tilted steel plate until it tripped a lever on the other side. This tilted the plate back in the opposite direction, reversed the direction of the ball and advanced the clock hands. Every year, the steel ball traveled some 2,500 miles back and forth, but never really went anywhere.

It's easy for us to feel trapped by our daily routine when we can't see a larger purpose. The apostle Paul longed to be effective in making the gospel of Christ known. "I do not run like someone running aimlessly; I do not fight like a boxer beating the air" (1 COR. 9:26). Anything can become monotonous—traveling, preaching, teaching, and especially being confined in prison. Yet Paul believed he could serve Christ his Lord in every situation.

Routine becomes lethal when we can't see a purpose in it. Paul's vision reached beyond any limiting circumstance because he was in the race of faith to keep going until he crossed the finish line. By including Jesus in every aspect of his life, Paul found meaning even in the routine of life.

And so can we.

DAVID MCCASLAND

Lord, give us renewed vision and energy to pursue the goal of making Christ known in the midst of our daily routine.

Jesus can transform our routine into meaningful service for Him.

Disappointing Heroes

Read: Hebrews 3:1–6

Think carefully about this Jesus whom we declare to be God's messenger and High Priest. —v. 1 NLT

A recent book that puts a fictional flavor on a slice of US history portrays Old West gunslingers Wyatt Earp and Doc Holliday as shiftless bums. In an interview with National Public Radio, the author said of the real Earp, "He didn't do anything remarkable his whole life, ever." Through the years, in books and Hollywood movies, they've become heroes. Yet reputable historical accounts show that they were not.

In contrast, the Bible is full of flawed people who became real heroes. But don't lose sight of the vital source of their heroic actions. The object of their faith was God, who chooses flawed human beings for His remarkable purposes.

As biblical heroes go, Moses stands tall. We tend to forget that he was a murderer and a reluctant leader who once directed a rant at God: "Why are you treating me, your servant, so harshly?" he demanded. "What did I do to deserve the burden of all these people? Did I give birth to them?" (NUM. 11:11–12 NLT).

How very human of Moses! And yet Hebrews reminds us: "Moses was certainly faithful in God's house as a servant. His work was an illustration of the truths God would reveal later" (HEB. 3:5 NLT).

Real heroes point to the Hero who never disappoints. "Jesus deserves far more glory than Moses" (v. 3 NLT).

TIM GUSTAFSON

Lord, thank you for being the only Hero we can rely on without fail. Help us not to conceal our flaws and mistakes, but to give them to you. We trust you to use us for your good purpose.

Looking for someone who won't disappoint you? Look to Jesus.

Baby Steps

Read: Psalm 18:31–36

He makes my feet like the feet of a deer. —v. 33

My baby is learning to walk. I have to hold her, and she clings to my fingers because she is still unsteady on her feet. She is afraid of slipping, but I'm there to steady her and watch over her. As she walks with my help, her eyes sparkle with gratitude, happiness, and security. But sometimes she cries when I don't let her take dangerous paths, not realizing that I am protecting her.

Like my baby girl, we often need someone to watch over us, to guide and steady us in our spiritual walk. And we have that someone—God our Father—who helps His children learn to walk, guides our steps, holds our hand, and keeps us on the right path.

King David knew all about the need for God's watchful care in his life. In Psalm 18 he describes how God gives us strength and guidance when we are lost or confused (v. 32). He keeps our feet steady, like the feet of the deer that can climb high places without slipping (v. 33). And if we do slip, His hand is there for us (v. 35).

Whether we are new believers just learning to walk in the faith or we are further along in our walk with God, all of us need His guiding, steadying hand.

Keila Ochoa

Dear Father, hold my hand and lead me in the paths of right living.

God watches over me every step of the way.

Verify the Truth

Read: Acts 17:10–13

[The Bereans] examined the Scriptures every day to see if what Paul said was true. —v. 11

"A deadly jungle spider has migrated to the US and is killing people." This was the story sent to me and to others on my friend's e-mail list. The story sounded plausible—lots of scientific names and real-life situations. But when I checked it out on reliable websites, I found it was not true—it was an Internet hoax. Its truth could only be verified by consulting a trusted source.

A group of first-century believers living in Macedonia understood the importance of confirming what they were hearing. The folks in Berea "received the message with great eagerness and examined the Scriptures every day to see if what Paul said was true" (ACTS 17:11). They were listening to Paul, and wanted to make sure what he was saying lined up with the teachings of the Old Testament. Perhaps he was telling them that there was evidence in the Old Testament that the Messiah would suffer and die for sin. They needed to verify that with the source.

When we hear spiritual ideas that disturb us, we need to be cautious. We can search the Scriptures for ourselves, listen to trustworthy sources, and seek wisdom from Jesus, our Lord. *DAVE BRANON*

Please give us discernment, Lord, to accept only truth that is rooted in your Word.
We praise you for preserving the inspired Scriptures for us—
now help us to use them to seek you.

God's truth stands any test.

Don't Delay

Read: Luke 9:57–62

For God so loved the world that he gave his one and only Son, that whoever believes in him shall not perish but have eternal life. –John 3:16

For many years I spoke to my distant cousin about our need of a Savior. When he visited me recently and I once again urged him to receive Christ, his immediate response was: "I would like to accept Jesus and join the church, but not yet. I live among people of other faiths. Unless I relocate, I will not be able to practice my faith well." He cited persecution, ridicule, and pressure from his peers as excuses to postpone his decision.

His fears were legitimate, but I assured him that whatever happened, God would not abandon him. I encouraged my cousin not to delay but to trust God for care and protection. He gave up his defenses, acknowledged his need of Christ's forgiveness, and trusted Him as his personal Savior.

When Jesus invited people to follow Him, they too offered excuses—all about being busy with the cares of this world (LUKE 9:59–62). The Lord's answer to them (vv. 60–62) urges us not to let excuses deprive us of the most important thing in life: the salvation of our souls.

Do you hear God calling you to commit your life to Him? Do not delay. "Now is the time of God's favor, now is the day of salvation" (2 COR. 6:2).

LAWRENCE DARMANI

Come to the Savior, make no delay—here in His Word He's shown us the way; here in our midst He's standing today, tenderly saying, "Come!" GEORGE F. ROOT

Today is the day of salvation.

Age Is Not a Factor

Read: 1 Corinthians 12:12–26

If one part suffers, every part suffers with it. –v. 26

After owning and working at his dental lab for 50 years, Dave Bowman planned to retire and take it easy. Diabetes and heart surgery confirmed his decision. But when he heard about a group of young refugees from Sudan who needed help, he made a life-changing decision. He agreed to sponsor five of them.

As Dave learned more about these young Sudanese men, he discovered that they had never been to a doctor or a dentist. Then one day in church someone mentioned the verse, "If one part suffers, every part suffers with it" (1 COR. 12:26). He couldn't get the verse out of his mind. Sudanese Christians were suffering because they needed medical care, and Dave sensed that God was telling him to do something about it. But what?

Despite his age and bad health, Dave began exploring the possibility of building a medical center in Sudan. Little by little, God brought together the people and the resources, and in 2008 Memorial Christian Hospital opened its doors to patients. Since then, hundreds of sick and injured people have been treated there.

Memorial Christian Hospital stands as a reminder that God cares when people suffer. And often He works through people like us to share His care—even when we think our work is done. *JULIE ACKERMAN LINK*

Do you see a need that God may be calling you to meet?
Pray and ask Him to help you step out in faith.

God cares when people suffer.

The Babel Project

Read: Genesis 11:1–9

Unless the LORD builds the house, the builders labor in vain. —Psalm 127:1

Two workmen were asked what they were building together. One said he was building a garage. The other replied that he was building a cathedral. A day later there was only one man laying bricks. When asked where the second was, the first replied, "Oh, he got fired. He insisted on building a cathedral instead of a garage."

Something similar happened on the ancient worksite of Babel. A group of people decided they would build a city and a tower that would reach to the heavens and unite their world (GEN. 11:4). But God didn't want them working on a grand, self-centered plan based on the idea that they could rise to the heights of God and solve all of their own problems. So He came down, stopped the project, scattered the people "over all the earth," and gave them different languages (VV. 8–9).

God wanted people to see Him as the solution to their problems, and He revealed His plan for them to Abraham (12:1–3). Through the faith of Abraham and his descendants, He would show the world how to look for a city "whose architect and builder is God" (HEB. 11:8–10).

Our faith does not rise out of our own dreams and solutions. The foundation of faith is in God alone and what He can do in and through us.

MART DEHAAN

Dear heavenly Father, forgive me for focusing on my own schemes and dreams. Help me to look to you for guidance in all that I do.

God wants to do what only He can do in and for us.

The Tyranny of the Perfect

Read: 1 John 1:5–2:2

If we claim to be without sin, we deceive ourselves and the truth is not in us. –v. 8

Dr. Brian Goldman obsessively tried to be perfect in treating his patients. But on a nationally broadcast show he admitted to mistakes he had made. He revealed that he had treated a woman in the emergency room and then made the decision to discharge her. Later that day a nurse asked him, "Do you remember that patient you sent home? Well, she's back." The patient had been readmitted to the hospital and then died. This devastated him. He tried even harder to be perfect, only to learn the obvious: Perfection is impossible.

As Christians, we may harbor unrealistic expectations of perfection for ourselves. But even if we can somehow manage the appearance of a flawless life, our thoughts and motives are never completely pure.

John the disciple wrote, "If we claim to be without sin, we deceive ourselves and the truth is not in us" (1 JOHN 1:8). The remedy is not to hide our sins and to strive harder, but to step into the light of God's truth and confess them. "If we walk in the light," said John, "as he is in the light, we have fellowship with one another, and the blood of Jesus, his Son, purifies us from all sin" (v. 7).

What if Christians were known not for hiding their sins but for loving and supporting each other with the truth and grace of our God? What if we practiced a risky yet healthy honesty with each other and with the watching world? *TIM GUSTAFSON*

Father, it's so difficult for us to share our faults with each other, but you call us to wholeness as your people. Empower us by your Spirit to live courageously in love and honesty.

Honesty with God about our sins brings forgiveness.

People Power

Read: Ephesians 4:7–16

The whole body . . . grows and builds itself up in love, as each part does its work. —v. 16

A man was boarding a train in Perth, Australia, when he slipped and his leg got caught in the gap between the train carriage and the station platform. Dozens of passengers quickly came to his rescue. They used their sheer might to tilt the train away from the platform, and the trapped man was freed! The train service's spokesman, David Hynes, said in an interview, "Everyone sort of pitched in. It was people power that saved someone from possibly quite serious injury."

In Ephesians 4, we read that people power is God's plan for building up His family. He has given each of us a special gift of His grace (v. 7) for the specific purpose that "the whole body, joined and held together by every supporting ligament, grows and builds itself up in love, as each part does its work" (v. 16).

Every person has a job to do in God's family; there are no spectators. In God's family we weep and laugh together. We bear each other's burdens. We pray for and encourage one another. We challenge and help each other to turn from sin. Show us, Father, our part in helping your family today.

POH FANG CHIA

Are you a spectator or a participant?
What gifts do you have?
In what ways can God use you to help others
grow closer to Him?

We need each other to get to where God wants us to go.

Love Locks

Read: Ephesians 4:29–5:2

Walk in the way of love, just as Christ loved us and gave himself up for us. —v. 2

"Love Locks" is a growing phenomenon. Thousands of people in love have attached these love padlocks to bridges, gates, and fences around the world, including France, China, Austria, Czech Republic, Serbia, Spain, Mexico, Northern Ireland. Couples engrave their names on a padlock and then attach it in a public place to symbolize their everlasting love. Authorities of some landmarks frown upon them because of the danger they can cause if too many are attached. Some think they are acts of vandalism, while others view them as beautiful art and a picture of committed love.

The Lord showed us true "everlasting love" in a public place. He displayed His love on the cross when He gave His life to provide forgiveness of sin. And He continues to show us His love on a daily basis. Salvation is not only a promise that we'll have eternity with God, but it is also a daily experience of forgiveness, assurance, provision, and grace in our relationship with Him. Jesus's love for us is the basis of Paul's challenge to "walk in the way of love" toward others (EPH. 5:2).

The love of our Father enables us to be patient and kind. In His Son He has given us the ultimate example and means of loving one another—forever.

ANNE CETAS

In what ways have you learned to love others?
What action could you take today to grow in love?

Jesus shows us how to love.

To Be Continued . . .

Read: 1 Cor. 15:50–58

Death has been swallowed up in victory. –v. 54

Growing up in the 1950s, I often attended the Saturday matinee at a local movie theater. Along with cartoons and a feature film, there was an adventure serial that always ended with the hero or heroine facing an impossible situation. There seemed to be no way out, but each episode concluded with the words "To Be Continued . . ."

The apostle Paul was no stranger to life-threatening situations. He was imprisoned, beaten, stoned, and shipwrecked as he sought to take the good news of Jesus Christ to people. He knew that someday he would die, but he never considered that to be the end of the story. Paul wrote to the followers of Jesus in Corinth, "When the perishable has been clothed with the imperishable, and the mortal with immortality, then the saying that is written will come true: 'Death has been swallowed up in victory'" (1 COR. 15:54). The passion of Paul's life was telling others that Jesus our Savior gave His life on the cross so that through faith in Him we can receive forgiveness for all our sins and have eternal life.

We are not like the movie hero who always escapes certain death. The day will come when our earthly lives will end either by death or Christ's return. But by God's grace and mercy, the story of your life and mine is "to be continued."

DAVID MCCASLAND

Father, we praise you for your gift of eternal life and say with Paul, "Thanks be to God! He gives us the victory through our Lord Jesus Christ" (1 COR. 15:57).

In life and death, Christ is our hope.

Ripples of Hope

Read: 1 Peter 1:3–9

In his great mercy he has given us new birth into a living hope through the resurrection of Jesus Christ. —v. 3

In 1966, U.S. Senator Robert Kennedy made an influential visit to South Africa. There he offered words of hope to opponents of apartheid in his famous "Ripple of Hope" speech at the University of Cape Town. In his speech, he declared, "Each time a man stands up for an ideal, or acts to improve the lot of others, or strikes out against injustice, he sends forth a tiny ripple of hope, and crossing each other from a million different centers of energy and daring, those ripples build a current which can sweep down the mightiest walls of oppression and resistance."

At times in this world, hope seems scarce. Yet there is an ultimate hope readily available for the follower of Christ. Peter wrote, "Praise be to the God and Father of our Lord Jesus Christ! In his great mercy he has given us new birth into a living hope through the resurrection of Jesus Christ from the dead" (1 PETER 1:3).

Through the certainty of Christ's resurrection, the child of God has a hope that is more than a ripple. It is an overwhelming current of confidence in the faithfulness of the One who conquered death for us. Jesus, in His victory over death—our greatest enemy—can infuse hope into the most hopeless of situations. *BILL CROWDER*

My hope is built on nothing less than Jesus' blood and righteousness;
I dare not trust the sweetest frame, but wholly lean on Jesus' name. EDWARD MOTE

In Christ the hopeless find hope.

SEPTEMBER 8

God's Plans

Read: Joshua 5:13–6:2

What do you want your servant to do? —v. 14 NLT

An army officer may have an overall plan, but before each battle he has to receive and give out new instructions. Joshua, a leader of the Israelites, had to learn this lesson. After God's people spent 40 years in the wilderness, God chose Joshua to lead them into the land He had promised to them.

The first stronghold they faced was the city of Jericho. Before the battle, Joshua saw the "commander of the LORD's army" (probably the Lord himself) standing opposite him with His sword drawn in His hand. Joshua fell on his face and worshiped. In other words, he recognized God's greatness and his own smallness. Then he asked, "What message does my Lord have for his servant?" (JOSH. 5:14). Joshua experienced victory at Jericho because he followed the Lord's instructions.

On another occasion, however, Joshua and his people "did not inquire of the LORD" (9:14). As a result, they were deceived into making a peace treaty with the people of Gibeon, enemies in the land of Canaan. This displeased the Lord (vv. 3–26).

We too are dependent on the Lord as we face life's struggles. He longs for us to come near to Him today in humility. And He'll be there again for us tomorrow.

KEILA OCHOA

In what area do you need God's guidance today?
Ask God to lead the way.

Spiritual victory comes to those who humble themselves and seek God's will.

A Fragrance and a Letter

Read: 2 Cor. 2:14–3:3

We are to God the pleasing aroma of Christ. —v. 15

Every time I get close to a rosebush or a bouquet of flowers, I'm unable to resist the temptation to pull a flower toward my nose to savor the fragrance. The sweet aroma lifts up my heart and triggers good feelings within me.

Writing to the Christians in Corinth centuries ago, the apostle Paul says that because we belong to Christ, God "uses us to spread the aroma of the knowledge of him everywhere" (2 COR. 2:14). Through His strength we can live a victorious life, exchanging our selfishness for His love and kindness and proclaiming the goodness of His salvation. When we do this, we are indeed a sweet fragrance to God.

Paul then switches to a second image, describing Christians as a "letter from Christ" (3:3). The letter of our lives is not written with ordinary ink, but by the Spirit of God. God changes us by writing His Word on our hearts for others to read.

Both word pictures encourage us to allow the beauty of Christ to be seen in us so we can point people to Him. He is the One who, as Paul wrote in Ephesians 5:2, "loved us and gave himself up for us as a fragrant offering and sacrifice to God." *LAWRENCE DARMANI*

Lord, let your splendor fill my life, that I may draw people to you.
Help me walk in the way that spreads the fragrance of
your love to others.

Our actions speak louder than our words.

Holding Me Up

Read: Psalm 34:1–7

I am the LORD your God who takes hold of your right hand and says to you, Do not fear; I will help you. —Isaiah 41:13

After I no longer went on family road trips with my parents, it became a rare occasion to visit my grandparents who lived hundreds of miles away from us. So one year, I decided to fly to visit them in the small town of Land O' Lakes, Wisconsin, for a long weekend. As we drove to the airport for my return flight, Grandma, who had never flown, began to express her fears to me: "That was such a small plane you flew on . . . . There's *nothing* really holding you up there, is there? . . . I would be so afraid to go up that high."

By the time I boarded the small aircraft, I was as fearful as the first time I had flown. *What exactly* is *holding up this plane, anyway?*

Irrational fears, or even legitimate ones, don't need to terrify us. David lived as a fugitive, afraid of King Saul who relentlessly pursued him because he was jealous of David's popularity with the people. David found true solace and comfort only in his relationship with God. In Psalm 34 he wrote: "I sought the LORD, and he answered me; he delivered me from all my fears" (v. 4).

Our Father in heaven is all-wise and all-loving. When fear starts to overwhelm us, we need to stop and remember that He is our God and He will always hold us up.

CINDY HESS KASPER

My fears sometimes overwhelm me, Father. Yet I know that you are here with me. May your perfect love cast out my fear and still my troubled heart!

When we believe that God is good, we can learn to release our fears.

In the Garden

Read: Matthew 26:36–42

My Father, . . . may your will be done. —v. 42

My forefathers were pioneers in Michigan. They cleared the land, planted crops, and cultivated gardens to raise food for their families. This agrarian bent has been passed down through the generations. My dad grew up on a Michigan farm and loved gardening, which may explain why I love gardening and the smell of fertile soil. Cultivating plants that bear beautiful flowers and tending roses that fragrantly grace our yard with beauty are enjoyable pastimes for me. If it weren't for the weeds it would be wonderful!

When I have to wrestle with the weeds, I am reminded of the garden of Eden; it was a perfect garden until Adam and Eve disobeyed God and thorns and thistles became a reality for them and every gardener since then (GEN. 3:17–18).

The Bible also mentions another garden—the garden of Gethsemane where Christ, in deep distress, pleaded with His Father to find another way to reverse sin's consequences that were born in Eden. In Gethsemane, Jesus surrendered to His Father by uttering words of full obedience in the face of great pain: "Your will be done" (MATT. 26:42).

Because Jesus surrendered in that garden, we now harvest the benefits of His amazing grace. May this lead us to surrender to His weeding of sin from our lives.

JOE STOWELL

Lord, thank you for the amazing price you paid to free me from sin. May the reality of the victory you won encourage me to reject the sin that entangles my ability to be fruitful for you.

Spiritual growth occurs when faith is cultivated.

The Two Bears

Read: Proverbs 13:10–20

Where there is strife, there is pride, but wisdom is found in those who take advice. —v. 10

Some years ago, my wife, Carolyn, and I spent a few days camping on the flanks of Mount Rainier in Washington State. When we were returning to our campsite one evening, we saw in the middle of a meadow two male bears boxing each other's ears. We stopped to watch.

There was a hiker nearby, and I asked him what the conflict was about. "A young female," he said.

"Where is she?" I asked.

"Oh, she left about 20 minutes ago," he chuckled. Thus, I gathered, the conflict at this point was not about the female bear but about being the toughest bear.

Most fights aren't about policy and principle, or about right and wrong; they're almost always about pride. The wise man of Proverbs swings his axe at the root of the problem when he writes: "Pride leads to conflict" (13:10 NLT). Quarrels are fueled by pride, by needing to be right, by wanting our way, or by defending our turf or our egos.

On the other side, wisdom resides with the well-advised—those who listen and learn, those who allow themselves to be instructed. There is wisdom in those who humble themselves—those who set aside their own selfish ambition; who acknowledge the limits of their own understanding; who listen to the other person's point of view; who allow their own ideas to be corrected. This is the wisdom from God that spreads peace wherever it goes.

DAVID ROPER

Dear heavenly Father, help me as I battle pride today. It's so easy to take my eyes off you and focus on myself. Give me a humble heart.

Humility brings wisdom.

God So Loved . . .

Read: John 3:13–19

Jesus said, "Father, forgive them, for they do not know what they are doing." –Luke 23:34

July 28, 2014, marked the 100th anniversary of the beginning of World War I. In the British media many discussions and documentaries recalled the start of that 4-year conflict. Even the TV program *Mr. Selfridge,* which is based on an actual department store in London, included an episode set in 1914 that showed young male employees lining up to volunteer for the army. As I observed these portrayals of self-sacrifice, I felt a lump in my throat. The soldiers they depicted had been so young, so eager, and so unlikely to return from the horror of the trenches.

Although Jesus didn't go off to war to defeat an earthly foe, He did go to the cross to defeat the ultimate enemy—sin and death. Jesus came to earth to demonstrate God's love in action and to die a horrendous death so that we could be forgiven of our sins. And He was even prepared to forgive the men who flogged and crucified Him (LUKE 23:34). He conquered death by His resurrection and now we can become part of God's forever family (JOHN 3:13–16).

Anniversaries and memorials remind us of important historical events and heroic deeds. The cross reminds us of the pain of Jesus's death and the beauty of His sacrifice for our salvation. *MARION STROUD*

Dear Lord, thank you for loving me so much that you left your home in heaven, came to earth, and willingly went to the cross for me. Thank you for paying the penalty for my sins and forgiving me.

The cross of Jesus is the supreme evidence of the love of God.

OSWALD CHAMBERS

Words and Actions

Read: Matthew 21:28–32

Let us not love with words or speech but with actions and in truth. –1 John 3:18

The e-mail from the student in my college writing class expressed urgency. It was the end of the semester, and he realized he needed a better grade to participate in sports. What could he do? He had missed some assignments, so I gave him two days to complete those papers and improve his grade. His response: "Thank you. I'll do it."

Two days—and the deadline—passed, and no papers appeared. He didn't back up his words with action.

Jesus told about a young man who did something similar. The boy's dad asked him to do some work in the vineyard. The son said, "I will, sir" (MATT. 21:30). But he was all talk and no action.

In commenting on this parable, Matthew Henry concluded: "Buds and blossoms are not fruit." The buds and blossoms of our words, which breed anticipation of what we might do, are empty without the fruit of our follow-through. Jesus's main application was to religious leaders who spoke of obedience yet refused to follow through with repentance. But the words apply to us as well. It is in following God "with actions and in truth" (1 JOHN 3:18)—not in making empty promises—that we honor our Lord and Savior.

Our actions in obeying God show Him more love, honor, and praise than any empty words we might say to try to appear good. *DAVE BRANON*

Dear Father, help me to follow through on my promises to you and to all who depend on me. Especially help me to do your will and not just talk about it.

Words are the blossoms, action the fruit.

God's Compass

Read: Psalm 119:105–112

Your word is a lamp for my feet, a light on my path. —v. 105

During World War II, small compasses saved the lives of 27 sailors 300 miles off the coast of North Carolina. Waldemar Semenov, a retired merchant seaman, was serving as a junior engineer aboard the SS *Alcoa Guide* when a German submarine surfaced and opened fire on the ship. The ship was hit, caught fire, and began to sink. Semenov and his crew lowered compass-equipped lifeboats into the water and used the compasses to guide them toward the shipping lanes closer to shore. After three days, the men were rescued.

The psalmist reminded God's people that His Word was a trustworthy "compass." He likened it to a lamp. In that day, the flickering light cast by an olive oil lamp was only bright enough to show a traveler his next step. To the psalmist, God's Word was such a lamp, providing enough light to illuminate the path for those pursuing God (PS. 119:105). When the psalmist was wandering in the dark on a chaotic path of life, he believed that God, through the guidance of His Word, would provide direction.

When we lose our bearings in life, we can trust our God who gives His trustworthy Word as our compass, using it to lead us into deeper fellowship with Him. *MARVIN WILLIAMS*

Heavenly Father, it is difficult to navigate life. I drift sometimes, but I will trust in you. Lead me and guide me by the faithfulness and reliability of your Word.

God has given us His Word to help us know and follow Him.

Feeling Forsaken

Read: Psalm 22:1–21

My God, my God, why have you forsaken me? —Matthew 27:46

In his book *The Screwtape Letters,* C. S. Lewis records an imaginary conversation between a senior devil and a junior devil as they discuss how to properly tempt a Christian. The two devils desired to destroy the believer's faith in God. "Be not deceived," the senior devil says to the junior. "Our cause is never more in jeopardy than when a human . . . looks round upon a universe in which every trace of [God] seems to have vanished, and asks why he has been forsaken, and still obeys."

The Bible gives us many examples of people who acted with faith despite their feelings of abandonment. Abram felt that God's promise of an heir had gone unheeded (GEN. 15:2–3). The psalmist felt ignored in his trouble (PS. 10:1). Job's troubles were so great that he thought God might even kill him (JOB 13:15). And Jesus from the cross cried out: "My God, my God, why have you forsaken me?" (MATT. 27:46). Yet in each instance God was shown to be faithful (GEN. 21:1–7; PS. 10:16–18; JOB 38:1–42:17; MATT. 28:9–20).

Although Satan may try to tempt you to think you are forsaken, God is always near. He never forsakes His own. "God has said, 'Never will I leave you; never will I forsake you' " (HEB. 13:5). We may boldly say, "The Lord is my helper; I will not be afraid" (v. 6).

DENNIS FISHER

Lord, although clouds and darkness sometimes shroud me,
I know that you are close by my side. Thank you.

God is always near in spite of our fears.

Doesn't God Care?

Read: Habakkuk 1:1–11

"For my thoughts are not your thoughts, neither are your ways my ways," declares the Lord. —Isaiah 55:8

Why does the intoxicated driver escape an accident unharmed while his sober victim is seriously injured? Why do bad people prosper while good people suffer? How often have you been so confused by things going on in your life that you have cried out, "Doesn't God care?"

Habakkuk struggled with this same question as he saw the distressing situation in Judah where wickedness and injustice were running rampant (HAB. 1:1–4). His confusion drove him to ask God when He would act to fix the situation. God's reply was nothing short of perplexing.

God said that He would use the Chaldeans as the means of Judah's correction. The Chaldeans were notorious for their cruelty (V. 7). They were bent on violence (V. 9) and worshiped nothing but their military prowess and false gods (VV. 10–11).

In moments when we don't understand God's ways, we need to trust His unchanging character. That's exactly what Habakkuk did. He believed that God is a God of justice, mercy, and truth (PS. 89:14). In the process, he learned to look at his circumstances from the framework of God's character instead of looking at God's character from the context of his own circumstances. He concluded, "The Sovereign LORD is my strength; he makes my feet like the feet of a deer, he enables me to tread on the heights" (HAB. 3:19).

POH FANG CHIA

Lord, it is easy to let my circumstances change how I understand you. Help me to remember that you are good and faithful, even though I can't see everything and may not understand how you are working.

Our situation may look very different from God's point of view.

2 A.M. Friends

Read: Colossians 4:2–15

He is always wrestling in prayer for you, that you may stand firm in all the will of God, mature and fully assured. —v. 12

A friend told me about a group of people who share a strong bond of faith in Christ. One of them, a 93-year-old woman, said, "I feel like I can call any of you at 2 a.m., and I don't even have to apologize if I feel the need for any type of assistance." Whether the need is prayer, practical help, or someone to be there during a time of need, these friends are unconditionally committed to each other.

The same sense of commitment shines through Paul's letter to the followers of Jesus in Colosse. Writing from prison in Rome, Paul says he is sending Tychicus and Onesimus to encourage them (COL. 4:7–9). Aristarchus, Mark, and Justus send their greetings (VV. 10–11). And Epaphras is "always wrestling in prayer for you, that you may stand firm in all the will of God, mature and fully assured" (V. 12). These are bold assurances of practical help and deep-seated love.

Are you part of a "2 a.m. group"? If so, give thanks for the faithfulness of friends. If not, ask the Lord to connect you with another person with whom you can share a commitment to pray and care. I suspect it will soon grow to include others. Share the love of Christ with one another. Anything. Anytime. Anywhere. All in Jesus's name! *DAVID MCCASLAND*

Jesus, thank you for friends who demonstrate your love to me.
Help me to do the same for them and those around me.
Most of all, thank you for being the friend who sticks closer than a brother.

Greater love has no one than this: to lay down one's life for one's friends.

JESUS

Lessons in Suffering

Read: 2 Cor. 11:21–30

If I must boast, I will boast of the things that show my weakness. –v. 30

The close-up image on the giant screen was big and sharp, so we could see the deep cuts on the man's body. A soldier beat him while an angry crowd laughed at the man whose face was now covered with blood. The scenes appeared so real that, in the silence of the open-air theater, I cringed and grimaced as if I could feel the pain myself. But this was only a film reenactment of Jesus's suffering for us.

Reminding us of Jesus's suffering, Peter wrote, "To this you were called, because Christ suffered for you, leaving you an example, that you should follow in his steps" (1 PETER 2:21). While suffering comes in different forms and intensity, it is to be expected. Ours may not be as intense as that experienced by Paul, who for the sake of Christ was beaten with rods, stoned, and shipwrecked. He was attacked by bandits, and he endured hunger and thirst (2 COR. 11:24–27). Likewise, we may not suffer like those who endure severe persecution in cultures where Christianity is not welcomed.

In some form or another, however, suffering will come our way as we deny ourselves, endure harassment, bear insults, or refuse to engage in activities that do not honor the Lord. Even exercising patience, avoiding revenge, and forgiving others in order to foster good relationships are forms of following in His steps.

Whenever we encounter suffering, may we remember what Jesus endured for us. *LAWRENCE DARMANI*

What have you learned about God through your trials?

The school of suffering teaches us lessons that we could learn in no other classroom.

Tissue Boxes

Read: Psalm 31:9–18

I trust in you, LORD; I say, "You are my God." My times are in your hands. –vv. 14–15

As I sat in the surgical waiting room, I had time to think. I had been here recently, when we received the jarring news that my only brother, much too young, was "brain dead."

And so on this day, waiting for news about my wife who was undergoing a serious surgical procedure, I waited and listened for the quiet voice of God.

Suddenly, news! The surgeon wanted to see me. I went to a secluded room to wait. There, on the table, sat two tissue boxes, conspicuously available. They weren't for the sniffles. They were for cold, hard phrases like I heard when my brother died—"brain dead" and "nothing we can do."

In such times of grief or uncertainty, the honesty of the psalms makes them a natural place to turn. Psalm 31 was the heart-cry of David, who endured so much that he wrote, "My life is consumed by anguish" (v. 10). Compounding that grief was the pain of abandonment by his friends and neighbors (v. 11).

But David had the bedrock of faith in the one true God. "I trust in you, LORD; I say, 'You are my God.' My times are in your hands" (vv. 14–15). His lament concludes with resounding hope. "Be strong and take heart, all you who hope in the LORD" (v. 24).

This time in the waiting room, the surgeon gave us good news: My wife could expect a full recovery. But even if she hadn't been "okay," our times still remain in God's hands. *TIM GUSTAFSON*

Lord, we give you our deepest grief as well as our joy. Thank you for your constant presence no matter what today holds. you alone are faithful!

When we put our problems in God's hands, He puts His peace in our hearts.

A Fly's Reminder

Read: Ecclesiastes 9:4–12

Anyone who is among the living has hope. —v. 4

When I first began working in the small office I now rent, the only inhabitants were a few mopey flies. Several of them had gone the way of all flesh, and their bodies littered the floor and windowsills. I disposed of all but one, which I left in plain sight.

That fly carcass reminds me to live each day well. Death is an excellent reminder of life, and life is a gift. Solomon said, "Anyone who is among the living has hope" (ECCL. 9:4). Life on earth gives us the chance to influence and enjoy the world around us. We can eat and drink happily and relish our relationships (VV. 7, 9).

We can also enjoy our work. Solomon advised, "Whatever your hand finds to do, do it with all your might" (V. 10). Whatever our vocation or job or role in life, we can still do things that matter, and do them well. We can encourage people, pray, and express love with sincerity each day.

The writer of Ecclesiastes says, "Time and chance happen to them all. . . . No one knows when their hour will come" (VV. 11–12). It's impossible to know when our lives on earth will end, but gladness and purpose can be found in this day by relying on God's strength and depending on Jesus's promise of eternal life (JOHN 6:47). *JENNIFER BENSON SCHULDT*

Dear God, help me to manage my time well and enjoy the gifts of this world today. Thank you for the promise of eternal life through your Son, Jesus Christ.

This is the day the Lord has made. Rejoice and be glad.

A Fishing Lesson

Read: 1 Peter 5:1–9

Resist [the devil], standing firm in the faith. —v. 9

I was fishing quietly on the clear, still waters of Piatt Lake, casting next to a lush weedbed. I watched a large smallmouth bass sneak out of the thick vegetation to investigate. He approached the tempting night crawler on the end of my line, stared at it, and backed into the weeds. This happened several times until he spotted the hook. Then he whipped his tail and disappeared into his lair, never to come out again.

Satan dangles temptation, like a fishhook, right in front of us. It looks tasty. It promises gratification. But Satan's power ends there. He cannot force us to take the hook. His power stops at the edge of our will—at our decision point. When we are warned by the Holy Spirit and decide to say no, Satan can do no more. James says he runs away (4:7).

As believers, we can receive great comfort from the words of the apostle Peter, who himself experienced great temptation (MATT. 26:33–35). In later life he wrote, "Be alert and of sober mind. Your enemy the devil prowls around like a roaring lion . . . . Resist him, standing firm in the faith" (1 PETER 5:8–9).

Just as that big old bass ignored my hook, we can in God's strength successfully resist Satan's most enticing tactics! *DAVE EGNER*

Father in heaven, thank you for the promise of your help when we are tempted and for the truth that Satan's power is limited. Give us the wisdom to recognize temptation and the humility to rely on your Spirit for the strength to resist.

Respond to the lies of Satan with the truth of God's Word.

No Wonder!

Read: Song of Sol. 1:1–4

We love Him because He first loved us. —1 John 4:19 NKJV

"He's perfect for you," my friend told me. She was talking about a guy she had just met. She described his kind eyes, his kind smile, and his kind heart. When I met him I had to agree. Today he's my husband, and no wonder I love him!

In the Song of Solomon the bride describes her lover. His love is better than wine and more fragrant than ointments. His name is sweeter than anything in this world. So she concludes that it's no wonder he is loved.

But there is Someone far greater than any earthly loved one, Someone whose love is also better than wine. His love satisfies our every need. His "fragrance" is better than any perfume because when He gave himself for us, His sacrifice became a sweet-smelling aroma to God (EPH. 5:2). Finally, His name is above every name (PHIL. 2:9). No wonder we love Him!

It is a privilege to love Jesus. It is the best experience in life! Do we take the time to tell Him so? Do we express with words the beauty of our Savior? If we show His beauty with our lives, others will say, "No wonder you love Him!"

KEILA OCHOA

Lord, you are beautiful! No wonder we love you!
Deepen our love for you today, we pray. Help us see your beauty
in new ways.

God's Word tells us of His love; our words tell Him of our love.

The Upside of Setbacks

Read: Psalm 27

Wait for the LORD; be strong and take heart and wait for the LORD. —v. 14

American swimmer Dara Torres had a remarkable career, appearing in five different Olympics from 1984 to 2008. Late in her career, Torres broke the US record for the 50-meter freestyle—25 years after she herself set that record. But it wasn't always medals and records. Torres also encountered obstacles in her athletic career: injuries, surgery, as well as being almost twice the age of most other competitors. She said, "I've wanted to win at everything, every day, since I was a kid. . . . I'm also aware that setbacks have an upside; they fuel new dreams."

"Setbacks have an upside" is a great life lesson. Torres's struggles motivated her to reach for new heights. They have a spiritual benefit too. As James said, "Consider it pure joy . . . whenever you face trials of many kinds, because you know that the testing of your faith produces perseverance" (JAMES 1:2–3).

Adopting this perspective on the difficulties of life is not easy, but it is worthwhile. Trials provide opportunity to deepen our relationship with God. They also provide the opening to learn lessons that success cannot teach by developing in us the kind of patience that waits on God and trusts Him for the strength to endure.

The psalmist reminds us, "Wait for the LORD; be strong and take heart and wait for the LORD" (PS. 27:14).

BILL CROWDER

In my times of trial, dear Lord, teach me to wait for you.
But please teach me even more to trust the love you have for me.
And as I do, may I learn your wisdom and have the patience to endure.

The setbacks of life can teach us to wait upon the Lord for His help and strength.

Keep on Asking

Read: Luke 11:1–13

Ask and it will be given to you; seek and you will find; knock and the door will be opened to you. —v. 9

I heard a woman say that she never prayed more than once for anything. She didn't want to weary God with her repeated requests.

The Lord's teaching on prayer in Luke 11 contradicts this notion. He told a parable about a man who went to his friend's house at midnight and asked for some bread to feed his unexpected visitors. At first the friend refused, for he and his family were in bed. Finally he got up and gave him the bread—not out of friendship but because the caller was so persistent (vv. 5–10).

Jesus used this parable to contrast this reluctant friend with our generous heavenly Father. If an irritated neighbor will give in to his friend's persistence and grant his request, how much more readily will our heavenly Father give us all we need!

It's true that God, in His great wisdom, may sometimes delay His answers to prayer. It's also true that we must pray in harmony with the Scriptures and God's will. But Jesus moved beyond those facts to urge us to persist in prayer. He told us to ask, seek, and knock until the answer comes (v. 9).

So don't worry about wearying God. He will never tire of your persistent prayer!

JOANIE YODER

Thank you, Lord, that you hear our every plea. We trust in you.

God never tires of our asking.

A New Creation

Read: Acts 9:10–22

If anyone is in Christ, the new creation has come. —2 Corinthians 5:17

Early in my work life I had a coworker who seemed to delight in using God's name as a profanity. He mercilessly taunted Christians who were new to their faith or who tried to talk with him about Jesus. On the day I left that job to move to another community and a new place of employment, I remember thinking that this man would never become a follower of Jesus.

Two years later I visited my old workplace. He was still there, but never have I witnessed such a dramatic change in a person! This man, so antagonistic to faith, was now a walking, talking example of what it means to be a "new creation" in Christ (2 COR. 5:17). And now, more than 30 years later, he's still telling others how Jesus "met him where he was—sin and all."

It occurs to me that the early Christians must have seen something similar in Paul, their fiery persecutor—a riveting example of what it means to become a new creation (ACTS 9:1–22). What great hope both of these lives are to those who think themselves beyond redemption!

Jesus sought Paul and my former coworker—and me. And He continues today to reach the "unreachable" and model for us just how we can reach people too.

RANDY KILGORE

Lord, I want to learn to reach out to others
and share your love and forgiveness.
Teach me and help me to step out in both faith and trust.

No one is beyond the reach of God.

Consider the Poor

Read: Matthew 25:31–40

The righteous considers the cause of the poor. —Proverbs 29:7 NKJV

The year was 1780, and Robert Raikes had a burden for the poor, illiterate children in his London neighborhood. He noticed that nothing was being done to help these children, so he set out to make a difference.

He hired some women to set up schools for them on Sunday. Using the Bible as their textbook, the teachers taught the poorest children of London to read and introduced them to the wisdom of the Bible. Soon about 100 children were attending these classes and enjoying lunch in a safe, clean environment. These "Sunday schools," as they were soon called, eventually touched the lives of thousands of boys and girls. By 1831, Sunday schools in Great Britain reached more than a million children—all because one man understood this truth: "The righteous considers the cause of the poor" (PROV. 29:7 NKJV).

It's no secret that Jesus cares greatly for those who struggle. In Matthew 25, He suggests that followers of Christ show a readiness for the Lord's return by helping the hungry to get food, helping the thirsty to get a drink, helping the homeless to find a home, helping the naked to get clothes, and helping the sick or imprisoned to receive comfort (vv. 35–36).

As we bear witness that Jesus Christ is in our hearts, we honor our compassionate Savior by considering those on God's heart. *DAVE BRANON*

Awaken my heart, Lord, to those you care about, including the poor and helpless, the hungry and homeless, the troubled and hopeless in our world.

Open your heart to God to learn compassion, and open your hand to give help.

SEPTEMBER 28

Give It Away

Read: Philippians 2:19–30

I think it is necessary to send back to you Epaphroditus, . . . whom you sent to take care of my needs. —v. 25

Many charities that help people with various needs depend on donations of unwanted clothing and household items from those who have more than enough. And it's good to give away unused things so they can benefit others. But we are often more reluctant to part with things of value that we use every day.

When Paul was imprisoned in Rome, he needed continuing encouragement and the companionship of trusted friends. Yet he sent two of his closest comrades to help the followers of Jesus in Philippi (PHIL. 2:19–30). "I hope in the Lord Jesus to send Timothy to you soon . . . . I have no one else like him, who will show genuine concern for your welfare" (vv. 19–20). And, "I think it is necessary to send back to you Epaphroditus, my brother, co-worker and fellow soldier, who is also your messenger, whom you sent to take care of my needs" (v. 25). Paul freely gave to others what he most needed himself.

Whatever we feel is "most valued" in our lives today could be of great benefit to someone we know. It may be our time, friendship, encouragement, a listening ear, or a helping hand. When we give away what the Lord has given to us, He is honored, others are helped, and we are blessed.

DAVID MCCASLAND

Lord, show me what I cling to. If someone needs it, open my heart and my hands and help me give it away today.

Giving freely honors the Lord, helps others, and blesses us.

Piercing the Darkness

Read: Isaiah 60:19–22

The LORD will be your everlasting light, and your God will be your glory. —v. 19

I caught my first glimpse of them as a college student. On a frosty, fall night, far from the lights of the city, I was riding on a hay wagon loaded with noisy friends when the sky lit up and colors flashed across the horizon. I was mesmerized. Ever since that night I have been fascinated with the phenomenon called *aurora borealis,* also known as northern lights. Mostly they are seen far north of where I live, but occasionally they appear in lower latitudes. Having seen them once, I long to see more. Whenever the conditions are favorable, I say to my equally fascinated friends, "Maybe tonight . . ."

Throughout Scripture, light and glory are used to describe the coming of the Lord. A time is coming when the sun and moon will be unnecessary (ISA. 60:19). And in describing God on His throne, the apostle John wrote, "The one who sat there had the appearance of jasper and ruby. A rainbow that shone like an emerald encircled the throne" (REV. 4:3).

An emerald circle is an apt description of the northern lights. So whenever I see glorious light displays in the skies above—whether in person or via picture or video—I think of it as a foretaste of what is to come, and I praise God that even now His glory pierces the darkness.

JULIE ACKERMAN LINK

Lord, the world around us is sometimes so dark that it is difficult to see your power and goodness. Thank you for the reminders that the darkness does not and will not last forever. Help us wait with great expectation for the day when we will see you on your throne.

Jesus came to give light to a dark world.

The Valley of Vision

Read: Jonah 2:1–10

I remembered you, LORD, and my prayer rose to you. –v. 7

The Puritan prayer "The Valley of Vision" speaks of the distance between a sinful man and his holy God. The man says to God, "Thou hast brought me to the valley of vision . . . ; hemmed in by mountains of sin I behold Thy glory." Aware of his wrongs, the man still has hope. He continues, "Stars can be seen from the deepest wells, and the deeper the wells the brighter Thy stars shine." Finally, the poem ends with a request: "Let me find Thy light in my darkness, . . . Thy glory in my valley."

Jonah found God's glory during his time in the ocean's depths. He rebelled against God and ended up in a fish's stomach, overcome by his sin. There, Jonah cried to God: "You cast me into the deep . . . . The waters surrounded me, even to my soul" (JONAH 2:3, 5 NKJV). Despite his situation, Jonah said, "I remembered you, LORD, and my prayer rose to you" (V. 7). God heard his prayer and caused the fish to free him.

Although sin creates distance between God and us, we can look up from the lowest points in our lives and see Him—His holiness, goodness, and grace. If we turn away from our sin and confess it to God, He will forgive us. God answers prayers from the valley. *JENNIFER BENSON SCHULDT*

Lord, in the daytime stars can be seen from deepest wells,
and the deeper the wells the brighter your stars shine;
let me find your light in my darkness.

The darkness of sin only makes the light of God's grace shine brighter.

We Can Know

Read: 1 John 5:10–15

I write these things to you . . . that you may know that you have eternal life. —v. 13

As I sat on a train headed for an important appointment, I began to wonder if I was on the right train. I had never traveled that route before and had failed to ask for help. Finally, overcome by uncertainty and doubt, I exited at the next station—only to be told I had indeed been on the right train!

That incident reminded me how doubt can rob us of peace and confidence. At one time I had struggled with the assurance of my salvation, but God helped me deal with my doubt. Later, after sharing the story of my conversion and my assurance that I was going to heaven, someone asked, "How can you be sure you are saved and going to heaven?" I confidently but humbly pointed to the verse that God had used to help me: "I write these things to you who believe in the name of the Son of God so that you may know that you have eternal life" (1 JOHN 5:13).

God promises that through faith in His Son, Jesus, we *already* have eternal life: "God has given us eternal life, and this life is in his Son" (v. 11). This assurance sharpens our faith, lifts us up when we are downhearted, and gives us courage in times of doubt. *LAWRENCE DARMANI*

Dear Lord, during my times of doubt help me remember
the promise of your Word. Since I have invited Jesus into my life
and placed my faith in His payment for my sins,
you have promised me eternal life with you.

Recalling God's promises destroys doubt.

We Have Fruit!

Read: Joshua 24:2, 8–14

I gave you a land on which you did not toil and cities you did not build. –v. 13

The young mother sighed as she scraped together lunch for her 3-year-old daughter. Spying the empty fruit basket on the table in their tiny kitchen, she sighed and said aloud, "If we just had a basket of fruit, I would feel rich!" Her little girl overheard her.

Weeks passed. God sustained the small family. Still, the struggling mom worried. Then one day her little girl bounded into the kitchen. "Look, Mommy, we're rich!" she exclaimed, pointing at the full fruit basket on the table. Nothing had changed except that the family had purchased a bag of apples.

When Joshua, the leader of the Israelites, was about to die, he shared a message from the Lord that recounted all God had done for them. And he noted, "You lived in the wilderness for a long time" (JOSH. 24:7). Then he said, "[God] gave you a land on which you did not toil and cities you did not build; and you live in them and eat from vineyards and olive groves that you did not plant" (v. 13). Joshua set up a large stone to remind Israel of God's provision (v. 26).

Like the Israelites, after a time of challenge and scarcity, that family now lives in a different place and enjoys fruit trees in a spacious yard, planted years earlier by a previous owner. If you visit them, you'll find a bowl of fruit in their kitchen. It reminds them of God's goodness and how a 3-year-old infused her family with faith, joy, and perspective. *TIM GUSTAFSON*

Thank God for how He has provided in the past. Thank Him for what He will do. Ask Him what He wants you to do. Then trust Him.

Remembering God's provision for yesterday gives hope and strength for today.

Better Than Waking Up

Read: Luke 23:33–43

Today you will be with me in paradise. –v. 43

Have you ever felt that your life was ruined as a result of having done something embarrassing, shameful, or even criminal—only to wake up and realize it was just a dream? But what if it wasn't just a nightmare? What if the situation was all too real—either for yourself or someone you love?

This is the situation confronted in George MacDonald's 19th-century novel *The Curate's Awakening*. It's the story of a parish minister who discovers that he's been speaking for a God he's not even sure he believes in. Later, he is called to the bedside of a young man who is losing his mind and dying, haunted by a murder he has committed.

In the heart-rending struggle that follows, the minister discovers what we all need to see. The relief of waking up from a bad dream is nothing compared to waking to the reality of God's forgiveness, which we once thought was too good to be true.

Where will we find the mercy we need? It is found in Jesus, who, from His own cross said to a dying criminal who turned to Him for help, "Today you will be with me in paradise" (LUKE 23:43). *MART DEHAAN*

Father in heaven, please help us to believe that our forgiveness is as real as the price you paid for our rescue.

We are saved by God's mercy, not by our merit.

Miracle Rain

Read: 1 Kings 18:1, 41–45

I am God, and there is no other. —Isaiah 46:9

Life is hard for the villagers who live on a hilly terrain in the Yunnan Province of China. Their main source of food is corn and rice. But in May 2012 a severe drought hit the region and the crops withered. Everyone was worried, and many superstitious practices were carried out as the people attempted to end the drought. When nothing worked, people started blaming the five Christians in the village for offending the spirits of the ancestors.

These five believers gathered to pray. Before long, the sky darkened and thunder was heard. A heavy downpour started and lasted the whole afternoon and night. The crops were saved! While most of the villagers did not believe God sent the rain, others did and desired to find out more about Him and Jesus.

In 1 Kings 17 and 18 we read of a severe drought in Israel. But in this case, we are told, it was a result of God's judgment on His people (17:1). They had begun to worship Baal, the god of the Canaanites, believing that this deity could send the rain for their crops. Then God, through His prophet Elijah, showed that He is the one true God who determines when rain falls.

Our all-powerful God desires to hear our prayers and answer our pleas. And though we do not always understand His timing or His purposes, God always responds with His best for our lives. *POH FANG CHIA*

In what ways have you seen God answer prayer in the past?
What needs do you have to bring before Him today?
What do you want to thank Him for?

Through prayer, we draw upon the power of the infinite God.

Seconds Count

Read: Psalm 39:4–13

Show me, Lord, my life's end. –v. 4

At the age of 59 my friend Bob Boardman wrote, "If the 70 years of a normal life span were squeezed into a single 24-hour day, it would now be 8:30 in the evening in my life. . . . Time is slipping by so rapidly."

The difficulty in admitting that our time on earth is limited inspired the creation of "Tikker," a wristwatch that tells you what time it is, calculates your estimated normal life span, and displays a running countdown of your remaining time. It is advertised as the watch "that counts down your life, just so you can make every second count."

In Psalm 39, David grappled with the brevity of his life, saying, "Show me, Lord, my life's end and the number of my days; let me know how fleeting my life is" (v. 4). He described his life span as no longer than the width of his hand, as only a moment to God, and merely a breath (v. 5). David concluded, "But now, Lord, what do I look for? My hope is in you" (v. 7).

The clock is ticking. Now is the time to seek God's power to help us become the people He wants us to be. Finding hope in our eternal God gives meaning for our lives today. *David McCasland*

In what ways am I wasting time?
In what ways am I making my days count?
In what areas do I need to make changes?

The time to live for Jesus is now.

Playing with Fire

Read: John 15:10–20

Whoever has my commands and keeps them is the one who loves me. . . . And I too will love them and show myself to them. –14:21

When I was a young boy, my mom warned me that I should never play with fire. Yet one day I decided to see what would happen if I did. Taking a book of matches and some paper, I went out into the backyard to experiment. With heart beating fast, I knelt on the ground, struck the match, and set the paper aflame.

Suddenly I saw my mother approaching. Not wanting to get caught, I put my legs over the flames to hide what I was doing. But Mom shouted, "Denny, move your legs! There's a fire underneath them!" Fortunately, I moved my legs quickly enough and was not burned. I realized then that my mother's rule about not playing with fire was not to spoil my fun but because of her concern to keep me safe.

Sometimes we don't understand the reasons behind God's commands. We may even think He is a cosmic killjoy, setting up rules and regulations to keep us from enjoying ourselves. But God asks us to obey Him because He has our best interests at heart. As we obey, we "remain in his love" and are filled with joy (JOHN 15:10–11).

So when God warns us not to sin, He does it for our own good. He really wants to protect us from "playing with fire" and getting burned.

DENNIS FISHER

Dear heavenly Father, may your Holy Spirit empower us to obey your Word. We thank you for the protection your precepts provide and the love and joy we find in obeying you.

God gives us loving warnings in His Word to protect us.

Unclear Vision

Read: Job 19:1–21

My ears had heard of you but now my eyes have seen you. —42:5

My friend Meaghan is an accomplished equestrian, and I've been learning some interesting things about horses from her. For instance, despite having the largest eyes of all land mammals, horses have poor eyesight and can see fewer colors than humans. Because of this, they can't always identify objects on the ground. When they see a pole, they don't know if it's a pole they can easily step over or a large snake that might harm them. For this reason, until they are properly trained horses are easily frightened and quick to run away.

We too may want to run from alarming circumstances. We may feel like Job who misunderstood his troubles and wished he'd never been born. Since he couldn't see that it was Satan who was trying to break him down, he feared that the Lord, in whom he had trusted, was trying to destroy him. Overwhelmed, he cried out, "God has wronged me and drawn his net around me" (JOB 19:6).

Like Job's vision, ours is limited. We want to run away from the difficult situations that scare us. From God's perspective, we are not alone. He understands what confuses and frightens us. He knows we are safe with Him by our side. This is our opportunity to trust His understanding rather than our own.

ANNE CETAS

In what ways have you doubted God's goodness?
How have you seen Him working in your life
during a difficult time?

Trusting God's faithfulness dispels our fearfulness.

Reckless Words

Read: 1 Peter 2:13–25

When they hurled their insults at him, he did not retaliate. —v. 23

I had been driving for almost half an hour when my daughter suddenly wailed from the backseat. When I asked, "What happened?" she said her brother had grabbed her arm. He claimed he had grabbed her arm because she had pinched him. She said she pinched him because he had said something mean.

Unfortunately, this pattern, which is common between children, can show up in adult relationships too. One person offends another, and the hurt person shoots back a verbal blow. The original offender retaliates with another insult. Before long, anger and cruel words have damaged the relationship.

The Bible says that "the words of the reckless pierce like swords," and that "a harsh word stirs up anger" but "a gentle answer turns away wrath" (PROV. 12:18; 15:1). And sometimes not answering at all is the best way to deal with mean or cruel words or comments.

Before Jesus's crucifixion, the religious authorities tried to provoke Him with their words (MATT. 27:41–43). Yet, "When they hurled their insults at him, he did not retaliate . . . . Instead, he entrusted himself to him who judges justly" (1 PETER 2:23).

Jesus's example and the Spirit's help offer us a way to respond to people who offend us. Trusting the Lord, we don't need to use words as weapons.

JENNIFER BENSON SCHULDT

Dear God, please give me self-control through your Holy Spirit when I am tempted to retaliate with words.

A soft answer has often been the means of breaking a hard heart.

The Song of Our Lives

Read: Job 29:1–6; 30:1–9

The LORD God is my strength and my song. —Isaiah 12:2 NLT

Everyone touched by a piece of music hears it differently. The composer hears it in the chamber of his imagination. The audience hears it with their senses and emotions. The members of the orchestra hear most clearly the sound of the instruments closest to them.

In a sense, we are the members of God's orchestra. Often we hear only the music closest to us. Because we don't hear a balanced work, we are like Job who cried as he suffered: "Now those young men mock me in song; I have become a byword among them" (JOB 30:9).

Job recalled how princes and officials had respected him. His life was "awash in cream, and the rocks gushed olive oil for me" (29:6 NLT). But now, he had become the target of mockers. "My harp plays sad music," he lamented (30:31 NLT). Yet there was much, much more to the symphony. Job simply couldn't hear the whole song.

Maybe today you can hear only the sad notes of your own violin. Don't lose heart. Every detail in your life is part of God's composition. Or perhaps you are listening to a cheerful flute. Praise God for it and share your joy with someone else.

God's masterpiece of redemption is the symphony we are playing, and ultimately everything will work together for His good purposes. God is the composer of our lives. His song is perfect, and we can trust Him.

KEILA OCHOA

Lord, help me to trust you, especially when my life seems discordant and out of tune. I thank you because I'm part of your symphony and your song is perfect.

Faith in God's goodness puts a song in the heart.

Love Comes First

Read: 1 John 4:7–19

We love [God] because he first loved us. –v. 19

One evening my friend showed me one of the three decorative plaques that would be part of a wall arrangement in her living room. "See, I've already got *Love*," she said, holding up the plaque with the word written on it. "*Faith* and *Hope* are on order."

So Love comes first, I thought. *Faith and Hope soon follow!*

Love did come first. In fact, it originated with God. First John 4:19 reminds us that "We love [God] because he first loved us." God's love, described in 1 Corinthians 13 (known as the "love chapter"), explains a characteristic of real love when it says, "Love never fails" (v. 8).

Faith and hope are essential to the believer. It is only because we are justified by *faith* that "we have peace with God through our Lord Jesus Christ" (ROM. 5:1). And *hope* is described in Hebrews 6 as "an anchor for the soul, firm and secure" (v. 19).

One day we will have no need of faith and hope. Faith will become sight and our hope will be realized when we see our Savior face to face. But love is eternal, for love is *of* God and God *is* love (1 JOHN 4:7–8). "Now these three remain: faith, hope and love. But the greatest of these is love"—it's first and last (1 COR. 13:13). *CINDY HESS KASPER*

Thank you, Lord, for your faithful love and for the love of family and friends. Please help me find ways to show your love to others today.

We love because God first loved us.

Spiritual Checkup

Read: Colossians 3:1–14

Love the Lord your God with all your heart and with all your soul and with all your mind and with all your strength. —Mark 12:30

To detect health problems before they become serious, doctors recommend a routine physical exam. We can do the same for our spiritual health by asking a few questions rooted in the great commandment (MARK 12:30) Jesus referred to.

Do I love God with all my heart because He first loved me? Which is stronger, my desire for earthly gain or the treasures that are mine in Christ? (COL. 3:1). He desires that His peace rule our hearts.

Do I love God with all my soul? Do I listen to God telling me who I am? Am I moving away from self-centered desires? (v. 5). Am I becoming more compassionate, kind, humble, gentle, and patient? (v. 12).

Do I love God with all my mind? Do I focus on my relationship with His Son or do I let my mind wander wherever it wants to go? (v. 2). Do my thoughts lead to problems or solutions? To unity or division? Forgiveness or revenge? (v. 13).

Do I love God with all my strength? Am I willing to be seen as weak so that God can show His strength on my behalf? (v. 17). Am I relying on His grace to be strong in His Spirit?

As we let "the message of Christ dwell among [us] richly . . . with all wisdom" (v. 16), He will equip us to build each other up as we become spiritually fit and useful to Him.

JULIE ACKERMAN LINK

Heavenly Father, when I rely on anything other than love in my efforts to initiate change in people, I am neglecting to love you with all my heart, soul, mind, and strength. I choose today to exchange my strength for yours.

To be spiritually fit, feed on God's Word and exercise your faith.

Not My Worry

Read: Isaiah 40:25–31

Cast your cares on the Lord and he will sustain you. —*Psalm 55:22*

A man worried constantly about everything. Then one day his friends heard him whistling happily and looking noticeably relaxed. "What happened?" they asked him in astonishment.

He said, "I'm paying a man to do my worrying for me."

"How much do you pay him?" they asked.

"Two thousand dollars a week," he replied.

"Wow! How can you afford that?"

"I can't," he said, "but that's his worry."

While this humorous way to handle stress doesn't work in real life, as God's children we can turn our worries over to Someone who has everything perfectly under control even—especially—when we feel it is not.

The prophet Isaiah reminds us that God brings out the stars and calls them all by name (40:25–26). Because of "his great power and mighty strength" not one of them is missing (v. 26). And just as God knows the stars by name, He knows us individually and personally. We are each under His watchful care (v. 27).

If we are inclined to worry, we can turn that worry over to the Lord. He is never too weary or too tired to pay attention to us. He has all wisdom and all power, and He loves to use it on our behalf. The Holy One who directs the stars has His loving arms around us. *Poh Fang Chia*

Lord, you know there are times when I get really scared.
And I forget that you have promised that you will never leave me
to face difficulty or loss alone. Help me to trust.

Worry ends where faith begins.

Burning Questions

Read: Exodus 3:1–6, 10–14

"I AM WHO I AM." —v. 14

An old Native American story tells of a young boy who was sent into the woods alone on an autumn night to prove his courage. Soon the sky darkened and the sounds of night filled the air. Trees creaked and groaned, an owl screeched, and a coyote howled. Even though he was frightened, the boy remained in the woods all night, as the test of courage required. Finally morning came, and he saw a solitary figure nearby. It was his grandfather, who had been watching over him all night long.

When Moses went deep into the desert, he saw a burning bush that didn't burn up. Then God began talking to him from the bush, commissioning him to go back to Egypt and lead the Israelites out of cruel slavery to freedom. A reluctant Moses began to ask questions: "Who am I that I should go?"

God simply answered, "I will be with you."

"Suppose I . . . say to them, 'The God of your fathers has sent me to you,' and they ask me, 'What is his name?' Then what shall I tell them?"

God replied, "I AM WHO I AM. . . . [Say to them], 'I AM has sent me to you'" (EX. 3:11–14). The phrase "I AM WHO I AM" can be interpreted, "I will be who I will be" and reveals God's eternal and all-sufficient character.

God has promised always to be present with those who believe in Jesus. No matter how dark the night, the unseen God is ready to respond appropriately to our need. *DAVE EGNER*

Dear Father, thank you for your never-changing character.

God is always present and at work.

All Safe! All Well!

Read: Hebrews 11:8–16

Now faith is confidence in what we hope for and assurance about what we do not see. —v. 1

In January 1915, the ship *Endurance* was trapped and crushed in the ice off the coast of Antarctica. The group of polar explorers, led by Ernest Shackleton, survived and managed to reach Elephant Island in three small lifeboats. Trapped on this uninhabited island, far from normal shipping lanes, they had one hope. On April 24, 1916, 22 men watched as Shackleton and five comrades set out in a tiny lifeboat for South Georgia, an island 800 miles away. The odds seemed impossible, and if they failed, they would all certainly die. What joy, then, when more than *four months* later a boat appeared on the horizon with Shackleton on its bow shouting, "Are you all well?" And the call came back, "All safe! All well!"

What held those men together and kept them alive over those months? Faith and hope placed in one man. They believed that Shackleton would find a way to save them.

This human example of faith and hope echoes the faith of the heroes listed in Hebrews 11. Their faith in the "substance of things hoped for, the evidence of things not seen" kept them going through great difficulties and trials (HEB. 11:1 NKJV).

As we look out upon the horizon of our own problems, may we not despair. May we have hope through the certainty of our faith in the One Man—Jesus, our God and Savior. *RANDY KILGORE*

Thank you, Father, for the promise of forgiveness made possible by Jesus. May that promise lighten the darkest of our days.

The hope of Jesus shines brightly even on our darkest day.

God's Direction

Read: Proverbs 3:1–8

In all your ways acknowledge Him, and He shall direct your paths. —v. 6 NKJV

A century ago, 41-year-old Oswald Chambers arrived in Egypt to serve as a YMCA chaplain to British Commonwealth troops during World War I. He was assigned to a camp at Zeitoun, six miles north of Cairo. On his first night there, October 27, 1915, Chambers wrote in his diary, "This [area] is absolutely desert in the very heart of the troops and a glorious opportunity for men. It is all immensely unlike anything I have been used to, and I am watching with interest the new things God will do and engineer."

Chambers believed and practiced the words of Proverbs 3:5-6: "Trust in the LORD with all your heart, and lean not on your own understanding; in all your ways acknowledge Him, and He shall direct your paths" (NKJV).

This is both a comfort and a challenge. There is security in knowing that the Lord will lead us each day, but we must not become so attached to our plans that we resist God's redirection or His timing.

"We have no right to judge where we should be put, or to have preconceived notions as to what God is fitting us for," said Chambers. "God engineers everything. Wherever He puts us, our one great aim is to pour out a whole-hearted devotion to Him in that particular work."

DAVID MCCASLAND

Lord, may I love and serve you with all my heart
where you have placed me today.

As we trust in God, He directs our steps.

Treasures in Heaven

Read: Matthew 6:19–24

Lay up for yourselves treasures in heaven, where neither moth nor rust destroys and where thieves do not break in and steal. —v. 20 NKJV

Poorly installed electric wiring caused a fire that burned down our newly built home. The flames leveled our house within an hour, leaving nothing but rubble. Another time, we returned home from church one Sunday to find our house had been broken into and some of our possessions stolen.

In our imperfect world, loss of material wealth is all too common—vehicles are stolen or crashed, ships sink, buildings crumble, homes are flooded, and personal belongings are stolen. This makes Jesus's admonition not to put our trust in earthly wealth very meaningful (MATT. 6:19).

Jesus told a story of a man who accumulated abundant treasures and decided to store up everything for himself (LUKE 12:16–21). "Take life easy," the man told himself; "eat, drink and be merry" (v. 19). But that night he lost everything, including his life. In conclusion, Jesus said, "This is how it will be with whoever stores up things for themselves but is not rich toward God" (v. 21).

Material wealth is temporary. Nothing lasts forever—except what our God enables us to do for others. Giving of our time and resources to spread the good news, visiting those who are lonely, and helping those in need are just some of the many ways to store up treasure in heaven (MATT. 6:20).

LAWRENCE DARMANI

In what ways are you storing up treasures in heaven?
How might you change and grow in this area of your life?

Our real wealth is what we invest for eternity.

The Rugged Road

Read: Psalm 25:4–11

Ask where the good way is, and walk in it, and you will find rest for your souls. –Jeremiah 6:16

A fishing buddy of mine told me about an alpine lake located high on the north flank of Jughandle Mountain here in Idaho. Rumor had it that large cutthroat trout lurked up there. My friend got a pencil and scrap of napkin and drew a map for me. Several weeks later I gassed up my truck and set out to follow his directions.

His map put me on one of the worst roads I've ever driven! It was an old logging road that had been bulldozed through the forest and never regraded. Washouts, fallen timber, deep ruts, and large rocks battered my spine and bent the undercarriage of my truck. It took half a morning to reach my destination, and when I finally arrived I asked myself, "Why would a *friend* send me up a road like this?"

But the lake was magnificent and the fish were indeed large and scrappy! My friend had put me on the right road—one I would have chosen myself and patiently endured had I known what I knew at the end.

There is a faithful saying: "All the ways of the Lord are loving and faithful toward those who keep the demands of his covenant" (PS. 25:10). Some of God's paths for us are rough and rugged, others tedious and boring, but all are filled with His love and faithfulness. When we come to the end of our journey and know what we then will know, we will say, "God's path was best for me."

DAVID ROPER

Father, we don't see the end of the road, but you do. We trust you for what we can't see. We know that you are bringing us through it.

Our path may have obstacles, but God will lead us.

The Cross and the Crown

Read: John 19:21–30

I am the resurrection and the life. The one who believes in me will live, even though they die. —11:25

Westminster Abbey in London has a rich historical background. In the 10th century, Benedictine monks began a tradition of daily worship there that still continues today. The Abbey is also the burial place of many famous people, and every English monarch since AD 1066 has been crowned at the Abbey. In fact, 17 of those monarchs are also buried there—their rule ending where it began.

No matter how grandiose their burial, world rulers rise and fall; they live and die. But another king, Jesus, though once dead, is no longer buried. In His first coming, Jesus was crowned with thorns and crucified as the "king of the Jews" (JOHN 19:3, 19). Because Jesus rose from the dead in victory, we who are believers in Christ have hope beyond the grave and the assurance that we will live with Him forever. Jesus said, "I am the resurrection and the life. The one who believes in me will live, even though they die; and whoever lives by believing in me will never die" (11:25–26).

We serve a risen King! May we gladly yield to His rule in our lives now as we look forward to the day when the "Lord God Almighty" will reign for all eternity (REV. 19:6).

BILL CROWDER

Thank you, Jesus, for rising from the dead and that you are alive forever.

Jesus's resurrection spelled the death of death.

Waiting for an Answer

Read: Psalm 9:1–10

Those who know your name trust in you, for you, Lord, have never forsaken those who seek you. —v. 10

When our daughter was 15, she ran away. She was gone more than 3 weeks. Those were the longest 3 weeks of our lives. We looked everywhere for her and sought help from law enforcement and friends. During those desperate days, my wife and I learned the importance of waiting on God in prayer. We had come to the end of our strength and resources. We had to rely on God.

It was on a Father's Day that we found her. We were in a restaurant parking lot, on our way to dinner, when the phone rang. A waitress at another restaurant had spotted her. Our daughter was only three blocks away. We soon had her home, safe and sound.

We have to wait on God when we pray. We may not know how or when He will answer, but we can put our hearts constantly before Him. Sometimes the answers don't come when we would hope. Things may even go from bad to worse. But we have to persevere, keep believing, and keep asking.

Waiting is never easy, but the end result, whatever it is, will be worth it. David put it this way: "Those who know your name trust in you, for you, Lord, have never forsaken those who seek you" (Ps. 9:10). Keep seeking. Keep trusting. Keep asking. Keep praying. *James Banks*

What's on your heart that you need to talk to God about today?
Will you trust Him and keep praying?

Time spent in prayer is always time well spent.

An Inside View

Read: 1 Samuel 16:1–7

The Lord looks at the heart. —v. 7

Retired physicist Arie van't Riet creates works of art in an unusual way. He arranges plants and deceased animals in various compositions and then x-rays them. He scans the developed x-rays into a computer and then adds color to certain parts of his pictures. His artwork reveals the inner complexity of flowers, fish, birds, reptiles, and monkeys.

An inside view of something is often more fascinating and more significant than an exterior view. At first glance, Samuel thought Eliab looked like he could be Israel's next king (1 SAM. 16:6). But God warned Samuel not to look at Eliab's physical traits. He told Samuel, "People look at the outward appearance, but the LORD looks at the heart" (v. 7). God chose David, instead of Eliab, to be Israel's next king.

When God looks at us, He is more interested in our hearts than our height, the state of our soul than the structure of our face. He doesn't see us as too old, too young, too small, or too big. He zeroes in on the things that matter—our response to His love for us and our concern for other people (MATT. 22:37–39). Second Chronicles 6:30 says that God alone knows the human heart. When the God who has done so much for us looks at our heart, what does He see?

JENNIFER BENSON SCHULDT

Dear God, help me to value what you value.
As I follow your example, I pray that you will be pleased
with what you see in my heart.

The true measure of a person is what's in the heart.

Pride at the Core

Read: Ezra 9:1–9

Ezra . . . was a teacher well versed in the Law of Moses. –7:6

"He thinks he's really something!" That was my friend's assessment of a fellow Christian we knew. We thought we saw in him a spirit of pride. We were saddened when we learned that he soon was caught in some serious misdeeds. By elevating himself, he had found nothing but trouble. We realized that could happen to us as well.

It can be easy to minimize the terrible sin of pride in our own hearts. The more we learn and the more success we enjoy, the more likely we are to think we're "really something." Pride is at the core of our nature.

In Scripture, Ezra is described as "a teacher well versed in the Law of Moses" (EZRA 7:6). King Artaxerxes appointed him to lead an expedition of Hebrew exiles back to Jerusalem. Ezra could have been a prime candidate to succumb to the sin of pride. Yet he didn't. Ezra didn't only know God's law; he lived it.

After his arrival in Jerusalem, Ezra learned that Jewish men had married women who served other gods, defying God's express directions (9:1–2). He tore his clothes in grief and prayed in heartfelt repentance (VV. 5–15). A higher purpose guided Ezra's knowledge and position: his love for God and for His people. He prayed, "Here we are before you in our guilt, though because of it not one of us can stand in your presence" (V. 15).

Ezra understood the scope of their sins. But in humility he repented and trusted in the goodness of our forgiving God. *TIM GUSTAFSON*

Lord, fill us with such a love for you that we think first of what will please you, not ourselves. Free us from the subtle captivity of our own pride.

Pride leads to every other vice: It is the complete anti-God state of mind.

C. S. LEWIS

The Joy of Your Presence

Read: Psalm 145:1–18

Great is the LORD and most worthy of praise; he is to be feared above all gods. –96:4

"Man's chief end is to glorify God and enjoy Him forever," says the Westminster Catechism. Much of Scripture calls for joyful gratitude and adoration of the living God. When we honor God, we celebrate Him as the Source from which all goodness flows.

When we praise God from our heart we find ourselves in that joyful state for which we were created. Just as a beautiful sunset or a peaceful pastoral scene points to the majesty of the Creator, so worship draws us into a close spiritual union with Him. The psalmist says, "Great is the LORD and most worthy of praise . . . . The LORD is near to all who call on him" (PS. 145:3, 18).

God does not need our praise, but we need to praise God. By basking in His presence we drink in the joy of His infinite love and rejoice in the One who came to redeem and restore us. "In your presence there is fullness of joy," the psalmist says. "At your right hand are pleasures forevermore" (PS. 16:11 ESV).

DENNIS FISHER

Dear Lord, you are the great and mighty God,
the Creator of the universe. I will praise your name always.
There is no God besides you.

Worship is a heart overflowing with praise to God.

October 23

For This I Have Jesus

Read: Isaiah 49:13–20

The LORD comforts his people and will have compassion on his afflicted ones. —v. 13

There is rarely a problem-free season in our lives, but sometimes the onslaught is terrifying.

Rose saw her entire family, except for her two little daughters, slaughtered in the Rwandan Genocide of 1994. Now she is a widow among many widows with little money. But she refuses to be defeated. She has adopted two orphans and simply trusts God to provide for the food and school fees for her family of five. She translates Christian literature into the local language and organizes an annual conference for other widows. Rose wept as she told me her story. But for every problem in her life she has one simple remedy. "For this," she said, "I have Jesus."

God knows exactly what you are facing today. Isaiah reminds us that God's knowledge of us is so intimate that it is as if our names were written on the palms of His hands (ISA. 49:16). We may sometimes neglect the needs of others, even those who are closest to us, but God is aware of every detail of our lives. And He has given us His Spirit to guide, to comfort, and to strengthen us.

Think of the challenges you face at this moment, and then write these words beside each one as a reminder of His faithfulness and care: "For this, I have Jesus." *MARION STROUD*

Thank you, Jesus, for being near to me right now.
I'm grateful for your faithfulness.

Life takes on perspective in the light of Christ.

Becoming Invisible

Read: Exodus 2:11–22

There is a time for everything, and a season for every activity under the heavens. —Ecclesiastes 3:1

Where I live, this is the time of year when plants defy death by remaining underground until it is safe to come out again. Before the snow comes and the ground freezes, they let go of their beautiful blooms and retreat to a place where they can rest and save energy for the next growing season. Contrary to the way it looks, they are not dead; they are dormant. When the snow melts and the ground thaws, they will again lift their heads toward heaven, greeting their Creator with brilliant colors and sweet fragrances.

The seasons of life require that we sometimes enter a period of dormancy. We are not dead, but we may feel we've become invisible. During such times we may feel useless, and we may wonder whether God will ever use us again. But periods like this are for our protection and preparation. When the time is right and the conditions are safe, God will call us once again to service and worship.

Moses experienced a period of time like this. After killing an Egyptian who harmed a fellow Hebrew, Moses had to flee for his life to the distant land of the Midianites (EX. 2:11–22). There, God protected him and prepared him for the biggest assignment of his life (3:10).

So be encouraged. We are never invisible to God.

JULIE ACKERMAN LINK

Savior, like a shepherd lead us, much we need Thy tender care;
in Thy pleasant pastures feed us, for our use Thy folds prepare.
DOROTHY A. THRUPP

No one is invisible to God.

Behind the Scenes

Read: John 3:22–31

He must become greater; I must become less. –v. 30

The outreach activities of our church culminated with a city-wide service. As the team that had organized and led the events—comprised of our youth music group, counselors, and church leaders—walked onto the stage, we all excitedly applauded and poured out our appreciation for their hard work.

One man, however, was hardly noticeable, yet he was the leader of the team. When I saw him a few days later, I thanked and congratulated him for his work and said, "We hardly noticed you during the program."

"I like to work in the background," he said. He was not concerned with getting recognition for himself. It was time for those who did the work to receive appreciation.

His quiet demeanor was an entire sermon to me. It was a reminder that when serving the Lord, I need not seek to be recognized. I can give honor to God whether or not I'm openly appreciated by others. A Christ-first attitude can subdue any petty jealousies or unhealthy competition.

Jesus, who is "above all" (JOHN 3:31), "must become greater; I must become less" (v. 30). When we have this attitude, we will seek the progress of God's work. It is Christ, not us, who should be the focus of all we do.

LAWRENCE DARMANI

Jesus, be the center of my thoughts, desires, and actions.
Control me and use me.

The spotlight is the place for Christ.

Hidden in My Heart

Read: Psalm 119:9–16

I have hidden your word in my heart. —v. 11

I'm getting used to reading digital magazines, and I feel good that I'm saving trees. Plus, I don't have to wait for the magazines to come in the mail. I do, however, miss the print editions because I like to run my fingers through the glossy pages and cut out my favorite recipes.

I also have a digital edition of the Bible on my reading device. But I still have my favorite printed Bible—the one I have underlined and read many times. We don't know the future of the printed page, but one thing we do know: The best place for God's Word is not on our cell phones, electronic reading devices, or bedside table.

In Psalm 119 we read about treasuring the Scriptures in our hearts: "I have hidden your word in my heart" (v. 11). Nothing compares to pondering God's Word, learning more of Him, and putting it into practice in our daily lives. The best place for His Word lies deep in our souls.

We may have many excuses for not reading, meditating, or memorizing, but we need God's Word. I pray that God will help us store His Word in the best place possible—our hearts. *KEILA OCHOA*

Lord, give me the desire to read your Word.
Then implant it in my heart and thoughts and help me live it out.

The best place for God's Word is our hearts.

You Missed the Chance

Read: 1 Corinthians 13

If I have the gift of prophecy and can fathom all mysteries and all knowledge, and if I have a faith that can move mountains, but do not have love, I am nothing. —v. 2

I heard the saddest words today. Two believers in Christ were discussing an issue about which they had differing opinions. The older of the two seemed smug as he wielded Scripture like a weapon, chopping away at the things he saw as wrong in the other's life. The younger man just seemed weary of the lecture, weary of the other person, and discouraged.

As the exchange drew to a close, the older man commented on the other's apparent disinterest. "You used to be eager," he started, and then abruptly quit. "I don't know what it is you want."

"You missed the chance to love me," the young man said. "In all the time you've known me, what has seemed to matter most to you is pointing out what you think is wrong about me. What do I want? I want to see Jesus—in you and through you."

Had this been said to me, I thought, *I would have been devastated.* In that moment I knew the Holy Spirit was telling me there had been people I had missed the chance to love. And I knew there were people who couldn't see Jesus in me either.

The apostle Paul tells us that love must be the underlying motive in anything we do; in *everything* we do (1 COR. 13:1–4). Let's not miss the next chance to show love. *RANDY KILGORE*

Ask the Holy Spirit to show you today who it is you've missed the chance to love. Then ask Him to give you another opportunity. Start your conversation with these words: "I'm sorry . . ."

Love beats lectures every time.

Where Is My Focus?

Read: Hebrews 10:32–39

You suffered . . . , because you knew that you yourselves had better and lasting possessions. —v. 34

Early in September 2011, a raging wildfire destroyed 600 homes in and around the city of Bastrop in central Texas. A few weeks later an article in the Austin *American-Statesman* newspaper carried this headline: "People who lost the most, focus on what wasn't lost." The article described the community's outpouring of generosity and the realization of those who received help that neighbors, friends, and community were worth far more than anything they lost.

The writer of Hebrews reminded first-century followers of Jesus to recall how they had bravely endured persecution early in their life of faith. They stood their ground in the face of insults and oppression, standing side by side with other believers (HEB. 10:32–33). "You suffered along with those in prison and joyfully accepted the confiscation of your property, because you knew that you yourselves had better and lasting possessions" (V. 34). Their focus was not on what they had lost but on eternal things that could not be taken from them.

Jesus told His followers, "Where your treasure is, there your heart will be also" (MATT. 6:21). As we focus on the Lord and all that we have in Him, even our most precious possessions can be held lightly. *DAVID MCCASLAND*

Lord, open our eyes to see you and to embrace what is most important each day.

Where is your focus today?

Don't Touch the Fence!

Read: Jeremiah 18:1–12

The LORD . . . sent word to them . . . again and again, because he had pity on his people. —2 Chronicles 36:15

As a young girl I went with my parents to visit my great-grandmother, who lived near a farm. Her yard was enclosed by an electric fence, which prevented cows from grazing on her grass. When I asked my parents if I could play outside, they consented, but explained that touching the fence would result in an electric shock.

Unfortunately I ignored their warning, put a finger to the barbed wire, and was zapped by an electrical current strong enough to teach a cow a lesson. I knew then that my parents had warned me because they loved me and didn't want me to get hurt.

When God saw the ancient Israelites in Jerusalem crafting and worshiping idols, He "sent word to them . . . again and again, because he had pity on his people" (2 CHRON. 36:15). God spoke through the prophet Jeremiah, but the people said, "We will continue with our own plans" (JER. 18:12). Because of this, God allowed Nebuchadnezzar to destroy Jerusalem and capture most of its inhabitants.

Maybe God is warning you today about some sin in your life. If so, be encouraged. That is proof of His compassion for us (HEB. 12:5–6). He sees what's ahead and wants us to avoid the problems that will come.

JENNIFER BENSON SCHULDT

Lord, give me the ability to hear not just your words but also your heart. Help me to learn from the mistakes of those whose stories you have given us. Help me to honor you with my life.

God's warnings are to protect us, not to punish us.

The Storms of Life

Read: Mark 4:35–5:1

You may have had to suffer grief in all kinds of trials. These have come so that the proven genuineness of your faith . . . may result in praise, glory and honor when Jesus Christ is revealed. –1 Peter 1:6-7

In the book of Mark we read about a terrible storm. The disciples were with Jesus on a boat crossing the Sea of Galilee. When a "furious squall came up," the disciples—among them some seasoned fishermen—were afraid for their lives (4:37–38). Did God not care? Weren't they handpicked by Jesus and closest to Him? Weren't they obeying Jesus who told them to "go over to the other side"? (v. 35). Why, then, were they going through such a turbulent time?

No one is exempt from the storms of life. But just as the disciples who initially feared the storm later came to revere Christ more, so the storms we face can bring us to a deeper knowledge of God. "Who is this," the disciples pondered, "even the wind and the waves obey him!" (v. 41). Through our trials we can learn that no storm is big enough to prevent God from accomplishing His will (5:1).

While we may not understand why God allows trials to enter our lives, we thank Him that through them we can come to know who He is. We live to serve Him because He has preserved our lives. *ALBERT LEE*

Lord, I know I don't need to fear the storms of life around me.
Help me to be calm because I stand secure in you.

The storms of life prove the strength of our anchor.

Repair or Replace?

Read: 2 Corinthians 5:14–21

If anyone is in Christ, he is a new creation. —v. 17 NKJV

It was time to fix the trim on the windows of our house. So I scraped, sanded, and applied wood filler to get the aging trim ready for paint. After all of my efforts—including a coat of primer and some too-expensive paint—the trim looks, well, pretty good. But it doesn't look new. The only way to make the trim look new would be to replace the old wood.

It's okay to have weather-damaged window trim that looks "pretty good" to our eye. But when it comes to our sin-damaged hearts, it's not enough to try to fix things up. From God's point of view, we need all things to become new (2 COR. 5:17).

That is the beauty of salvation through faith in Jesus. He died on the cross as a sacrifice for our sin and rose from the dead to display His power over sin and death. The result is that in God's eyes, faith in Christ's work makes us a "new creation" (2 COR. 5:17) and replaces the old with a "new life" (ACTS 5:20). Looking through Jesus and His work on the cross for us, our heavenly Father sees everyone who has put his or her faith in Him as new and unblemished.

Sin has caused great damage. We can't fix it ourselves. We must trust Jesus as Savior and let Him give us a brand-new life. *DAVE BRANON*

Heavenly Father, I understand that sin has damaged my heart.
I put my trust in the Savior's sacrifice and ask you to
wash away my sins and make me a new person.
Thank you for what Jesus did for me.

Only Jesus can give you a new life.

Water and Life

Read: John 4:1–15

Jesus answered, "Everyone who drinks this water will be thirsty again, but whoever drinks the water I give them will never thirst." —vv. 13–14

As Dave Mueller reached down and turned the handle, water rushed from the spigot into a blue bucket. Around him people applauded. They celebrated as they saw fresh, clean water flowing in their community for the first time. Having a clean source of water was about to change the lives of this group of people in Kenya.

Dave and his wife, Joy, work hard to meet people's needs by bringing them water. But they don't stop with H_2O. As they help bring people clean water, they also tell them about Jesus Christ.

Two thousand years ago, a man named Jesus stood at a Samaritan well and talked with a woman who was there to get clean drinking water for her physical health. But Jesus told her that what she needed even more than that was living water for her spiritual health.

As history has marched on and humanity has become more sophisticated, life still filters down to two truths: Without clean water, we will die. More important, without Jesus Christ, the source of living water, we are already dead in our sins.

Water is essential to our existence—both physically with H_2O and spiritually with Jesus. Have you tasted of the water of life that Jesus, the Savior, provides? *DAVE BRANON*

Thank you, Jesus, for being our living water. Thank you for your willingness to die on the cross and for your power to rise from the dead in order to provide us that water.

Only Jesus has the living water to quench our spiritual thirst.

Words of the Wise

Read: Ecclesiastes 9:13–18

Words of the wise, spoken quietly, should be heard. —v. 17 NKJV

My niece's husband recently wrote these words on a social media site: "I would say a lot more online if it weren't for this little voice that prompts me not to. As a follower of Jesus, you might think that little voice is the Holy Spirit. It isn't. It's my wife, Heidi."

With the smile comes a sobering thought. The cautions of a discerning friend can reflect the wisdom of God. Ecclesiastes 9 says that the "words of the wise, spoken quietly, should be heard" (v. 17 NKJV).

Scripture warns us not to be wise in our own eyes or proud (PROV. 3:7; ISA. 5:21; ROM. 12:16). In other words, let's not assume that we have all the answers! Proverbs 19:20 says, "Listen to advice and accept discipline, and at the end you will be counted among the wise." Whether it is a friend, a spouse, a pastor, or a co-worker, God can use others to teach us more of His wisdom.

"Wisdom reposes in the heart of the discerning," declares the book of Proverbs (14:33). Part of recognizing the Spirit's wisdom is discovering how to listen and learn from each other. *CINDY HESS KASPER*

Dear Lord, thank you for your Word that teaches me how to love you and others. Thank you also for the people you place in my life to remind me of your truth.

True wisdom begins and ends with God.

The Daily Grind

Read: Ephesians 6:5–9

Whatever you do, work at it with all your heart, as working for the Lord, not for human masters. —Colossians 3:23

The high school I attended required 4 years of Latin instruction. I appreciate the value of that discipline now, but back then it was a grind. Our teacher believed in drill and repetition. *"Repetitio est mater studiorum,"* she intoned over us several times a day, which simply means, "Repetition is the mother of learning." *"Repetitio est absurdum,"* we muttered under our breath. "Repetition is absurd."

I realize now that most of life is simply that: repetition—a round of dull, uninspiring, lackluster things we must do again and again. "Repetition is both as ordinary and necessary as bread," said Danish philosopher Søren Kierkegaard. But he went on to say, "It is the bread that satisfies with benediction."

It's a matter of taking up each duty, no matter how mundane, humble, or trivial, and asking God to bless it and put it to His intended purposes. In that way we take the drudgeries of life and turn them into holy work, filled with unseen, eternal consequence.

The poet Gerard Manley Hopkins said, "To lift up the hands in prayer gives God glory, but a man with a [pitchfork] in his hand, a woman with a slop pail, give Him glory, too. God is so great that all things give Him glory if you mean that they should."

If whatever we do is done for Christ, we'll be amazed at the joy and meaning we'll find in even the most ordinary tasks. *DAVID ROPER*

Remind us, Lord, that you are in the dull and ordinary tasks in a most extraordinary way. May we do even the smallest tasks for you.

A willing spirit changes the drudgery of duty into a labor of love.

Our Jealous God

Read: 2 Corinthians 11:1–4

The LORD, whose name is Jealous, is a jealous God. —Exodus 34:14

In 2014 a University of California researcher used a stuffed dog to show that animals are capable of jealousy. Professor Christine Harris asked dog owners to show affection for a stuffed animal in the presence of their pet. She found that three-fourths of the dogs responded with apparent envy. Some tried to get attention with touch or a gentle nudge. Others tried to push between their owner and the toy. A few went so far as to snap at their stuffed rival.

In a dog, jealousy seems heartwarming. In people, it can lead to less admirable results. Yet, as Moses and Paul remind us, there is also another jealousy—one that beautifully reflects the heart of God.

When Paul wrote to the church at Corinth, he said he was "jealous for you with a godly jealousy" (2 COR. 11:2). He didn't want them to be "led astray from [their] sincere and pure devotion to Christ" (v. 3). Such jealousy reflects the heart of God, who told Moses in the Ten Commandments, "I, the LORD your God, am a jealous God" (EX. 20:5).

God's jealousy is not like our self-centered love. His heart expresses His protective zeal for those who are His by creation and salvation. He made us and rescued us to know and enjoy Him forever. How could we ask for anything more than a God who is so zealous—and jealous—for our happiness?

MART DEHAAN

Father, help me shun anything that distracts me from you, so that I may always find enjoyment in who you are and in your plan for me.

God loves every one of us as if there were but one of us to love. AUGUSTINE

Angry Prayers

Read: Psalm 86:1–13

Fools give full vent to their rage, but the wise bring calm in the end. —Proverbs 29:11

The neighbors probably didn't know what to think as they looked out their windows at me one wintry day. I was standing in the driveway with a garden shovel clutched in my hands, whacking wildly and angrily at a clump of ice that had formed beneath a corner gutter. With each smack, I was uttering prayers that were variations on one theme: "I can't do this." "I don't have the strength to do this." As a caregiver, with a long list of responsibilities to handle, I now had this ice to deal with, and I had had enough!

My anger was wrapped around a bundle of lies: "I deserve better than this." "God isn't enough after all." "Nobody cares anyway." But when we choose to cling to our anger, we become mired in the trap of bitterness, never moving forward. And the only cure for anger is truth.

The truth is that God does not give us what we deserve; He gives us mercy instead. "You, Lord, are forgiving and good, abounding in love to all who call to you" (PS. 86:5). The truth is that God is more than enough, despite what we see. The truth is that His strength is sufficient (2 COR. 12:9). Yet before we can find such reassurance, we may need to step back, lay down the shovel of our own efforts, and take Jesus's hand that's extended to us in mercy and grace.

God is big enough to listen to our anger and loving enough to show us, in His time, the path forward. *SHELLY BEACH, GUEST WRITER*

Loving God, forgive me for my outbursts of anger. Today I choose to lay down my sinful anger and accept your mercy and grace.

SHELLY BEACH IS THE AUTHOR OF SEVERAL BOOKS, INCLUDING *PRECIOUS LORD, TAKE MY HAND: MEDITATIONS FOR CAREGIVERS.*

Grace: Getting what we don't deserve. Mercy: Not getting what we do deserve.

He Trains My Hands

Read: Exodus 4:10–17

Praise be to the Lord my Rock, who trains my hands for war, my fingers for battle. –Psalm 144:1

When former NBA player David Wood was playing for Taugrés de Baskonia, I was with him at a Spanish Basketball Cup final. Before one game, he read Psalm 144:1: "Praise be to the Lord my Rock, who trains my hands for war, my fingers for battle." He turned to me and said, "You see? It's as if God has written this verse just for me! He trains my hands to catch rebounds and my fingers to shoot!" David felt called to play basketball and had learned that God takes us as we are and enables us to do what He calls us to do.

We can easily dismiss ourselves as having little use to God because we feel we have nothing to offer. When God appeared to Moses and assigned him the task of telling the Israelites that He would deliver them from the Egyptians (EX. 3:16–17), Moses felt inadequate. He said to the Lord, "I have never been eloquent . . . . I am slow of speech and tongue" (4:10). Perhaps Moses had some kind of speech impediment, or he was just afraid, but God overcame his inadequacy with His sufficiency. God said, "Now go; I will help you speak and will teach you what to say" (v. 12).

All God wants from us is to follow His plans. He will sort out the rest. In His mighty hands, you can be a blessing to others.

JAIME FERNÁNDEZ GARRIDO, GUEST WRITER

Here I am, Lord, ready to serve you in whatever way you desire. Lead me.

DR. JAIME FERNÁNDEZ GARRIDO IS DIRECTOR OF THE EVANGELICAL RADIO AND TELEVISION PROGRAM *BORN AGAIN*, AUTHOR OF VARIOUS BOOKS, AND COMPOSER OF MORE THAN 400 HYMNS AND CHORUSES.

God's call to a task includes His strength to complete it.

Mention the Name

Read: Acts 4:5–20

I am in the Father, and . . . the Father is in me. –John 14:10

A church group invited a speaker to address their meeting. "Talk about God," the group leader told him, "but leave out Jesus."

"Why?" the man asked, taken aback.

"Well," the leader explained, "some of our prominent members feel uncomfortable with Jesus. Just use God and we'll be fine."

Accepting such instructions, however, was a problem for the speaker who said later, "Without Jesus, I have no message."

Something similar was asked of followers of Jesus in the days of the early church. Local religious leaders conferred together to warn the disciples not to speak about Jesus (ACTS 4:17). But the disciples knew better. "We cannot help speaking about what we have seen and heard," they said (v. 20).

To claim to believe in God and not in His Son Jesus Christ is a contradiction in terms. In John 10:30, Jesus clearly describes the unique relationship between himself and God: "I and the Father are one"—thus establishing His deity. That is why He could say, "You believe in God; believe also in me" (JOHN 14:1). Paul knew that Jesus is the very nature of God and equal with God (PHIL. 2:6).

We need not shy away from the name Jesus, for "salvation is found in no one else, for there is no other name under heaven given to mankind by which we must be saved" (ACTS 4:12). *LAWRENCE DARMANI*

Jesus, you are God. Thank you for showing yourself to us in the Bible and in our lives. You have done so much for us. Help us to share with others what we know of you and have experienced of you.

The name of Jesus is at the heart of our faith and our hope.

Bringing Our Friends to Jesus

Read: Mark 2:1–12

When Jesus saw their faith, he said to the paralyzed man, "Son, your sins are forgiven." –v. 5

During my childhood, one of the most feared diseases was polio, often called "infantile paralysis" because most of those infected were young children. Before a preventive vaccine was developed in the mid-1950s, some 20,000 people were paralyzed by polio and about 1,000 died from it each year in the United States alone.

In ancient times, paralysis was viewed as a permanent, hopeless condition. But one group of men believed Jesus could help their paralyzed friend. While Jesus was teaching in the village of Capernaum, four of the men carried the man to Him. When they couldn't reach Jesus because of the crowd, "they made an opening in the roof above Jesus by digging through it and then lowered the mat the man was lying on" (MARK 2:1–4).

"When Jesus saw their faith, he said to the paralyzed man, 'Son, your sins are forgiven'" (v. 5), followed by "Get up, take your mat and go home" (v. 11). How remarkable that in response to the faith of the men who brought their friend, Jesus forgave his sins and healed his incurable condition!

When someone we know is facing serious physical difficulty or a spiritual crisis, it is our privilege to join together in prayer, bringing our friends to Jesus—the only One who can meet their deepest needs.

DAVID MCCASLAND

Lord Jesus, we know that you can speak the words of eternal life and healing to people in great need. We bring them to you in prayer today.

Praying for others is a privilege—and a responsibility.

Charity Island

Read: Psalm 107:23–32

The LORD is good, a refuge in times of trouble. He cares for those who trust in him. —Nahum 1:7

Charity Island is the largest island in Saginaw Bay in the Michigan waters of Lake Huron. For many years the island has provided a lighthouse for navigational aid and a safe harbor for those sailing these waters. The island received its name because sailors believed it was there "through the charity of God."

Sometimes in life we have to navigate through seas of troubling circumstances. Like those sailors we need guidance and a place of safety; we might wish for our own Charity Island. The psalmist understood that God is the one who can bring tranquility to troubled waters and guide us to safe harbors. He wrote, "He stilled the storm to a whisper; the waves of the sea were hushed. They were glad when it grew calm, and he guided them to their desired haven" (PS. 107:29–30).

While no one asks for the storms of life, they can multiply our appreciation for the guidance and refuge God provides. He offers the light of His Spirit and His Word to guide us. It is the safe harbor of His love that we long for. He alone can be our ultimate "Charity Island." *DENNIS FISHER*

Father, help me to seek your light to guide me through the storms of life.

The living God will always be our shelter.

Gentle Lights

Read: 1 Peter 3:13–17

Let your light shine before others, that they may see your good deeds and glorify your Father in heaven. —Matthew 5:16

Wang Xiaoying (pronounced Shao-ying) lives in a rural area of China's Yunnan province. Due to health problems, her husband couldn't find work in the fields, causing hardship for the family. Her mother-in-law attributed the trouble to Xiaoying's faith in God. So she mistreated Xiaoying and urged her to go back to the traditional religion of her ancestors.

But because Xiaoying's husband had observed her transformed life, he said, "Mother, it isn't enough for Xiaoying alone to believe in God; we too should put our faith in God!" Because of the noticeable change in his wife, he is now considering the good news of Jesus.

People will watch our walk before listening to our talk. The best witness combines good behavior with appropriate words, reflecting the difference Christ makes in our lives.

This was the apostle Peter's instruction on how we can introduce Jesus to a hostile world. He challenged his readers to be "eager to do good" (1 PETER 3:13), to live obediently in Christ, to have a good conscience, and to be prepared to explain to others why we have such hope (v. 15). If we do this, we have no reason to fear when people mistreat or slander us because of our beliefs.

Whatever our situation, let's shine for Jesus where we are. He can provide the grace we need to reach even those who don't agree with us.

POH FANG CHIA

Lord, we tend to react defensively when people shun us or attack us for our faith. Give us your courage to offer wise and gentle responses.

The more we live like Jesus, the more others will be drawn to Him.

Crumbs of Time

Read: Daniel 6:10–23

Three times a day he got down on his knees and prayed, giving thanks to his God, just as he had done before. —v. 10

A friend was coming to town. He is a very busy man and his schedule was tight, but after a difficult day in important meetings, he managed to see my family for half an hour for a quick and late dinner. We enjoyed his visit, but I remember looking at my plate and thinking, "We only got the crumbs of his time."

Then I remembered how many times God gets the crumbs of my time—sometimes just the last minutes before I fall asleep.

Daniel was a busy man. He held a high government position in the ancient kingdom of Babylon, and I'm sure he had a full schedule. However, he had developed the habit of spending time with God—praying three times a day, praising God, and thanking Him. This routine helped him develop a strong faith that did not waver when he faced persecution (DAN. 6).

God desires a relationship with us. In the morning we can invite Him into our day, and then we can praise Him and ask Him for His help throughout the day. At other times we can treasure some time alone with Him and reflect on His faithfulness. As we spend time with God in prayer and in His Word, we grow in our relationship with Him and learn to become more and more like Him. As time with God becomes a priority, we enjoy His company more and more. *KEILA OCHOA*

Dear Father, I want to have an intimate relationship with you. I invite you to be part of my entire day—from the time I awake until I go to sleep.

Those who hope in the LORD will renew their strength. ISAIAH 40:31

Of Geese and Difficult People

Read: Romans 12:14–21

If it is possible, as far as it depends on you, live at peace with everyone. —v. 18

When we first moved into our present home, I enjoyed the beauty of the geese that nest nearby. I admired the way they cared for each other and the way they moved in straight lines in the water and in majestic V-formations in the air. It was also a joy to watch them raise their young.

Then summer came, and I discovered some less beautiful truths about my feathered friends. You see, geese love to eat grass, and they don't really care if it ruins the look of the lawn. Worse, what they leave behind makes a stroll across the yard a messy adventure.

I think of these geese when I'm dealing with difficult people. Sometimes I wish I could simply shoo them out of my life. It's then that God usually reminds me that there is beauty in even the most difficult person if we can get close enough to discover it, and the pain they're giving out may be reflective of the pain they are feeling. The apostle Paul says in Romans, "If it is possible, as far as it depends on you, live at peace with everyone" (12:18). So I ask God to help me be patient with the "hard side" of others. This doesn't always produce a happy outcome, but it is remarkable how often God redeems these relationships.

As we encounter difficult people, by God's grace we can see and love them through His eyes. *RANDY KILGORE*

By your grace, Lord, help me to live peaceably with others. And help me to recognize when I'm the difficult person in other people's lives and need your intervention. Give me the will and desire to change.

Peace can come if we respond with a gentle answer.

The Big Stink

Read: Genesis 3:6–13, 22–24

God knows that when you eat from it your eyes will be opened, and you will be like God, knowing good and evil. —v. 5

In August 2013, large crowds gathered at the Phipps Conservatory in Pittsburgh, Pennsylvania, to witness the blooming of the tropical plant known as the corpse flower. Since the flower is native to Indonesia, and may flower only once every several years, its blooming is a spectacle. Once open, the huge spiky, beautiful, red bloom smells like rotten meat. Because of its putrid fragrance, the flower attracts flies and beetles that are looking for rotting meat. But there is no nectar.

Like the corpse flower, sin holds out promises but in the end offers no rewards. Adam and Eve found this out the hard way. Eden was beautiful until they ruined it by doing the one thing God urged them not to do. Tempted to doubt God's goodness, they ignored their Creator's loving warning and soon lost their innocence. The God-given beauty of the tree of the knowledge of good and evil became like a corpse flower to them. The reward for their disobedience was alienation, pain, emptiness, toil, and death.

Sin looks inviting and may feel good, but it doesn't compare with the wonder, beauty, and fragrance of trusting and obeying God, who has made us to share His life and joy. *MARVIN WILLIAMS*

What temptations are you facing today?
Remember that God promises to help you fight against temptation.
Ask Him to help you remember to rely on Him.

God's commands can overpower Satan's suggestions.

The Mighty Finns

Read: Isaiah 37:30–38

Lord our God, deliver us from his hand, so that all the kingdoms of the earth may know that you, Lord, are the only God. —v. 20

It began as a distant, foreboding hum, then grew into an ominous, earth-rattling din. Soon hundreds of tanks and thousands of enemy infantrymen swarmed into view of the badly outnumbered soldiers in Finland. Assessing the murderous wave, an anonymous Finn lent some perspective. Courageously, he wondered aloud about the enemy: "Where will we find room to bury them all?"

Some 2,600 years before Finland showed such pluck in that World War II battle, an anxious Judean citizenry reacted quite differently to their own overwhelming situation. The Assyrian armies had trapped the people of Jerusalem inside its walls, where they faced the hopeless prospect of a starvation-inducing siege. Hezekiah nearly panicked. But then he prayed, "Lord Almighty, the God of Israel, enthroned between the cherubim, you alone are God over all the kingdoms of the earth" (ISA. 37:16).

Through the prophet Isaiah, the Lord answered with strong words for Assyria's King Sennacherib. "Against whom have you raised your voice and lifted your eyes in pride? Against the Holy One of Israel!" (v. 23). Then God comforted Jerusalem. "I will defend this city and save it, for my sake and for the sake of David my servant!" (v. 35). The Lord defeated Sennacherib and destroyed the Assyrian army (vv. 36–38).

No matter what dangers loom on your horizon today, the God of Hezekiah and Isaiah still reigns. He longs to hear from each of us and show himself powerful. *TIM GUSTAFSON*

In what ways has God shown himself strong in the past?

God is greater than our greatest problem.

Who We Are

Read: Psalm 100

You are . . . God's special possession, that you may declare the praises of him who called you out of darkness into his wonderful light. –1 Peter 2:9

In her autobiography, Corrie ten Boom described her and her sister Betsie's horrific time in a Nazi concentration camp in the early 1940s. On one occasion they were forced to take off their clothes during an inspection. Corrie stood in line feeling defiled and forsaken. Suddenly, she remembered that Jesus had hung naked on the cross. Struck with wonder and worship, Corrie whispered to her sister, "Betsie, they took His clothes too." Betsie gasped and said, "Oh, Corrie, . . . and I never thanked Him."

It is easy for us to live thanklessly in a world that is full of trouble, struggles, and woes. On any given day we can find many reasons to complain. However, Psalm 100 exhorts God's people to be glad, joyful, and thankful for "it is he who made us, and we are his; we are his people, the sheep of his pasture" (v. 3). As we remember who we are, we can respond in thanksgiving. For even in the worst of times, we can remember Christ's love and sacrifice for us.

Don't let the brutality of the world take away your thankful heart. Remember you are God's child, and He has shown you His goodness and mercy through His work on the cross. *ALBERT LEE*

I thank you, Lord, that though my heart can grow cold at times,
when I remember that I am yours and you are mine,
I'm encouraged yet again. Thank you for your love for me,
for your mercy, and your sacrifice.

Praise comes naturally when you count your blessings.

Shared Struggles

Read: Galatians 6:1–10

Share each other's burdens, and in this way obey the law of Christ. v. 2 NLT

April 25, 2015, marked the 100th commemoration of Anzac Day. It is celebrated each year by both Australia and New Zealand to honor the members of the Australian and New Zealand Army Corps (ANZAC) who fought together during World War I. It marks a time when neither country had to face the dangers of war alone; soldiers from both countries engaged in the struggle together.

Sharing life's struggles is fundamental to the way followers of Christ are called to live. As Paul challenged us, "Share each other's burdens, and in this way obey the law of Christ" (GAL. 6:2 NLT). By working together through life's challenges we can help to strengthen and support one another when times are hard. By expressing toward one another the care and affections of Christ, the difficulties of life should draw us to Christ and to each other—not isolate us in our suffering.

By sharing in the struggles of another, we are modeling the love of Christ. We read in Isaiah, "Surely He has borne our griefs and carried our sorrows" (ISA. 53:4 NKJV). No matter how great the struggle we face, we never face it alone.

BILL CROWDER

Thank you, Father, that I don't have to walk my life's journey alone. you are near.

We can go a lot further together than we can alone.

Safe in His Arms

Read: Isaiah 66:5–13

As a mother comforts her child, so will I comfort you. —v. 13

I sat next to my daughter's bed in a recovery room after she had undergone surgery. When her eyes fluttered open, she realized she was uncomfortable and started to cry. I tried to reassure her by stroking her arm, but she only became more upset. With help from a nurse, I moved her from the bed and onto my lap. I brushed tears from her cheeks and reminded her that she would eventually feel better.

Through Isaiah, God told the Israelites, "As a mother comforts her child, so will I comfort you" (ISA. 66:13). God promised to give His children peace and to carry them the way a mother totes a child around on her side. This tender message was for the people who had a reverence for God—those who "tremble at his word" (v. 5).

God's ability and desire to comfort His people appears again in Paul's letter to the Corinthian believers. Paul said the Lord is the one "who comforts us in all our troubles" (2 COR. 1:3–4). God is gentle and sympathetic with us when we are in trouble.

One day all suffering will end. Our tears will dry up permanently, and we will be safe in God's arms forever (REV. 21:4). Until then, we can depend on God's love to support us when we suffer. *JENNIFER BENSON SCHULDT*

Dear God, help me to remember that nothing can separate me from your love. Please assure me of your care through the power of the Holy Spirit.

God comforts His people.

Reflecting the Son

Read: Matthew 5:14–16

The light shines in the darkness, and the darkness has not overcome it. –John 1:5

Due to its location among sheer mountains and its northern latitude, Rjukan, Norway, does not see natural sunlight from October to March. To lighten up the town, the citizens installed large mirrors on the mountainside to reflect the sunrays and beam sunlight into the town square. The continuous glow is made possible because the giant mirrors rotate with the rising and setting sun.

I like to think of the Christian life as a similar scenario. Jesus said His followers are "the light of the world" (MATT. 5:14). John the disciple wrote that Christ the true light "shines in the darkness" (JOHN 1:5). So too, Jesus invites us to reflect our light into the darkness around us: "Let your light shine before others, that they may see your good deeds and glorify your Father in heaven" (MATT. 5:16). That is a call for us to show love in the face of hatred, patience in response to trouble, and peace in moments of conflict. As the apostle Paul reminds us, "For you were once darkness, but now you are light in the Lord. Live as children of light" (EPH. 5:8).

Jesus also said, "I am the light of the world. Whoever follows me will never walk in darkness, but will have the light of life" (JOHN 8:12). Our light is a reflection of Jesus the Son. Just as without the sun the large mirrors of Rjukan would have no light to reflect, so too we can do nothing without Jesus.

LAWRENCE DARMANI

Teach us, Lord, what it is to reflect your light, especially when life's demands can tempt us to live selfishly. Help us today to live in your love.

Reflect the Son and shine for Him.

As It Is Written

Read: Ezra 3:1–6

[They] built the altar . . . to offer burnt offerings on it, as it is written. —v. 2 NKJV

When it comes to putting things together—electronics, furniture, and the like—my son and I have differing approaches. Steve is more mechanically inclined, so he tends to toss the instructions aside and just start in. Meanwhile, I'm poring over the "Read This Before Starting" warning while he has already put the thing halfway together.

Sometimes we can get by without the instructions. But when it comes to putting together a life that reflects the goodness and wisdom of God, we can't afford to ignore the directions He's given to us in the Bible.

The Israelites who had returned to their land after the Babylonian captivity are a good example of this. As they began to reestablish worship in their homeland, they prepared to do so "in accordance with what is written in the Law of Moses" (EZRA 3:2). By building a proper altar and in celebrating the Feast of Tabernacles as prescribed by God in Leviticus 23:33–43, they did exactly what God's directions told them to do.

Christ gave His followers some directions too. He said, "Love the Lord your God with all your heart and with all your soul and with all your mind." And "love your neighbor as yourself" (MATT. 22:37, 39). When we believe in Him and come to Him, He shows us the way to live. The One who made us knows far better than we do how life is supposed to work. *DAVE BRANON*

Remind us, Lord, as we start each day that you have already shown us by your example how to live. Help us to read your Word and follow the directions you so graciously provide for us.

If we want God to lead us, we must be willing to follow Him.

Our Main Concern

Read: Galatians 1:6–10

If I were still trying to please people, I would not be a servant of Christ. –v. 10

Peer pressure is part of everyday life. Sometimes we base our decisions on what other people will think or say rather than on our convictions and on what will please God. We're worried that we'll be judged or made fun of.

The apostle Paul experienced his fair share of peer pressure. Some Jewish Christians believed that Gentiles should be circumcised to be truly saved (GAL. 1:7; SEE 6:12–15). However, Paul stood his ground. He continued to preach that salvation is by grace through faith alone; no further works are required. And for that he was accused of being a self-appointed apostle. They further asserted that his version of the gospel had never received the apostles' approval (2:1–10).

Despite the pressure, Paul was very clear about whom he served—Christ. God's approval mattered most, not man's. He made it his goal not to win the approval of people, but of God (1:10).

Similarly, we are Christ's servants. We serve God whether people honor or despise us, whether they slander or praise us. One day "each of us will give an account of ourselves to God" (ROM. 14:12). That doesn't mean that we shouldn't consider what people think or say, but ultimately, we make pleasing God our main concern. We want to hear our Savior say, "Well done, good and faithful servant!" (MATT. 25:23).

JAIME FERNÁNDEZ GARRIDO, GUEST WRITER

Dear Lord, no matter what others may say or do,
give me the courage to be faithful to you today.

DR. JAIME FERNÁNDEZ GARRIDO IS DIRECTOR OF THE EVANGELICAL RADIO AND TELEVISION PROGRAM *BORN AGAIN*, AUTHOR OF VARIOUS BOOKS, AND COMPOSER OF MORE THAN 400 HYMNS AND CHORUSES.

Keep following Jesus.

Winning the Big One

Read: Philippians 3:7–14

I press on toward the goal to win the prize for which God has called me heavenward in Christ Jesus. —v. 14

In every field of endeavor, one award is considered the epitome of recognition and success. An Olympic gold medal, a Grammy, an Academy Award, or a Nobel Prize are among "the big ones." But there is a greater prize that anyone can obtain.

The apostle Paul was familiar with first-century athletic games in which competitors gave their full effort to win the prize. With that in mind, he wrote to a group of followers of Christ in Philippi: "Whatever were gains to me I now consider loss for the sake of Christ" (PHIL. 3:7). Why? Because his heart had embraced a new goal: "I want to know Christ—yes, to know the power of his resurrection and participation in his sufferings" (v. 10). And so, Paul said, "I press on to take hold of that for which Christ Jesus took hold of me" (v. 12). His trophy for completing the race would be the "crown of righteousness" (2 TIM. 4:8).

Each of us can aim for that same prize, knowing that we honor the Lord in pursuing it. Every day, in our ordinary duties, we are moving toward "the big one"—"the heavenly prize for which God, through Christ Jesus, is calling us" (PHIL. 3:14 NLT).

DAVID MCCASLAND

Dear Lord, when I get discouraged,
help me to keep pressing on,
looking ahead to when I will be with you forever.

What is done for Christ in this life will be rewarded in the life to come.

The Main Event

Read: Luke 10:38–42

One thing is needed, and Mary has chosen that good part. —v. 42 NKJV

While watching a fireworks display during a celebration in my city, I became distracted. Off to the right and the left of the main event, smaller fireworks occasionally popped up in the sky. They were good, but watching them caused me to miss parts of the more spectacular display directly above me.

Sometimes good things take us away from something better. That happened in the life of Martha, whose story is recorded in Luke 10:38–42. When Jesus and His disciples arrived in the village of Bethany, Martha welcomed them into her home. Being a good host meant that someone had to prepare the meal for the guests, so we don't want to be too hard on her.

When Martha complained that her sister Mary wasn't helping, Jesus defended Mary's choice to sit at His feet. But the Lord wasn't saying that Mary was more spiritual than her sister. On occasion Martha seems to have shown more trust in Jesus than Mary did (JOHN 11:19–20). And He wasn't being critical of Martha's desire to look after their physical needs. Rather, what the Lord wanted Martha to hear is that in the busyness of our service, listening to Him is the main event. *ANNE CETAS*

Dear Lord, help me to remember that
my service for you is important,
but it can never take the place of
intimate fellowship with you.

Jesus longs for our fellowship.

The Sounds of Silence

Read: Proverbs 10:19–21

The lips of the righteous nourish many. –v. 21

A fishing buddy of mine observed, "Shallow streams make the most noise," a delightful turn on the old adage, "Still waters run deep." He meant, of course, that people who make the most noise tend to have little of substance to say.

The flip side of that problem is that we don't listen well either. I'm reminded of the line in the old Simon and Garfunkel song "The Sound of Silence" about folks hearing without listening. Oh, they hear the words, but they fail to silence their own thoughts and truly listen. It would be good if we all learned to be silent and still.

There is "a time to be silent and a time to speak" (ECCL. 3:7). Good silence is a listening silence, a humble silence. It leads to right hearing, right understanding, and right speaking. "The purposes of a person's heart are deep waters," the proverb says, "but one who has insight draws them out" (PROV. 20:5). It takes a lot of hard listening to get all the way to the bottom.

And while we listen to others, we should also be listening to God and hearing what He has to say. I think of Jesus, scribbling with His finger in the dust while the Pharisees railed on the woman caught in adultery (SEE JOHN 8:1–11). What was He doing? May I suggest that He could have been simply listening for His Father's voice and asking, "What shall we say to this crowd and this dear woman?" His response is still being heard around the world.

DAVID ROPER

Father, today may your Spirit remind us to seek the quiet
so that we may listen first to your voice and then understand the hearts of others.
Teach us when to speak and when to be quiet.

Well-timed silence can be more eloquent than words.

NOVEMBER 24

Beyond Disappointment

Read: Genesis 29:14–30

Hope in the LORD and keep his way. —Psalm 37:34

Perhaps you've seen the video of the little boy who learns he's getting another sister. In the middle of his meltdown he laments, "It's always girls, girls, girls, girls!"

It is an amusing glimpse into human expectations, but there's nothing funny about disappointment. It saturates our world. One story from the Bible is steeped in disappointment. Jacob agreed to work 7 years for the right to marry his boss's daughter Rachel. But after fulfilling his contract, Jacob got a wedding night surprise. In the morning he discovered not Rachel but her sister Leah.

We focus on Jacob's disappointment, but imagine how Leah must have felt! What hopes and dreams of hers began to die that day as she was forced to marry a man who did not love or want her?

Psalm 37:4 tells us, "Take delight in the LORD, and he will give you the desires of your heart." Are we to believe that God-fearing people are never disappointed? No, the psalm clearly shows that the writer sees injustice all around him. But he takes the long view: "Be still before the LORD and wait patiently for him" (v. 7). His conclusion: "The meek will inherit the land" (v. 11).

In the end, it was Leah whom Jacob honored and buried in the family grave plot with Abraham and Sarah, Isaac and Rebekah (GEN. 49:31). And it was through the lineage of Leah—who in life thought she was unloved—that God blessed the world with our Savior. Jesus brings justice, restores hope, and gives us an inheritance beyond our wildest dreams. *TIM GUSTAFSON*

Lord, it's hard to wait patiently for good things. Forgive us for comparing ourselves to others and complaining about what we don't have. Help us to meet you in a new way.

Jesus is the only friend who never disappoints.

With Us and in Us

Read: John 14:15–21

I will ask the Father, and he will give you another advocate to help you and be with you forever. —v. 16

My son had just started nursery school. The first day he cried and declared, "I don't like school." My husband and I talked to him about it. "We may not be physically there, but we are praying for you. Besides, Jesus is with you always."

"But I can't see Him!" he reasoned. My husband hugged him and said, "He lives in you. And He won't leave you alone." My son touched his heart and said, "Yes, Jesus lives in me."

Kids are not the only ones who suffer from separation anxiety. In every stage of life we face times of separation from those we love, sometimes because of geographical distance and sometimes because of death. However, we need to remember that even if we feel forsaken by others, God hasn't forsaken us. He has promised to be with us always. God sent the Spirit of truth—our Advocate and Helper—to dwell with us and in us forever (JOHN 14:15–18). We are His beloved children.

My son is learning to trust, but so am I. Like my son, I can't see the Spirit, but I feel His power as each day He encourages me and guides me as I read God's Word. Let us thank God for His wonderful provision, the Spirit of Christ who is with us and in us. We are certainly not alone! *KEILA OCHOA*

Lord, thank you for your Holy Spirit who lives in me.

We are never alone.

No Peas!

Read: Psalm 118:1–14

In every situation, by prayer and petition, with thanksgiving, present your requests to God. —Philippians 4:6

When our kids were young, one of them bluntly said "no" when we passed him some peas for dinner. To which we replied, "No what?" We hoped he would say, "No, thank you." Instead he said, "No peas!" That led to a discussion about the importance of good manners. In fact, we had similar discussions on numerous occasions.

Beyond good manners—which are external—our Lord reminds us that we are to have a heart of gratitude. Scripture contains dozens of reminders that expressing gratitude is of primary importance in our relationship with God. Psalm 118 begins and ends with the exhortation to "give thanks to the LORD" (vv. 1, 29). We are to give thanks when we come into His presence (100:4). And the requests we bring to Him are to be wrapped in a spirit of thanksgiving (PHIL. 4:6). Such an attitude of gratitude will help us remember our abundant blessings. Even in the midst of trouble and despair, God's presence and love are our constant companions.

It's no wonder, then, that the psalmist reminds us to "give thanks to the LORD, for he is good; his love endures forever" (PS. 118:1). *JOE STOWELL*

Lord, your goodness is enough to make me thankful every day. Teach me to live with a thankful heart and remind me to regularly thank you for your goodness and steadfast love.

It is only with gratitude that life becomes rich.

DIETRICH BONHOEFFER

Help from the Outside

Read: Jeremiah 17:7–13

God is greater than our hearts, and he knows everything. –1 John 3:20

On a business trip, my husband had just settled into his hotel room when he heard an unusual noise. He stepped into the hall to investigate and heard someone yelling from a nearby room. With the help of a hotel worker, he discovered that a man had become trapped in the bathroom. The lock on the bathroom door had malfunctioned and the man trapped inside started to panic. He felt like he couldn't breathe and began yelling for help.

Sometimes in life we feel trapped. We are banging on the door, pulling on the handle, but we can't get free. We need help from the outside, just like the man in the hotel.

To get that outside assistance, we have to admit that we are helpless on our own. Sometimes we look inward for the answers to our problems, yet the Bible says "the heart is deceitful" (JER. 17:9). In truth, we are often the source of our problems in life.

Thankfully, "God is greater than our hearts, and he knows everything" (1 JOHN 3:20). Because of this, He knows exactly how to help us. Lasting heart-level change and real progress with our problems originate with God. Trusting Him and living to please Him means we can flourish and be truly free.

JENNIFER BENSON SCHULDT

Heavenly Father, I humble myself before you.
I can't solve my problems on my own.
Please help me to seek your help and perspective.

God helps those who know they are helpless.

Seeing Ourselves

Read: 1 Corinthians 11:23–34

Everyone ought to examine themselves. –v. 28

Long ago, before the invention of mirrors or polished surfaces, people rarely saw themselves. Puddles of water, streams, and rivers were one of the few ways they could see their own reflection. But mirrors changed that. And the invention of cameras took fascination with our looks to a whole new level. We now have lasting images of ourselves from any given time throughout our entire life. This is good for making scrapbooks and keeping family histories, but it can be detrimental to our spiritual well-being. The fun of seeing ourselves on camera can keep us focused on outward appearance and leave us with little interest in examining our inner selves.

Self-examination is crucial for a healthy spiritual life. God wants us to see ourselves so that we can be spared the consequences of sinful choices. This is so important that Scripture says we are not to participate in the Lord's Supper without first examining ourselves (1 COR. 11:28). The point of this self-examination is not only to make things right with God but also to make sure we are right with one another. The Lord's Supper is a remembrance of Christ's body, and we can't celebrate it properly if we're not living in harmony with other believers.

Seeing and confessing our sin promotes unity with others and a healthy relationship with God. *JULIE ACKERMAN LINK*

Dear Lord, help me to be more concerned with the reflection of my heart than with my physical reflection. Change me through the power of your Spirit.

When we look into the mirror of God's Word, we see ourselves more clearly.

The Low Point

Read: Psalm 40

You are my help and my deliverer. —v. 17

C. S. Lewis and his older brother, Warren (Warnie), endured several terms at Wynyard, an English boarding school for boys. The headmaster was a cruel man who made life unbearable for everyone there. Decades later, Warnie wrote in his understated dry wit, "I am now sixty-four and a bit, and have never yet been in a situation in which I have not had the consolation of reflecting that at any rate I was better off than I was at Wynyard." Most of us can recall a similar dark and difficult time in our lives and be grateful that we're better off now than we were then.

Psalm 40:1–5 records a low point of David's life when he cried out to the Lord who rescued him. God brought him up from "the slimy pit" and "the mud and mire" and set his feet on a rock (v. 2). "He put a new song in my mouth," David says, "a hymn of praise to our God" (v. 3).

But deliverance from depression and despair are seldom one-time events. Psalm 40 continues with David's renewed plea for God's mercy, lovingkindness, and truth to deliver him from his own sin and the threats of his enemies (vv. 11–14).

Along with David, we can say at every low point, "I am poor and needy; may the Lord think of me. You are my help and my deliverer" (v. 17).

DAVID MCCASLAND

How does recalling a low point in your life encourage you to trust God for His help today?

The One who holds the universe will never let you down.

The Heavenly Manifest

Read: Luke 10:17–24

Rejoice that your names are written in heaven. –v. 20

At the Kenya Airways check-in counter, I presented my passport for verification. When the agents searched for my name on their manifest—the document that lists names of passengers—my name was missing. The problem? Overbooking and lack of confirmation. My hope of reaching home that day was shattered.

The episode reminded me of another kind of manifest—the Book of Life. In Luke 10, Jesus sent His disciples on an evangelistic mission. On their return, they happily reported their success. But Jesus told them: "Do not rejoice that the spirits submit to you, but rejoice that your names are written in heaven" (v. 20). The focus of our joy is not merely that we are successful but that our names are inscribed in God's book.

But how can we be sure of that? God's Word tells us, "If you declare with your mouth, 'Jesus is Lord,' and believe in your heart that God raised him from the dead, you will be saved" (ROM. 10:9).

In Revelation 21, John makes a breathtaking description of the Holy City that awaits those who trust Christ. Then he writes, "Nothing impure will ever enter it, nor will anyone who does what is shameful or deceitful, but only those whose names are written in the Lamb's book of life" (v. 27).

The Book of Life is God's heavenly manifest. Is your name written in it?

LAWRENCE DARMANI

Father in heaven, thank you for the gift of your Son, who promised to prepare a place for us. Thank you too, that you are preparing us for that place.

God opens the gates of heaven to those who open their hearts to Him.

The Meaning of a Name

Read: Matthew 1:18–25

You are to give him the name Jesus. —v. 21

According to a *New York Times* article, children in many African countries are often named after a famous visitor, special event, or circumstance that was meaningful to the parents. When doctors told the parents of one child that they could not cure the infant's illness and only God knew if he would live, the parents named their child Godknows. Another man said he was named Enough, because his mother had 13 children and he was the last one! There's a reason for everyone's name, and in some cases it also conveys a special meaning.

Before Jesus was born, an angel of the Lord told Joseph, "[Mary] will give birth to a son, and you are to give him the name Jesus, because he will save his people from their sins" (MATT. 1:21). Jesus is the Greek form of *Joshua*, which means "the Lord saves." In that day and culture, many children would have been named Jesus, but only one came into this world to die so that all who receive Him might live eternally, forgiven and freed from the power of sin.

Charles Wesley wrote these words we often sing as Christmas nears: "Come, Thou long-expected Jesus, born to set Thy people free; from our fears and sins release us; let us find our rest in Thee."

Jesus came to turn our darkness into light, to transform our despair into hope, and to save us from our sins. *DAVID MCCASLAND*

Heavenly Father, in Jesus we see your loving purpose and boundless grace.
We humbly acknowledge your Son as the One who came to save us from our sins.

Jesus's name and mission are the same—He came to save us.

Glass Beach

Read: 1 Thess. 5:23–24

"On the day when I act," says the LORD Almighty, "they will be my treasured possession." –Malachi 3:17

Early 20th-century residents of Fort Bragg, California, disposed of their trash by throwing it over a cliff and onto a nearby beach. Cans, bottles, tableware, and household garbage accumulated in huge, disgusting piles. Even when residents stopped depositing trash on the beach, it remained an embarrassment—a dump seemingly beyond reclamation.

Over the years, however, wave action broke up the glass and pottery and washed the rubbish out to sea. The pounding surf rolled and tumbled the glass fragments in the sand on the ocean floor, frosting and smoothing the surface and creating gemlike "sea glass," which it then deposited back onto the beach. The surf created a kaleidoscopic beauty at which visitors to Glass Beach now stare in wonder.

Perhaps you feel as though your life has become a dump—a mess beyond hope. If so, you need to know that there is someone who loves you and waits to redeem and reclaim you. Give Jesus your heart and ask Him to make you pure and clean. He may tumble you a bit, and it may take time to smooth away the rough edges. But He will never give up on you. He will make you into one of His jewels!

DAVID ROPER

Lord, when we have nothing left but you, we are right where you want us. You can use any situation for your glory and our good. You never give up on us. Help us to relax in your love.

God loves us too much to let us remain as we are.

When Not to Rejoice

Read: Ezek. 25:1–7; Matt. 5:43–48

Do not gloat when your enemy falls. —Proverbs 24:17

The Akan people of Ghana have a proverb: "The lizard is not as mad with the boys who threw stones at it as with the boys who stood by and rejoiced over its fate!" Rejoicing at someone's downfall is like participating in the cause of that downfall or even wishing more evil on the person.

That was the attitude of the Ammonites who maliciously rejoiced when the temple in Jerusalem "was desecrated and over the land of Israel when it was laid waste and over the people of Judah when they went into exile" (EZEK. 25:3). For spitefully celebrating Israel's misfortunes, the Ammonites experienced God's displeasure, which resulted in grim consequences (vv. 4–7).

How do we react when disaster befalls our neighbor or when our neighbor gets into trouble? If she is a nice and friendly neighbor, then, of course, we will sympathize with her and go to her aid. But what if he is an unfriendly, trouble-making neighbor? Our natural tendency may be to ignore him or even secretly rejoice at his downfall.

Proverbs warns us: "Do not gloat when your enemy falls; when they stumble, do not let your heart rejoice" (24:17). Instead, Jesus tells us that we show His love in action when we "love [our] enemies and pray for those who persecute [us]" (MATT. 5:44). By so doing, we imitate the perfect love of our Lord (5:48).

LAWRENCE DARMANI

Lord, open my eyes and my heart to be honest about my attitude toward those who are unkind or unfair to me. Fill my heart with your love, Lord, and help me pray for them.

Love your neighbor as yourself.

Worry-Free

Read: Psalm 37:1–9

Do not fret because of those who are evil. —v. 1

Trying to stay aware of current events has its downside because bad news sells better than good news. It's easy to become overly concerned about the criminal acts of individuals, crowds, or governments over whom we have no control.

Psalm 37 gives perspective to the daily news. David begins by saying, "Do not fret because of those who are evil" (v. 1). Then he proceeds to outline for us some alternatives to becoming overly anxious. In essence, David suggests a better way of thinking about negative news in our world.

What would happen if, instead of worrying about events beyond our control, we chose to trust in the Lord? (v. 3). Wouldn't we be better off to "take delight in the LORD" (v. 4) rather than fret without limits? Imagine the freedom from worry we could have if we would "commit [our] way to the LORD" (v. 5). And how calm we could be by learning to "be still before the LORD and wait patiently for him"! (v. 7).

News of trouble we cannot change offers us an opportunity to set boundaries for our concerns. As we trust God, commit our ways to Him, and rest in Him, our outlook brightens. The struggles and trials may not disappear, but we will discover that He gives us His peace in the midst of them.

DAVE BRANON

Lord, we see danger and trouble all around us. Help us not to worry but instead to trust and rest in you. Show us the peace that comes from waiting patiently on you.

Obstacles give us the opportunity to trust God.

What Christmas Is All About

Read: Luke 2:8–14

There were shepherds living out in the fields nearby, keeping watch over their flocks at night. —v. 8

More than 50 years ago *A Charlie Brown Christmas* was first broadcast on American television. Some network executives thought it would be ignored, while others worried that quoting the Bible would offend viewers. Some wanted its creator, Charles Schulz, to omit the Christmas story, but Schulz insisted it stay in. The program was an immediate success and has been rebroadcast every year since 1965.

When Charlie Brown, the frustrated director of the children's Christmas play, is discouraged by the commercial spirit of the holiday season, he asks if anyone can tell him the real meaning of Christmas. Linus recites Luke 2:8-14 including the words, "For unto you is born this day in the city of David a Saviour, which is Christ the Lord. And this shall be a sign unto you; ye shall find the babe wrapped in swaddling clothes, lying in a manger. And suddenly there was with the angel a multitude of the heavenly host praising God, and saying, Glory to God in the highest, and on earth peace, good will toward men" (vv. 11–14 KJV). Then Linus says, "That's what Christmas is all about, Charlie Brown."

During this season filled with our own doubts and dreams, it's good to ponder afresh God's great love expressed in the familiar story of Joseph, Mary, the baby Jesus, and the angels who announced the Savior's birth.

That's what Christmas is all about. *DAVID MCCASLAND*

Father in heaven, as we approach Christmas, may we grasp in a deeper way your amazing gift to us.

God broke into human history to offer us the gift of salvation!

The Birth of Christmas

Read: Luke 1:26–38

When Joseph woke up, he did what the angel of the Lord commanded him and took Mary home as his wife. —Matthew 1:24

When the angel Gabriel appeared to Mary and then to shepherds with good news for the world (LUKE 1:26–27; 2:10), was it good news to this teenage girl? Perhaps Mary was thinking: *How do I explain my pregnancy to my family? Will my fiancé Joseph call off the betrothal? What will the townspeople say? Even if my life is spared, how will I survive as a mother all alone?*

When Joseph learned about Mary's pregnancy, he was troubled. He had three options. Go ahead with the marriage, divorce her publicly and allow her to be publicly scorned, or break off the engagement quietly. Joseph chose option three, but God intervened. He told Joseph in a dream, "Do not be afraid to take Mary home as your wife, because what is conceived in her is from the Holy Spirit" (MATT. 1:20).

For Mary and Joseph, Christmas began with submitting themselves to God in spite of the unthinkable emotional challenges before them. They entrusted themselves to God and in doing so demonstrated for us the promise of 1 John 2:5: "If anyone obeys his word, love for God is truly made complete in them."

May God's love fill our hearts this Christmas season—and every day—as we walk with Him.

ALBERT LEE

Fill my heart, Lord, with rejoicing at the gift of your love and forgiveness found in your Son Jesus.

Obedience to God flows freely from a heart of love.

A Faithful Servant

Read: Joshua 14:6–15

If anyone serves, they should do so with the strength God provides, so that in all things God may be praised through Jesus Christ. —1 Peter 4:11

Madaleno is a bricklayer. From Monday to Thursday he builds walls and repairs roofs. He is quiet, reliable, and hardworking. Then from Friday to Sunday he goes up to the mountains to teach the Word of God. Madaleno speaks *Nahuatl* (a Mexican dialect), so he can easily communicate the good news of Jesus to the people in that region. At age 70, he still works with his hands building houses, but he also works to build the family of God.

His life has been threatened several times. He has slept under the stars and faced death from car accidents and falls. He has been kicked out of towns. But he thinks that God has called him to do what he does, and he serves happily. Believing that people need to know the Lord, he relies on God for the strength he needs.

Madaleno's faithfulness reminds me of the faithfulness of Caleb and Joshua, two of the men Moses sent to explore the Promised Land and report back to the Israelites (NUM. 13; JOSH. 14:6–13). Their companions were afraid of the people who lived there, but Caleb and Joshua trusted in God and believed He would help them conquer the land.

The work entrusted to us may be different than Madaleno's or Caleb's and Joshua's. But our confidence can be the same. In reaching out to others, we rely not on ourselves but on the strength of our God. *KEILA OCHOA*

Where has God placed you to serve? Are you being faithful?

We grow strong when we serve the Lord.

The Perfect Gift

Read: Romans 12:1–8

Ascribe to the LORD the glory due his name; bring an offering and come into his courts. –Psalm 96:8

Every year our local botanical garden hosts a celebration of Christmas around the world. My favorite display is a French nativity. Instead of the traditional scene showing shepherds and wise men with gifts of gold, frankincense, and myrrh gathered around the manger, it shows French villagers bringing their gifts to baby Jesus. They bring bread, wine, cheese, flowers, and other items that God has given them the ability to produce. This reminds me of the Old Testament command to bring the firstfruits of our labor to the house of the Lord (EX. 23:16–19). This depiction of the nativity illustrates that everything we have comes from God, so the only thing we have to give is something that God has given us.

When Paul instructed the Romans to present themselves as a living sacrifice, he was telling them to give back to God what God had given them—their own selves (ROM. 12:1). This includes the gifts He gave them, even their ability to earn a living. We know that God gives people special abilities. Some, like David, were skilled in music (1 SAM. 16:18). Some, like Bezalel and Oholiab, were skilled in artistic works (EX. 35:30–35). Others have skill in writing, teaching, gardening, and many other things.

When we give back to God what He has first given to us, we give Him the perfect gift—ourselves. *JULIE ACKERMAN LINK*

What can you *offer Jesus?*

Give your all to Christ who gave His all for you.

Just the Ticket

Read: Ephesians 1:1–10

In him we have . . . the forgiveness of sins, in accordance with the riches of God's grace. —v. 7

When a police officer stopped a woman because her young daughter was riding in a car without the required booster seat, he could have written her a ticket for a traffic violation. Instead, he asked the mother and daughter to meet him at a nearby store where he personally paid for the needed car seat. The mother was going through a difficult time and could not afford to buy a seat.

Although the woman should have received a fine for her misdemeanor, she walked away with a gift instead. Anyone who knows Christ has experienced something similar. All of us deserve a penalty for breaking God's laws (ECCL. 7:20). Yet, because of Jesus, we experience undeserved favor from God. This favor excuses us from the ultimate consequence for our sin, which is death and eternal separation from God (ROM. 6:23). "In [Jesus] we have . . . the forgiveness of sins, in accordance with the riches of God's grace" (EPH. 1:7).

Some refer to grace as "love in action." When the young mother experienced this, she later remarked, "I will be forever grateful! . . . And as soon as I can afford it I will be paying it forward." This grateful and big-hearted response to the officer's gift is an inspiring example for those of us who have received the gift of God's grace! *JENNIFER BENSON SCHULDT*

Dear Father, thank you for giving us what we don't deserve.
You have forgiven my sins and provided a way for me to be
reconciled to you through the gift of your Son.
Help me to always be grateful for your grace.

God's gift is grace.

Like Shooting a Fly

Read: 2 Corinthians 4:1–6

Christ's love compels us, because we are convinced that one died for all, and therefore all died. –5:14

Macarena Valdes's skill in mapping underground mines made a real difference in the rescue of the 33 Chilean miners trapped after an explosion in October 2010. Drilling to find the exact place where the men were located was like "trying to shoot a fly from 700 meters away," she said. With her mining experience, Valdes was able to guide the probe to where the miners were entombed, which helped bring about their dramatic rescue.

In efforts to carry out spiritual rescues, it's easy to become discouraged. Although the apostle Paul faced even greater obstacles, he said, "We do not lose heart" (2 COR. 4:1). Even though "the god of this age" had "blinded the minds of unbelievers, so that they cannot see the light of the gospel," he continued to proclaim the gospel of salvation (VV. 4–5). Compelled by God, who lovingly spoke light into his own darkness (V. 6), Paul knew that what God had done for him God could do for others.

You and I may have a similar story. Compelled by the love of God, we too have reason not to lose heart. As Macarena led in the rescue of the miners, the Spirit of God can carry the light of our love and words into the hearts of those who need a rescue they may not yet understand. *C. P. HIA*

Lord Jesus, thank you for coming to our rescue when we were lost and helpless in our sin. Help those of us who have been rescued to share the lifeline of your love with those who are still trapped.

When you've been rescued, you want to rescue others.

Paradogs

Read: Psalm 143:7–12

In You do I trust; cause me to know the way in which I should walk. —v. 8 NKJV

I am amazed by the story of the World War II paradogs. In preparing for D-Day (June 6, 1944), the Allied troops needed the sharp senses of dogs to sniff their way through minefields and to warn troops of approaching danger. And the only way to get these dogs to troops behind enemy lines was by parachute. But dogs are instinctively afraid of doing this—and let's be honest, they are not alone. Yet after weeks of training, the dogs learned to trust their masters enough to jump at their command.

I wonder if any of us trust our Master enough to do challenging things we would never instinctively do or things that might make us fearful. We may not be instinctively generous or forgiving or patient with those who annoy us. Yet Jesus commands us to trust Him enough to do things that may be difficult but that will advance His kingdom. To say, "In You do I trust; cause me to know the way in which I should walk" (PS. 143:8 NKJV).

Paradogs often received medals for their bravery. I believe we too will someday hear "well done" because we have trusted our Master enough to jump when He said, "Go!"

JOE STOWELL

Is God asking you to do something that you are afraid to do?
Will you trust Him to lead you and walk with you?

Trust Jesus to show you how you can be used by Him.

A Hunger for God

Read: Deut. 4:9–14

All Scripture is God-breathed and is useful for teaching, rebuking, correcting and training in righteousness. –2 Timothy 3:16

A-poe-la-pi is an elderly member of the Akha, a hill tribe people who live on the mountain ranges of Yunnan Province in China. As we visited him on a recent missions trip, A-poe-la-pi told us that he had missed the weekly Bible study because of heavy rains. So he implored us, "Could you share God's Word with me?"

A-poe-la-pi can't read, so the weekly gathering is vital to him. As we read the Bible to him, he listened intently. His earnest attitude reminded me that when we listen carefully to the story of the inspired Scriptures, we honor the Lord.

In Deuteronomy 4, Moses urged the Israelites to listen carefully to the rules and regulations he was teaching them (v. 1). He reminded them that the source and inspiration behind the teaching was none other than God himself, who had spoken to them "out of the fire" of Sinai (v. 12). Moses said, "He declared to you his covenant . . . which he commanded you to follow" (v. 13).

May A-poe-la-pi's hunger to hear God's Word encourage a similar desire in us. As the apostle Paul reminds us in 2 Timothy 3:15-16, the inspired Scriptures have been given for our good and growth—to make us wise in the salvation and ways of God. POH FANG CHIA

Lord, give us a hunger to hear and understand the truth of your Word. Help us show your love to others by faithfully living out its instructions for us.

To know Christ, the Living Word, is to love the Bible, the written Word.

How to Be Perfect

Read: Romans 3:20–26

For by one sacrifice he has made perfect forever those who are being made holy.
—Hebrews 10:14

Christmas is the time of year when the pressure to be perfect intensifies. We imagine the perfect celebration and then put forth our best effort to make it happen. We shop for the perfect gifts. We plan the perfect Christmas Day meal. We choose the perfect greeting cards or write the perfect family letter. But our striving leads to discouragement and disappointment when our ability to imagine perfection exceeds our ability to implement it. The carefully chosen gift receives only a halfhearted thank you. Part of the meal is overcooked. We find a typo in our Christmas greeting after we've mailed the cards. Children fight over toys. Adults resurrect old arguments.

Instead of being discouraged, however, we can use our disappointment to remind ourselves of the reason Christmas is so important. We need Christmas because none of us is or can be all that we want to be—not for a month, a week, or even a day. How much more meaningful our celebrations of Christ's birth would be if we would give up our faulty concept of perfection, then focus instead on the perfection of our Savior, in whom we are made righteous (ROM. 3:22).

If your Christmas celebration this year is less than ideal, relax and let it be a reminder that the only way to be "made perfect forever" (HEB. 10:14) is to live by faith in the righteousness of Christ. *JULIE ACKERMAN LINK*

What expectations do you have for the Christmas season?
Are they idealistic or realistic? Think about what you can do to focus more on Christ and the meaning of His birth.

Dressed in His righteousness alone, faultless to stand before His throne.

EDWARD MOTE

Let's Celebrate

Read: Psalm 150

Praise him with timbrel and dancing, praise him with the strings and pipe. —v. 4

After Ghana's Asamoah Gyan scored a goal against Germany in the 2014 World Cup, he and his teammates did a coordinated dance step. When Germany's Miroslav Klose scored a few minutes later, he did a running front flip. "Soccer celebrations are so appealing because they reveal players' personalities, values, and passions," says Clint Mathis, who scored for the US at the 2002 World Cup.

In Psalm 150, the psalmist invites "everything that has breath" to celebrate and praise the Lord in many different ways. He suggests that we use trumpets and harps, stringed instruments and pipes, cymbals and dancing. He encourages us to creatively and passionately celebrate, honor, and adore the Lord. Because the Lord is great and has performed mighty acts on behalf of His people, He is worthy of all praise. These outward expressions of praise will come from an inner wellspring overflowing with gratitude to God. "Let everything that has breath praise the LORD," the psalmist declares (150:6).

Though we may celebrate the Lord in different ways (I'm not encouraging back flips in our worship services), our praise to God always needs to be expressive and meaningful. When we think about the Lord's character and His mighty acts toward us, we cannot help but celebrate Him through our praise and worship.

MARVIN WILLIAMS

How has this psalm challenged you to be more expressive in your praise to God? Spend some time thinking about the greatness of the Lord's mighty works. Then give Him your praise.

Praise is the song of a soul set free.

The Importance of How

Read: Numbers 4:17–32

Assign to each man his work and what he is to carry. —v. 19

While attending Bible college, my friend Charlie and I worked for a furniture store. We often made deliveries accompanied by an interior decorator who talked with the people who had purchased the furniture while we brought it from the truck into the house. Sometimes we had to carry the furniture up several flights of stairs in an apartment building. Charlie and I often wished we had the decorator's job instead of ours!

During Israel's 40 years of wandering in the wilderness, three clans from the priestly tribe of Levi—the Kohathites, Gershonites, and Merarites—were assigned the job of transporting the Tent of Meeting (tabernacle). They put it up, took it down, and carried it to the next place, then repeated the process again and again. Their job description was simple: "Carry the things assigned to you" (SEE NUM. 4:32).

I wonder if these "custodians" ever envied the "clergymen" who offered sacrifices and incense using the holy articles in the sanctuary (vv. 4–5, 15). That job must have looked much easier and more prestigious. But both assignments were important and came from the Lord.

Many times we don't get to select the work we do. But all of us can choose our attitude toward the tasks we're given. How we do the job God gives us is the measure of our service to Him. *DAVID MCCASLAND*

Father in heaven, our work in life often causes us to wonder if we are accomplishing anything worthwhile. Give us eyes to see the importance of the tasks you have given us so that we may honor you by the way we do them.

Humble work becomes holy work when it's done for God.

Holy Is Your Name

Read: Exodus 20:1–7

You shall not misuse the name of the LORD your God. —v. 7

One afternoon I was having a discussion with a friend I considered my spiritual mentor about misusing God's name. "You shall not misuse the name of the LORD your God," says the third commandment (EX. 20:7). We may think this only refers to attaching God's name to a swear word or using His name flippantly or irreverently. But my mentor rarely missed an opportunity to teach me about real faith. He challenged me to think about other ways we profane God's name.

When I reject the advice of others and say, "God told me to go this way," I misuse His name if all I am doing is seeking approval for my own desires.

When I use Scripture out of context to try to support an idea I want to be true, I am using God's name in vain.

When I teach, write, or speak from Scripture carelessly, I misuse His name.

Author John Piper offers this reflection on what it means to take God's name in vain: "The idea is . . . 'don't empty the name.' . . . Don't empty God of His weight and glory." We misuse His name, Piper says, when we "speak of God in a way that empties Him of His significance."

My friend challenged me to honor God's name and to pay closer attention to using His Word carefully and accurately. Anything less dishonors Him.

RANDY KILGORE

Heavenly Father, help me to glorify your name
and to honor you always in what I say and do.

God's name: handle with care.

Christmas Rest

Read: Matthew 11:28–12:8

Come to me, all you who are weary and burdened. —v. 28

As a boy I delivered newspapers in order to earn money. Since it was a morning newspaper, I was required to get up at 3:00 every morning, 7 days a week, in order to have all 140 of my papers delivered to their appropriate homes by 6:00 a.m.

But one day each year was different. We would deliver the Christmas morning newspaper on Christmas Eve—meaning that Christmas was the only morning of the year I could sleep in and rest like a normal person.

Over the years, I came to appreciate Christmas for many reasons, but one that was special in those days was that, unlike any other day of the year, it was a day of rest.

At that time, I didn't fully understand the meaning of the true rest that Christmas brings. Christ came so that all who labor under the weight of a law that can never be fulfilled might find rest through the forgiveness Christ offers. Jesus said, "Come to me, all you who are weary and burdened, and I will give you rest" (MATT. 11:28).

In a world that is too much for us to bear alone, Christ has come to bring us into a relationship with Him and give us rest. *BILL CROWDER*

What burdens would you like the Lord to carry for you?
Ask Him today.

Our soul finds rest when it rests in God.

Reaching Out in the Darkness

Read: Psalm 139:7–12

The night will shine like the day, for darkness is as light to you. –v. 12

Our old dog—a West Highland white terrier—sleeps curled up at the foot of our bed. That's been her place for 13 years.

Normally she doesn't move or make a sound, but lately she's been pawing us gently in the middle of the night. At first we thought she wanted to go outside, so we tried to accommodate her. But we realized she just wants to know we are there. She's nearly deaf and partially blind now. She can't see in the darkness and can't hear us move or breathe. Naturally, she gets confused and reaches out for reassurance. So I just reach down and pat her on the head to assure her that I'm there. That's all she wants to know. She takes a turn or two, settles down, and goes back to sleep.

"Where can I flee from your presence?" David asked God (PS. 139:7). David took this as an immense comfort. "If I settle on the far side of the sea, even there your hand will guide me," he noted. "Even the darkness will not be dark to you" (VV. 9–12).

Lost in darkness? Grieving, fearful, guilty, doubting, discouraged? Not sure of God? The darkness is not dark to Him. Though unseen, He is at hand. He has said, "Never will I leave you; never will I forsake you" (HEB. 13:5). Reach out your hand for His. He is there. *DAVID ROPER*

Lord, you promised never to leave us or forsake us.
We know your word is true, but so often we see the obstacles and the challenges
and lose sight of you. Help us today to see more of you
and less of our problems.

Dark fears flee in the light of God's presence.

DECEMBER 19

The Seventh Stanza

Read: Luke 2:8–14

Today in the town of David a Savior has been born to you; he is the Messiah, the Lord. —v. 11

In the summer of 1861, Henry Wadsworth Longfellow's wife, Frances, died tragically in a fire. That first Christmas without her, he wrote in his diary, "How inexpressibly sad are the holidays." The next year was no better, as he recorded, " 'A merry Christmas,' say the children, but that is no more for me."

In 1863, as the American Civil War was dragging on, Longfellow's son joined the army against his father's wishes and was critically injured. On Christmas Day that year, as church bells announced the arrival of another painful Christmas, Longfellow picked up his pen and began to write, "I Heard the Bells on Christmas Day."

The poem begins pleasantly, lyrically, but then takes a dark turn. The violent imagery of the pivotal fourth verse ill suits a Christmas carol. "Accursed" cannons "thundered," mocking the message of peace. By the fifth and sixth verses, Longfellow's desolation is nearly complete. "It was as if an earthquake rent the hearth-stones of a continent," he wrote. The poet nearly gave up: "And in despair I bowed my head; 'There is no peace on earth,' I said."

But then, from the depths of that bleak Christmas day, Longfellow heard the irrepressible sound of hope. And he wrote this seventh stanza.

Then pealed the bells more loud and deep: "God is not dead, nor doth He sleep! The wrong shall fail, the right prevail, with peace on earth, good-will to men!"

The war raged on and so did memories of his personal tragedies, but it could not stop Christmas. The Messiah is born! He promises, "I am making everything new!" (REV. 21:5). *TIM GUSTAFSON*

Immanuel—God with us!

Pax Romana

Read: Isaiah 9:1–7

To us a child is born, to us a son is given, and the government will be on his shoulders. –v. 6

No one can afford the price of war. Many nations are currently involved in armed conflicts. When and how will they end? We want peace, but not at the expense of justice.

Jesus was born during a time of "peace," but it came at the cost of heavy-handed oppression. The *Pax Romana* ("Roman Peace") existed only because Rome squashed all dissent.

Seven centuries before that time of relative peace, hostile armies prepared to invade Jerusalem. From the shadow of war, God made a remarkable pronouncement. "On those living in the land of deep darkness a light has dawned," the prophet declared (ISA. 9:2). "For to us a child is born, to us a son is given . . . . Of the greatness of his government and peace there will be no end" (VV. 6–7). Matthew tells us that Isaiah's prophecy found fulfillment in the Christ-child (MATT. 1:22–23; SEE ALSO ISA. 7:14).

We adore the tiny baby in the manger scene. Yet that helpless babe is also the Lord Almighty, "the LORD of Heaven's Armies" (ISA. 13:13 NLT). He will one day "reign on David's throne and over his kingdom, establishing and upholding it with justice and righteousness" (9:7). Such a regime will be no oppressive *Pax Romana*. It will be the reign of the Prince of Peace.

TIM GUSTAFSON

Father, we can never sufficiently thank you that your Son came to bring us peace with you through His death and resurrection. Thank you that He will rule in both peace and righteousness.

The Lamb of God is also the Lion of Judah.

Amazing Love

Read: John 6:32–40

I have come down from heaven not to do my will but to do the will of him who sent me. –v. 38

Approaching the first Christmas after her husband died, our friend Davidene wrote a remarkable letter in which she pictured what it might have been like in heaven when Jesus was born on earth. "It was what God always knew would happen," she wrote. "The three were one, and He had agreed to allow the fracturing of His precious unity for our sake. Heaven was left empty of God the Son."

As Jesus taught and healed people on earth, He said, "I have come down from heaven not to do my will but to do the will of him who sent me. . . . For my Father's will is that everyone who looks to the Son and believes in him shall have eternal life, and I will raise them up at the last day" (JOHN 6:38, 40).

When Jesus was born in Bethlehem, it was the beginning of His mission on earth to demonstrate God's love and give His life on the cross to free us from the penalty and power of sin.

"I cannot imagine actually choosing to let go of the one I loved, with whom I was one, for the sake of anyone else," Davidene concluded. "But God did. He faced a house much emptier than mine, so that I could live in His house with Him forever."

"For God so loved the world that he gave his one and only Son" (JOHN 3:16).

DAVID MCCASLAND

Father in heaven, we are in awe of your amazing love for us.
Thank you for giving your only Son to save us from our sins.

The birth of Christ brought God to man;
the cross of Christ brings man to God.

The Drummer Boy

Read: Luke 21:1–4

She out of her poverty put in all she had to live on. —v. 4

"The Little Drummer Boy" is a popular Christmas song written in 1941. It was originally known as "Carol of the Drum" and is based on a traditional Czech carol. Although there isn't any reference to a drummer boy in the Christmas story in Matthew 1–2 and Luke 2, the point of the carol goes straight to the heart of the meaning of worship. The carol describes how a boy is summoned by the Magi to the scene of Christ's birth. Unlike the wise men, however, the drummer has no gift—so he gives what he has. He plays his drum, saying, "I played my best for Him."

This echoes the worship Jesus described when He told of the widow and her two coins: " 'Truly I tell you,' he said, 'this poor widow has put in more than all the others. All these people gave their gifts out of their wealth; but she out of her poverty put in all she had to live on' " (LUKE 21:3–4).

All the drummer boy had was his drum and all the poor widow had were her two coins, but the God they worshiped was worthy of their all. He is worthy of our all as well, having given His all for us. *BILL CROWDER*

All to Jesus, I surrender, all to Him I freely give;
I will ever love and trust Him, in His presence daily live.
JUDSON W. VAN DE VENTER

Your little is a lot when you give your all.

One Size Fits All

Read: John 3:10–21

Whoever believes in him shall not perish but have eternal life. —v. 16

Like most children, I thoroughly enjoyed Christmas. With great anticipation, I would snoop under the tree to see what toys and games awaited my eager grasp. So I felt deflated when I started getting things like shirts and pants. Grownup gifts were no fun! Then last Christmas, my kids gave me some cool socks with bright colors and designs. I almost felt young again! Even grownups could wear these socks, as the label reassured me: "One size fits all."

That welcome phrase "one size fits all" reminds me of the best gift of Christmas—the good news that Jesus is for everyone. The point was proven when the first invitation sent by angel choirs was to shepherds on the bottom rung of the social ladder. The news was underscored further when the VIPs—the wealthy and powerful Magi—followed the star to come and worship the Christ-child.

After Jesus began His ministry, an influential member of the Jewish ruling council came to Him at night. In the course of their conversation, Jesus invited "whoever believes" to come to Him. The simple act of faith in Christ grants eternal life to those who trust in Him (JOHN 3:16).

If Jesus were just for the poor and marginalized, or only for the famous and fortunate, many of us would not qualify. But Christ is for everyone, regardless of status, financial situation, or social standing. He is the only gift truly fit for all.

JOE STOWELL

Thank you, Lord, that no one is unqualified for the gift of your love. Teach us to rejoice in the fact that your love was just right for us, and help us to share that love with others.

God's gift to a dying world is the life-giving Savior.

Christmas Mystery

Read: 1 Timothy 3:14–16

The mystery from which true godliness springs is great. —v. 16

As Charles Dickens's story *A Christmas Carol* begins, there is mystery surrounding Ebenezer Scrooge. Why is he so mean-spirited? How did he become so selfish? Then, slowly, as the Christmas spirits marched Scrooge through his own story, things become clearer. We see the influences that changed him from a happy youth into a selfish miser. We observe his isolation and his brokenness. As the mystery is solved, we also glimpse the path to restoration. Concern for others pulls Scrooge from his self-absorbed darkness into a new joy.

A far more important mystery, and one much harder to explain, is that which Paul spoke of in 1 Timothy 3:16: "Beyond all question, the mystery from which true godliness springs is great: He appeared in the flesh, was vindicated by the Spirit, was seen by angels, was preached among the nations, was believed on in the world, was taken up in glory." Extraordinary! God "appeared in the flesh."

The mystery of Christmas is how God could become man while remaining fully God. It defies human explanation, but in the perfect wisdom of God, it was the plan of the ages.

"What child is this?" He is Jesus Christ—God revealed in the flesh.

BILL CROWDER

This, this is Christ the King, whom shepherds guard and angels sing: Haste, haste to bring Him laud, the babe, the son of Mary.

TRADITIONAL CAROL

God made His home with us so that we might make our home with Him.

A Fragile Gift

Read: Luke 2:1–7

Thanks be to God for his indescribable gift! —2 Corinthians 9:15

When we give a fragile gift, we make sure it is marked on the box that contains it. The word FRAGILE is written with big letters because we don't want anyone to damage what is inside.

God's gift to us came in the most fragile package: a baby. Sometimes we imagine Christmas day as a beautiful scene on a postcard, but any mother can tell you it wasn't so. Mary was tired, probably insecure. It was her first child, and He was born in the most unsanitary conditions. She "wrapped Him in swaddling cloths, and laid Him in a manger, because there was no room for them in the inn" (LUKE 2:7 NKJV).

A baby needs constant care. Babies cry, eat, sleep, and depend on their caregivers. They cannot make decisions. In Mary's day, infant mortality was high, and mothers often died in childbirth.

Why did God choose such a fragile way to send His Son to earth? Because Jesus had to be like us in order to save us. God's greatest gift came in the fragile body of a baby, but God took the risk because He loves us. Let us be thankful today for such a gift! *KEILA OCHOA*

Dear Lord, the Strong and Mighty One, I thank you for becoming small and fragile on that day long ago. It amazes me that you did that for me and the rest of your world.

May you know the peace of Christmas every day of the year.

Christmas Sacrifice

Read: Galatians 4:1–7

When the set time had fully come, God sent his Son. –v. 4

O. Henry's classic tale "The Gift of the Magi" tells of Jim and Della, a young married couple who are struggling financially. As Christmas approaches they want to give special gifts to each other, but their lack of money drives them to drastic measures. Jim's prized possession is a gold watch, while Della's is her long, beautiful hair. So Jim sells his watch in order to buy combs for Della's hair, while Della sells her hair to buy a chain for Jim's watch.

The story has deservedly become beloved, for it reminds us that sacrifice is at the heart of true love, and sacrifice is love's truest measure. This idea is particularly appropriate for Christmas, because sacrifice is the heartbeat of the story of the birth of Christ. Jesus Christ was born to die, and He was born to die for us. That is why the angel told Joseph, "You are to give him the name Jesus, because he will save his people from their sins" (MATT. 1:21).

Long before Christ's birth, it had been determined that He would come to rescue us from our fallenness—which means that we can never fully appreciate the manger unless we see it in the shadow of the cross. Christmas is completely about Christ's love, seen most clearly in His sacrifice for us.

BILL CROWDER

In what ways would you like to say thanks to Jesus for what He has done?

The essential fact of Christianity is that God thought all humanity worth the sacrifice of His Son. WILLIAM BARCLAY

Diamond Dust

Read: Isa. 1:18–20; Ps. 51:7

Wash me and I will be whiter than snow. —Psalm 51:7

During a bitterly frigid winter in our part of Michigan, there were many mixed emotions about the weather. As the snowy winter season pressed on into March, most people had long before fallen out of love with snow and were bemoaning long-range forecasts of low temperatures.

Yet the majestic beauty of the snow continued to amaze me. Even as I threw endless shovelsful of it from my driveway onto the over-my-head snowbanks, I was enthralled with the white stuff. One particular day, ice crystals filtered down from the sky to fall atop old snow. As my wife and I took a walk through this sparkling scene, it looked as if diamond dust had been sprinkled across the landscape.

In Scripture, snow seems to have varied purposes. God sends it as an indicator of His creative greatness (JOB 37:6; 38:22–23). Snow-capped mountains irrigate the arid valleys below. But more significantly, God gives snow as a picture of our forgiveness. The gospel of Jesus provides a way for us to be cleansed of our sins and for our hearts to be made much "whiter than snow" (PS. 51:7; ISA. 1:18).

The next time you see snow—in life or in photos—thank God for the forgiveness and the freedom from sin's penalties that this beautiful, natural gift pictures for all who have put their trust in our Savior. *DAVE BRANON*

Thank you for forgiving us and for turning our filthiness into the beauty of forgiveness. Help us to display the beauty of our forgiveness to all we encounter.

When Christ forgives us, our hearts are as clean as new-fallen snow.

A Place of Shelter

Read: Psalm 61

I long to . . . take refuge in the shelter of your wings. –v. 4

Homeless people in Vancouver, British Columbia, have a new way to find nighttime accommodations. A local charity, RainCity Housing, has created specialized benches that convert into temporary shelters. The back of the bench pulls up to create a roof that can shield a person from wind and rain. At night, these sleeping spaces are easy to find because they feature a glow-in-the-dark message that reads: THIS IS A BEDROOM.

The need for shelter can be physical, and it can be spiritual as well. God is a refuge for our souls when we are troubled. King David wrote, "I call as my heart grows faint; lead me to the rock that is higher than I" (PS. 61:2). When we're emotionally overloaded, we are more vulnerable to the Enemy's tactics—fear, guilt, and lust are a few of his favorites. We need a source of stability and safety.

If we take refuge in God, we can have victory over the Enemy as he tries to influence our hearts and minds. "You have been my refuge, a strong tower against the foe," David said to the Lord. "I long to . . . take refuge in the shelter of your wings" (VV. 3–4).

When we are overwhelmed, peace and protection are ours through God's Son, Jesus Christ. "In me you may have peace," Jesus said. "In this world you will have trouble. But take heart! I have overcome the world" (JOHN 16:33).

JENNIFER BENSON SCHULDT

*Dear God, I am frail and defenseless, but you are mighty and powerful.
Please help me find peace and rest in you when I am overwhelmed.*

God is our refuge.

Reject Apathy

Read: Nehemiah 1:1–10

Whatever you did for one of the least of these brothers and sisters of mine, you did for me. —Matthew 25:40

The room was splashed with an assortment of enchanting colors as women in beautiful saris scurried around, completing the final touches for a fundraising event. Formerly from India, these women now live in the USA. Yet they remain concerned for their native country. Upon hearing about the financial situation of a Christian school for autistic children in India, they not only heard the need, but they also took it to heart and responded.

Nehemiah did not allow his comfortable position in life as cupbearer and confidant to the most powerful man at that time to nullify his concerns for his countrymen. He talked to people who had just come from Jerusalem to find out the condition of the city and its citizens (NEH. 1:2). He learned that "those who survived the exile . . . are in great trouble and disgrace. The wall of Jerusalem is broken down, and its gates have been burned with fire" (v. 3).

Nehemiah's heart broke. He mourned, fasted, and prayed, asking God to do something about the terrible conditions (v. 4). God enabled Nehemiah to return to Jerusalem to lead the rebuilding effort (2:1–8).

Nehemiah accomplished great things for his people because he asked great things of a great God and relied on Him. May God open our eyes to the needs of those around us, and may He help us to become passionate and creative problem-solvers who bless others. *POH FANG CHIA*

Father, there are great needs all around us. We choose not to give in to despair or apathy, but look to you for help in doing the task at hand.

Those who walk with God won't run from the needs of others.

An Invitation to Rest

Read: Revelation 21:1–5

I will give you rest. —Matthew 11:28

At a friend's bedside in a hospital emergency ward, I was moved by the sounds of suffering I heard from other patients in pain. As I prayed for my friend and for the ailing patients, I realized anew how fleeting our life on earth is. Then I recalled an old country song by Jim Reeves that talks about how the world is not home for us—we're "just a-passin' through."

Our world is full of weariness, pain, hunger, debt, poverty, disease, and death. Because we must pass through such a world, Jesus's invitation is welcome and timely: "Come to me, all you who are weary and burdened, and I will give you rest" (MATT. 11:28). We need this rest.

There is hardly a funeral ceremony I've attended where John's vision of "a new heaven and a new earth" (REV. 21:1–5) is not quoted, and it certainly holds relevance for funerals.

But I believe the passage is more for the living than the dead. The time to heed Jesus's invitation to come rest in Him is while we are still living. Only then can we be entitled to the promises in Revelation. God will dwell among us (v. 3). He will wipe away our tears (v. 4). There will be "no more death or mourning or crying or pain" (v. 4).

Accept Jesus's invitation and enter His rest! *LAWRENCE DARMANI*

Father in heaven, this life can be wonderful, but it can also be so hard. Thank you for your Spirit's presence with us now. And thank you too for the reality of eternal life with you.

When you're weary in life's struggles, find your rest in the Lord.

On the Wing

Read: Matthew 10:27–31

So don't be afraid; you are worth more than many sparrows. —v. 31

In his book *On the Wing,* Alan Tennant chronicles his efforts to track the migration of the peregrine falcon. Valued for their beauty, swiftness, and power, these amazing birds of prey were favorite hunting companions of emperors and nobility. Sadly, the wide use of the pesticide DDT in the 1950s interfered with their reproductive cycle and placed them on the endangered species list.

Interested in the recovery of this species, Tennant attached transmitters to a select number of falcons to track their migration patterns. But when he and his pilot flew their Cessna behind the birds, they repeatedly lost signal from the transmitters. Despite their advanced technology, they were not always able to track the birds they wanted to help.

It's good to know that the God who cares for us never loses track of us. In fact, Jesus said that not even one sparrow "will fall to the ground outside your Father's care. . . . So don't be afraid; you are worth more than many sparrows" (MATT. 10:29–31).

When we face difficult circumstances, fear may cause us to wonder if God is aware of our situation. Jesus's teaching assures us that God cares deeply and is in control. His tracking of our lives will never fail.

DENNIS FISHER

Father, I'm putting my longings and burdens on you at the end of this year because I know you care for me and can work powerfully. Thank you that I and my loved ones are in your care.

If God cares for birds, will He not care for His children?

The *Our Daily Bread* Writers

Dr. **James Banks** and his wife have two adult children and live in Durham, North Carolina, where he is the pastor of Peace Church. He is the author of Discovery House books *The Lost Art of Praying Together, Praying the Prayers of the Bible, Prayers for Prodigals*, and *Prayers for Your Children.*

If you've read articles by **Dave Branon** over the years, you know about his family and the lessons learned from father- (and now grandfather-) hood. After serving for 18 years as managing editor of *Sports Spectrum* magazine, Dave is now an editor for Discovery House. A freelance writer for many years, he has authored 15 books. Dave and his wife, Sue, love rollerblading and spending time with their children and grandchildren. Dave also enjoys traveling overseas with students on ministry trips.

Anne Cetas became a follower of Jesus in her late teens after a friend invited her to a Bible conference. At 19, she began reading *Our Daily Bread* and studying Our Daily Bread Ministries Discovery Series booklets. Six years later she joined the editorial staff of *Our Daily Bread.* Anne began writing for the devotional booklet in September 2004 and serves as senior editor. Anne and her husband, Carl, enjoy bicycling, taking long walks, and serving as mentors in an urban ministry.

Poh Fang Chia never dreamed of being in a language-related profession; chemistry was her first love. The turning point came when she received Jesus as her Savior as a 15-year-old and expressed to Jesus that she would like to create books that touch lives. She serves with Our Daily Bread Ministries at the Singapore office as an editor and is also a member of the Chinese editorial review committee. Poh Fang says: "I really enjoy exploring the Scripture and finding passages that bring a fresh viewpoint, answer a question that is burning in my mind, or deal with a life issue I'm facing. My prayer is to write so that readers will see how presently alive the Bible is and will respond to the life-transforming power of the Word."

Bill Crowder joined the Our Daily Bread Ministries staff after more than 20 years in the pastorate. Bill serves as vice president of teaching content and spends much of his time in a Bible-teaching ministry for Christian leaders around the world. He has written many booklets for the Discovery Series, and he has published several books with Discovery House. Bill and his wife, Marlene, have five children as well as several grandchildren he'd be thrilled to tell you about.

Lawrence Darmani is a Ghanaian novelist and publisher. His first novel, *Grief Child*, won the Commonwealth Writers' Prize as best first book from Africa. He is editor of *Step* magazine, and CEO of Step Publishers. He is married and lives in Accra with his family. Lawrence enjoys church life and volunteers at other Christian ministry activities. He says that he derives writing ideas "out of personal experiences, reading, testimonies, and observing the world around me."

Tim Gustafson writes for *Our Daily Bread* and *Our Daily Journey* and serves as an editor for Discovery Series. As the adopted son of missionaries to Ghana, Tim has an unusual perspective on life in the West. He and his wife, Leisa, are the parents of one daughter and seven sons. Perhaps not surprisingly, his life verses say: "Father to the fatherless, defender of widows—this is God, whose dwelling is holy. God places the lonely in families; he sets the prisoners free and gives them joy" (PS. 68:5–6 NLT).

Mart DeHaan, grandson of Our Daily Bread Ministries founder, Dr. M. R. DeHaan, and son of former president, Richard W. DeHaan, has served with the ministry for more than 40 years. Mart is heard regularly on the *Discover the Word* radio program. Mart is also an author of many booklets for the Discovery Series. He and his wife, Diane, have two children. Mart enjoys spending time outdoors, especially with fishing pole in hand.

David Egner is retired from Our Daily Bread Ministries. During his years with the ministry, Dave was editor of *Discovery Digest* and *Campus Journal* (now called *Our Daily Journey*). He has written many Discovery Series booklets, and his work has appeared in a variety of other Our Daily Bread Ministries publications. Dave was a college writing professor for many years and has enjoyed occasional guest-professor stints at Bible colleges in Russia. He and his wife, Shirley, live in Grand Rapids, Michigan.

Dennis Fisher received Jesus as his Savior at a church meeting in Southern California. He says, "I came under terrible conviction of sin. After receiving Christ, I felt like I had taken a shower on the inside." Dennis was a professor of evangelism and discipleship at Moody Bible Institute before joining Our Daily Bread Ministries in 1998 where he currently serves as senior research editor. Dennis has two adult children and one grandson and lives with his wife, Janet, in DeWitt, Michigan.

Chek Phang (C. P.) Hia brings a distinctive flavor to *Our Daily Bread.* He and his wife, Lin Choo, reside in the island nation of Singapore. C. P. came to faith in Jesus Christ at the age of 13. During his early years as a believer, he was privileged to learn from excellent Bible teachers. Those godly mentors instilled in him a love for God's Word and a desire to teach it. He serves in the Singapore office as special assistant to the Our Daily Bread president. He and his wife enjoy traveling and going for walks.

Cindy Hess Kasper has served for more than 40 years at Our Daily Bread Ministries, where she is associate editor for *Our Daily Journey.* An experienced writer, she penned youth devotional articles for more than a decade before writing for *Our Daily Bread.* She is a daughter of longtime senior editor Clair Hess, from whom she learned a love for singing and working with words. Cindy and her husband, Tom, have three grown children and seven grandchildren, in whom they take great delight.

Randy Kilgore spent most of his 20-plus years in business as a senior human resource manager before returning to seminary. Since finishing his Master of Divinity in 2000, he has served as a writer and workplace chaplain. He wrote a weekly Internet devotional at madetomatter.org, and a collection of those devotionals appears in the Discovery House book *Made to Matter: Devotions for Working Christians.* Randy and his wife, Cheryl, founded Desired Haven Ministries in 2007 and work together in Massachusetts, where they live with their two children.

Albert Lee was director of international ministries for Our Daily Bread Ministries for many years, and he lives in Singapore. Albert's passion, vision, and energy expanded the work of the ministry around the world. He continues to oversee a number of projects for the ministry. Albert grew up in Singapore, and took a variety of courses from Singapore Bible College, as well as served with Singapore Youth for Christ from 1971–1999, and taught a course on youth evangelism at Taylor University in Indiana. Albert appreciates art and collects paintings. He and his wife, Catherine, have two children.

After a lengthy battle with cancer, **Julie Ackerman Link** went to be with the Lord on April 10, 2015. Since 2000, Julie had written articles each month for *Our Daily Bread*. She is a popular author with *Our Daily Bread* readers, and her insightful and inspiring articles have touched millions of lives around the world. Julie also wrote the books *Above All, Love* and *A Heart for God*, published by Discovery House.

David McCasland began writing for *Our Daily Bread* in 1995. His books *Oswald Chambers: Abandoned to God* and *Eric Liddell: Pure Gold* are published by Discovery House. David and his wife, Luann, live in Colorado Springs, Colorado. They have four daughters and six grandchildren.

Keila Ochoa and her husband live in Mexico and have two young children. She helps Media Associates International with their training ministry for writers around the world and has written several books in Spanish for children, teens, and women. She serves in her church in the areas of youth, missions, and women's ministry.

David Roper was a pastor for more than 30 years and now directs Idaho Mountain Ministries, a retreat dedicated to the encouragement of pastoral couples. He enjoys fishing, hiking, and being streamside with his wife, Carolyn. His favorite fictional character is Reepicheep, the tough little mouse that is the "soul of courage" in C. S. Lewis's Chronicles of Narnia. His favorite biblical character is Caleb—that rugged old saint who never retired, but who "died climbing."

Jennifer Benson Schuldt has been writing professionally since 1997 when she began her career as a technical writer with an international consulting firm. She writes for *Our Daily Journey* and first appeared in *Our Daily Bread* in October 2010. Jennifer lives in the Chicago suburbs with her husband, Bob, and their children. One of her favorite verses is Micah 6:8: "This is what he requires of you: to do what is right, to love mercy, and to walk humbly with your God" (NLT).

You may know **Joe Stowell** as the former president of Moody Bible Institute. Currently he serves as president of Cornerstone University in Grand Rapids, Michigan. Dr. Stowell also serves on the board of the Billy Graham Evangelistic Association. An internationally recognized speaker, Joe's first love is Jesus Christ and preaching His Word. He has also written numerous books. He and his wife, Martie, have three children and several grandchildren.

Marion Stroud went to be with her Savior on August 8, 2015. Since 2014 Marion had been writing devotional articles for *Our Daily Bread* that touched the lives of readers around the world. Two of her popular books of prayers, *Dear God, It's Me and It's Urgent* and *It's Just You and Me, Lord* were published by Discovery House. As an international author and writing mentor, Marion worked as a cross-cultural trainer for Media Associates International, helping writers produce books for their own culture. She was an encourager and role model for writers for many years and will be mourned by hundreds of friends around the world. Marion is survived by her husband, Gordon, and their five children and sixteen grandchildren.

Marvin Williams began writing for *Our Daily Bread* in 2007. He also writes for *Our Daily Journey*. Marvin is senior teaching pastor at Trinity Church in Lansing, Michigan. Educated at Bishop College in Dallas, Texas, and Trinity Evangelical Divinity School in Deerfield, Illinois, he has also served in several pastoral positions in Grand Rapids, Michigan. He and his wife, Tonia, have three children.

Joanie Yoder, a favorite among *Our Daily Bread* readers, went home to be with her Savior in 2004. She and her husband established a Christian rehabilitation center for drug addicts in England many years ago. Widowed in 1982, she learned to rely on the Lord's help and strength. She wrote with hope about true dependence on God and His life-changing power.

Topic Index

About the Publisher

Our Daily Bread Ministries

Our Daily Bread Ministries is a nondenominational, nonprofit organization with more than 600 staff and 1,000 volunteers serving in 37 countries. Together we distribute more than 60 million resources every year in over 150 countries. Our mission is to make the life-changing wisdom of the Bible understandable and accessible to all.

Beginning in 1938 as a Bible class aired on a small radio station in Detroit, Michigan, USA, Our Daily Bread Ministries now offers radio programs and videos; devotional, instructional, evangelistic, and apologetic print and digital resources; and a biblical correspondence ministry. You can access our online resources at ourdailybread.org. Our signature publication, *Our Daily Bread,* is published in nearly 50 languages and is read by people in almost every country around the world.

Discovery House

Discovery House was founded in 1988 as an extension of Our Daily Bread Ministries. Our goal is to produce resources that feed the soul with the Word of God, and we do this through books, music, video, audio, software, greeting cards, and downloadable content. All our materials focus on the never-changing truths of Scripture, so everything we produce shows reverence for God and His Word, demonstrates the relevance of vibrant faith, and equips and encourages people in their everyday lives.

Note to the Reader

The publisher invites you to share your response to the message of this book by writing Discovery House, P.O. Box 3566, Grand Rapids, MI 49501, USA. For information about other Discovery House books, music, or DVDs, contact us at the same address or call 1-800-653-8333. Find us online at dhp.org or send e-mail to books@dhp.org.

Notes